Andrea Gremels, Maren Scheurer, Frank Schulze-Engler, Jarula M.I. Wegner (eds.)

Entanglements:
Envisioning World Literature from the Global South

I0801712

Studies in World Literature

Editors:

Prof Janet Wilson, University of Northampton, UK
Dr Chris Ringrose, Monash University, Australia

Advisory Board:

Dr Gerd Bayer, University of Erlangen, Germany
Dr Fiona Tolan, Liverpool John Moores University, UK

The book series Studies in World Literature is devoted to the analysis of global literature, and the multiple, sometimes contradictory, tendencies it accommodates. Its field of enquiry is the 'new' world literature, a category currently emerging through multiple changes from the old Romantic concept of *Weltliteratur*, attuned to the challenges posed by postcolonialism and multiculturalism, the increasing globalisation of literature (but also its reverse trend, regionalisation), and the diversification of the market place. Studies in World Literature encourages research which celebrates and critically assesses a phenomenon that can be understood, as Pheng Cheah points out, as the 'literature of the world—imaginings and stories [...] that track and account for contemporary globalization as well as older historical narratives of worldhood'.

World literature can be brought into dialogue with postcolonial writing through scrutiny of how it is written, read, circulated, and received transnationally within the contemporary circuit of global cultural capital. The series also responds to the need to examine the inherent contradictions in the concept of a world literature and dependence on a hegemonic (often English-centred) literary and critical discourse.

The series seeks to address these tensions, and consequently welcomes:

1) volumes which debate such matters theoretically (including definitions of what counts as 'world literature' and the place of postcolonial literary production within this larger category);
2) comparative studies of texts and genres from different countries and cultures under common headings or concepts such as memory, ethics, and human rights.

Volumes on national literatures, when these are set in a world/comparative or generic context, will also be considered, and the series will include discussions of other complementary aspects of discourse, narratology, and media. While writing by 'canonical' authors will be covered, the series will additionally propose wider cultural and intellectual genealogies for 'minor' or occluded writers. A key aim of this series is to redeploy the familiar rhetoric of postcolonial theory and discourse in relation to concepts relevant to world literature by introducing arguments that will be integrated with the evidence of individual literary practice. This emphasis on contesting definitions of 'diasporic' or 'postcolonial' writing, 'transnational' or 'transcultural' literatures and 'world' literature as used by writers, critics and thinkers may lead to a reconsideration of the boundaries that divide and intersections that link these related fields.

Recent volumes:

6 *Gerri Kimber, Janet Wilson (Eds.)*
Re-forming World Literature
Katherine Mansfield and the Modernist Short Story
ISBN 978-3-8382-1163-3

7 *Flair Donglai Shi, Gareth Guanming Tan (Eds.)*
World Literature in Motion
Institution, Recognition, Location
ISBN 978-3-8382-1163-3

8 *Patricia Neville*
Janet Frame's World of Books
ISBN 978-3-8382-1242-5

9 *Chandani Lokuge, Chris Ringrose (Eds.)*
Creative Lives
Interviews with Contemporary South Asian Diaspora Writers
ISBN 978-3-8382-1544-0

Andrea Gremels, Maren Scheurer, Frank Schulze-Engler,
Jarula M.I. Wegner (eds.)

ENTANGLEMENTS

Envisioning World Literature from the Global South

ibidem
Verlag

Bibliographic information published by the Deutsche Nationalbibliothek
Die Deutsche Nationalbibliothek lists this publication in the Deutsche Nationalbibliografie; detailed bibliographic data are available in the Internet at http://dnb.d-nb.de.

Bibliografische Information der Deutschen Nationalbibliothek
Die Deutsche Nationalbibliothek verzeichnet diese Publikation in der Deutschen Nationalbibliografie; detaillierte bibliografische Daten sind im Internet über http://dnb.d-nb.de abrufbar.

Cover image: Photo 108127499 © Kts | Dreamstime.com

ISBN-13: 978-3-8382-1593-8
© *ibidem*-Verlag, Stuttgart 2022
All rights reserved.

No part of this publication may be reproduced, stored in or introduced into a retrieval system, or transmitted, in any form, or by any means (electronical, mechanical, photocopying, recording or otherwise) without the prior written permission of the publisher. Any person who does any unauthorized act in relation to this publication may be liable to criminal prosecution and civil claims for damages.

Alle Rechte vorbehalten. Das Werk einschließlich aller seiner Teile ist urheberrechtlich geschützt. Jede Verwertung außerhalb der engen Grenzen des Urheberrechtsgesetzes ist ohne Zustimmung des Verlages unzulässig und strafbar. Dies gilt insbesondere für Vervielfältigungen, Übersetzungen, Mikroverfilmungen und elektronische Speicherformen sowie die Einspeicherung und Verarbeitung in elektronischen Systemen.

Printed in the United States of America

Table of Contents

Introduction

Andrea Gremels, Maren Scheurer, Frank Schulze-Engler and Jarula M.I. Wegner

In recent years, "world literature" has become a hotspot of international academic debate. At the centre of the manifold and diverse attempts to turn the concept into a viable framework for engaging with literature in the 21st century lies a widely shared urge to overcome the Eurocentric limitations that so long bedevilled literary studies. It is in this context that the idea of a "Global South" has re-emerged as a powerful point of attraction in global literary debates. Like many variants of postcolonialism, the idea of a "Global South" has often relied on a victimological perspective: what defines societies, cultures and literatures in Africa, Asia and Latin America, it is habitually assumed, is a common history of colonial oppression and anticolonial resistance (Ngũgĩ wa Thiong'o 1981). Other currents in this debate have sought to establish the "Global South" as a new world historical subject, as a successor term for the once powerful idea of a "Third World" or as an avenue of reviving the "Bandung Spirit" of the erstwhile Nonaligned Movement (Yoon 2015). Half a century after the end of colonial rule in many parts of the world, however, this perspective increasingly clashes with the new realities of a globalized world and arguably needs to be redefined to allow for a fruitful encounter with the complexity of contemporary cultures and literatures.

The present volume moves beyond a theorizing of the Global South and the Global North "as simplified oppositions and homogenous entities" (Kloß 2018), as it considers the transcultural and transregional relationalities of world literature from the Global South. We encounter such relationalities throughout the contemporary literary world, when, for instance, Moroccan writer Tahar Ben Jelloun introduces the Argentinian writer Jorge Luis Borges as a protagonist into his 1985 novel *L'enfant de sable* (*The Sand Child*), the Indian writer Rabindranath Tagore influenced the literary scene of Buenos Aires of the 1920s through his friendship with Victoria Ocampo, and the voice of the Chilean poet Pablo Neruda resonates in the work of many contemporary Indian writers such as Namwar Singh (see Maurya 2016, 52–56). V.S. Naipaul's early novels inspired many writers, not only in the Caribbean, but also in Africa, to make non-European lifeworlds—that had hitherto been regarded as insignificant and "beyond the pale" of serious literature—the subject of their own writings, while Maryse Condé's literary exploration of the unsettling history of colonial entanglements in Mali is a collaborative South Atlantic work the Afro-Caribbean writer created with the help of her West African colleagues, e.g. by relying on their unedited family testimonies. South-South linkages have been further enhanced by literary festivals and periodicals as well as transcultural flows generated by and through popular music.

Entanglements: Envisioning World Literature from the Global South scrutinizes current debates that bring historical and contemporary South–South entanglements to the fore and aim to develop a new understanding of world literature in a multipolar world of globalized modernity. The volume suggests that we rethink the idea of world literature along the notion of "entanglements": as a field of variously criss-crossing relations of literary activity beyond the confines of literary canons, cultural containers or national borders. This lens sharpens our view for (re-)envisionings of world literature from a range of Global South perspectives and new transnational imaginaries emerging from these literatures. The chapters in this volume present individual case studies from a variety of language traditions that focus on particular literary relationships and practices across Africa, the Americas, Asia, and Europe as well as new fictional and theoretical imaginaries of world literature in order to broaden our understanding of the cultural and literary connectivities that shape our globalized world.

World Literature and the Global South: Debates and Problems

Early during the resurgence of world literature as a subject of critical debate, Christopher Prendergast (2004) noted that its "determinate shape and content are as yet far from clear" (vii). And so, scholars have continued to try and define what world literature is and how texts attain world literary status. In their introduction to *The Cambridge Companion to World Literature*, Ben Etherington and Jarad Zimbler (2018) summarize what they hold to be the dominant models of world literature:

> For some, world literature means exotic literature, verbal art of the world beyond their own; and, given the dominance of North American and European academic and literary institutions, such usage typically refers to literature produced beyond "the West". For others, world literature means a universal canon of masterpieces: the proverbial best that has been thought and said across histories and cultures. For still others, world literature consists of innumerable works that travel globally, exposing themselves to readers in new places and languages and taking part in the flows of transcultural interaction and exchange. In their contemporary manifestations, such notions inevitably take us into the web of the global market. World literature, some therefore insist, compels us to reflect on the ways in which works are caught up in an unequal world-system made up of highly developed centres and underdeveloped peripheries. (1)

This summary is revealing, given that all of these models are tied to the notion of a corpus or canon: a specific set of texts produced beyond the west; a canon of masterpieces; innumerable (and yet, presumably, potentially countable) travelling works; and works that fend for themselves in an uneven global system.

For several reasons, these attempts at defining a canon of world literature have been unsatisfactory. Thus, corpus-driven conceptualizations of world literature such as Damrosch's (2003) popular definition that "a work enters into world literature by a double process: first, by being read as literature; second by circulating out into a broader world beyond its linguistic and cultural point of origin" (6) often hinge on questionable premises. Damrosch's search for the conditions that 'make' world literature, for example, implies that there is one world, one vast globality of world literature which can be "entered".

The charge of the Eurocentrism of world literary canons has by now become another critical commonplace, but it is nevertheless surprising how tenacious a European or western focus remains within even the most well-meaning projects. Prendergast's (2004) volume *Debating World Literature*, for instance, seeks to make migrations "one of the principal themes" of its investigation (x), but these migrations still follow modern European colonial routes. Another, more recent example, Dieter Lamping and Galin Tihanov's (2019) *Vergleichende Weltliteraturen/Comparative World Literatures*, is open to a plural understanding of "world literature" that includes an opening toward non-European contexts (7–8) but constantly betrays its adherence to a Goethean understanding of the term and a decidedly European point of view, for example, when it is noted that

> even before Africans and Asians took note of European literature, the Europeans had already, more or less thoroughly, acknowledged theirs. The French poet Adelbert von Chamisso [. . .], for instance, discovered Malay poetry during a tour of the world in which he participated, and Goethe discovered Persian and Chinese poetry for himself. (5, our translation)

Although several recent publications seek to remedy the Eurocentric focus of world literature through the integration of non-western literatures and perspectives and by considering texts and theories from all over the world (Thomson 2009; Damrosch 2014), such supplementation ultimately does not do away with the discontents of the canon. Their emphasis on multilingual and multipolar formations and the need to break away from considering Europe or North America as exclusive cultural centres provide important starting points for renewing the debate, but paradoxically, in such "breaking away", Europe remains the necessary centre, in the very critical gesture of departing from it. Such discussions often remain tied to traditional categories like the classic or the canon as well as to established concepts and institutions.

In *Mapping World Literature*, for example, Mads Rosendahl Thomson (2009) develops a "paradigm of constellations" with which to approach world literature "based on formal and thematic similarities in international canons" (139). This empirical method approaches existing literary histories, anthologies and canons more generally in order to identify significant elements "reflecting an identity that has been built up and evolved over centuries" (140). Thomson analyses literary works to identify the criteria that potentially led to their canonization. This allows him to discuss world literature independently of national or linguistic "containers". His aim is "to connect less circulated literature with the most internationally canonized works" (141), but in this regard the notion of constellations reaffirms already established concepts and institutions of world literature. Is it, for instance, necessary to emphasize that canonical writers of world literature, such as James Joyce, T.S. Eliot and Ezra Pound, "were all migrants" (76) in order to justify a focus on migrant writers? In a similar vein, Jean Bessière and Gerald Gillespie's *Contextualizing World Literature* (2015), while problematizing Comparative Literature's lingering habit of considering "Europe as the standard measure against which to assess other cultural complexes" (10) and gesturing towards "a network of cross-cultural 'interferences'" (11), considers the circulation of literature through the problematic notion of "universalism", tracing empires of "World History" (12) rather than developing alternative routes and viewpoints that offer potential counterpoints. These examples show that simply pointing to and including other traditions within the corpus of world literature is not effective if we do not at the same time shed the canon and container mentality which has been dominant in World Literature and Cultural Studies. On the one hand, thinking in canons or corpora, however much we expand them, will always by definition be exclusive. And on the other, thinking in containers or fixed, binary structures does not actually do justice to the way cultures and literary relations work.

Nevertheless, a significant portion of the world literature debate has in recent times sought stability in the centre/periphery binary. In her influential book *The World Republic of Letters*, Pascale

Casanova (2004) argues that writers from the "periphery" have to reach to the "centre", either by adapting its literary norms, or by rebelling against them, in order to gain terrain in the asymmetrical and competitive field of world literature (12). Although the contributions to the present volume acknowledge continuing asymmetries in the field of world literature, their aim is to question a strictly systemic point of view that fixates structural hierarchies, such as the ones formulated by Casanova, Franco Moretti (2000), or the Warwick Research Collective (2015). As valuable as analyses of abiding inequalities may be, this volume argues that the predominant focus on economic or sociological models is too narrow to capture the cultural dynamics of world literature.

Therefore, even innovative variants of this type of reasoning that seek to inverse the centre/periphery model by putting the Global South in the "centre" of attention do not necessarily produce radically altered results (Müller and Siskind 2019, 4). Neither the attempt at *Re-Mapping World Literature* through perspectives of the Global South, as suggested by Gesine Müller, Jorge Locane and Benjamin Loy (2018), nor the questioning of rigid hierarchical models in Gesine Müller and Mariano Siskind's (2019) collection, *World Literature, Cosmopolitanism, Globality: Beyond, Against, Post, Otherwise*, are exempt from residual traces of an approach that classifies Latin America as "periphery", especially when it comes to analysing global literary markets.

The centre/periphery model has another shortcoming that links it with a number of postcolonial approaches to the problem of world literature. Postcolonial literature and world literature have often been held in "false opposition" (Nickels 2018, 1), as for example by Robert J.C. Young (2011), who distinguishes between the aesthetically defined category of world literature and postcolonial literature, whose "basis [...] has never been, in the first instance, aesthetic criteria, but rather, the effect that it seeks to achieve—it is a literature written against something" (216). Both the centre/periphery model and this postcolonial approach tend to lock literatures of the so-called "periphery" in a position of resistance and victimhood while overlooking aesthetic and creative approaches that may allow us to re-envision the aesthetics and the politics of Global South literatures.

In contrast to Young, Elke Sturm-Trigonakis's (2020) volume *World Literature and the Postcolonial* considers world and postcolonial literature not in opposition but in conjunction to reverse the old centre/periphery model and provincialize Europe. She contends that postcolonialism created an awareness of the "geopolitical asymmetries of power" (11) underlying the concept of world literature and thus pushed the conceptual boundaries in order to "always keep an eye on the whole world" (10). In this way, she shows that world literature was entangled with the history of colonization from the very start. Yet by holding on to classical concepts of the local, regional and global, she reiterates old centres and peripheries and thus misses an opportunity to confront the complex realities of a multipolar world in which nations, regions and continents do not necessarily circumscribe cultural relations and literary exchanges.

The Nobel Prize for Literature awarded to Abdulrazak Gurnah in 2021 has thrown many of these issues into stark relief. The prize motivation quoted by the Nobel Committee for their excellent decision ("for his uncompromising and compassionate penetration of the effects of colonialism and the fate of the refugee in the gulf between cultures and continents", [Nobel Prize 2021]) already remained somewhat unimaginative given the fact that many of Gurnah's novels explore not only "the effects of colonialism", but also the aftermath of hundreds of years of shared histories across East Africa, Arabia and Asia. This demonstrates that the supposed "gulf between cultures and continents" on closer scrutiny reveals centuries of cultural entanglements.

The response to the Nobel Prize for Gurnah also provides instructive examples of the persistence of a hierarchically inspired Eurocentrism both among "mainstream" critics and some commentators inspired by post- or decolonial theory. Thus the response in German-speaking countries (to take only one salient example) included a scathing critique in the *Neue Zürcher Zeitung* of the Nobel

Committee's decision to award the prize to an author largely unknown in Europe that signalled "the thunderous leave-taking into insignificance"[1] of the Nobel Prize for Literature (Bucheli 2021), but also a dismissal of Gurnah in the *Süddeutsche Zeitung* as a harmless author who fits well "into the European literary tradition" and whose writings do not "hurt" his audiences (Pollatschek 2021, 9).[2] Interestingly enough, Pollatschek's implied "post"- or "decolonial" disdain regarding Gurnah's alleged failure to effectively contribute to a "decolonization of the canon" or the "blasting of western criteria of quality" is firmly wedded to a brazen neo-Orientalist assumption that literary values such as "soft realism", "ambivalence", "fine humour" or "understatement" are typically "British" literary qualities naturally shared by European readers (9),[3] but not appropriate for "postcolonial" authors, from whom presumably more undomesticated, feral or visceral literary products are to be expected.

The reaction to Gurnah's unexpected canonization through the Nobel Prize is a perfect illustration of the contradictions inherent in stratified models of world literature: the "gulf" between European and non-European literature can, supposedly, only be bridged if either a "peripheral" author is undeservedly put centre stage or if this author is already playing according to the rules of the centre. Gurnah's own writing, in contrast, highlights relations that contradict and transcend such binary models. Taking its cue from Gurnah as well as countless other literary voices from across the world, this collection seeks to capture this complexity by analysing economic and sociological aspects of world literary activity alongside aesthetic,

1 Original: "Die krachende Verabschiedung in die Bedeutungslosigkeit" (our translation).

2 Original: "Und wenn man jetzt doch eine Kritik an Gurnah üben möchte, dann wäre es diese: Er tut nicht weh. Weder den Nachfahren der kolonialen Täter noch den Kriterien der europäischen Literaturtradition" (All translations from this text are ours).

3 Original: "Gurnah ist gut wie ein guter Brite. [. . .]. Dass es sich, um eine Forderung der postkolonialen Literaturkritik aufzugreifen, nicht um eine Dekolonisierung des Kanons und ein Sprengen westlicher Qualitätskriterien handelt, sondern um eine Assimilation, vielleicht sogar noch um eine Erweiterung."

epistemological as well as theoretical perspectives in order to begin to envision a multipolar web of literary entanglements reaching within and out of the Global South.

This volume's contribution to the debate is not just an opening up of the perspective to incorporate new authors into the canon or new areas of literary production into research and teaching. Pluralization and inclusion are important, but they remain tied to the idea of a corpus of texts that needs to be better described, managed, expanded, or confined. Thus, the chapters presented in this volume do not simply attempt to expand the European canon but seek instead to show how it is just one, increasingly entangled, element within a global literary field that engages with but also transcends traditional notions of literary canonization. They are thus offering a variety of approaches that think through the dynamics of world literature without privileging the traditional structures and concepts that have plagued the debate for so long. Instead of "adding" new literatures to an ever-expanding canon, this volume argues, we should understand world literature as a dynamic field of transcultural exchanges in which diverse literatures and cultures are already closely entangled within and beyond the Global South. The challenge, in other words, is to move beyond the idea of world literature as a set of texts, however expansive, and to develop the theoretical perspectives and methodological tools that are necessary to grasp world literature as a practice. It can be read as grounded in a complex set of interactions, exchanges and connectivities which generate new forms of transnational, transregional and transcultural worldliness in a world of "overlapping territories" and "intertwined histories" (Said 1993, 3). World literature is thus a matter of texts in contexts, including literary and artistic practices, procedures and relationships.

The chapters included here suggest that these world literary dynamics can best be observed by shifting the focus to South-South relations. Such relations have increasingly garnered the attention of scholars, especially within Latin American Studies (Klengel and Ortiz Wallner 2016; Müller, Locane and Loy 2018; Müller and Siskind 2019), and their investigations have produced detailed surveys of particular literary scenes and generated a vast amount of knowledge on previously neglected relations. However, in order to bring into focus the multipolar (Iliro 2010), transareal (Ette 2016) and transregional (Achenbach et al. 2020) connections we are advocating, a larger purview is needed. For this reason, the volume brings together contributions from Anglophone, Romance and Comparative Literary Studies on a range of different examples from all over the Global South. These case studies deal not only with the novel, which is often another "centre" of the world literature debate, but also with other genres such as the essay and oral poetry as well as platforms of performance and debate, bringing to light the wealth and vibrancy of South-South entanglements.

Entanglements and South-South Relations: Re-Envisioning World Literature

Before we turn to the contributions to this volume, however, we would like to discuss in more detail the two fundamental shifts in point of view that inform the enquiries assembled here. The first highlights the idea that world literature may be re-envisioned from the Global South, relationally and across cultures. Russell West-Pavlov (2018) has drawn attention to the "protean" nature of the term "Global South", which "refers simultaneously to a geopolitical area, a global economic process, a collective actor, a discursive event, and a body of theories, paradigms, and texts" (2). In order to remain relevant to the complex patterns of economic, social, political and cultural interdependencies and connectivities that characterize the 21st-century world, the idea of the "Global South" arguably needs to leave behind connotations of territoriality (as symbolized by the "Brandt Line" dividing "North" and "South" proposed in the 1970s). This volume thus aims to embrace the internal diversity, heterogeneity and contradictions of societies and cultures in a "Global South" that—through the mobilities generated by migration, commerce and communication—has long since become entangled with the "Global North".

Regarding world literature as an ongoing practice rather than a set of works corresponds to an understanding of the Global South as a "shifty, shifting term" (West-Pavlov 2018, 7). According to Sinah Kloß (2018), it cannot be identified as an entity, "but as something that is created, imagined, invented, maintained and recreated" (7). Conceptualized as a practice or a process, world literature from the Global South also embraces new forms and "transcultural modes" (14) of knowledge production beyond the binary of North and South, or "the west" and "the rest".

Such knowledge production often takes place in explicit and implicit relations and connections across multiple locations. South-South relationships may thus offer new ways of rethinking the Global South, as Mukoma wa Ngugi (2012) has suggested. He seeks to "facilitate conversation among writers and scholars from Africa, the Middle East, Latin America, and Asia as well as minority groups in the West" (7). These conversations do not necessarily exclude the Global North, since the "goal is to be in relation with the West as with everyone else" (6–7) and to explore "other ways of knowing and relating" (7). Knowing and relating "otherwise" drastically change how we look at established patterns and leads us to new material, which, as Mukoma wa Ngugi acknowledges, can at first seem like we are losing hold of what we know and what we can rely on.

> To think about South-to-South relations is to enter a place of great intellectual vulnerability. Once we leave the relationship of, let's say, Africa and Europe via colonialism, the world suddenly becomes very vast, complicated, and scary as the knowledge of how just little [sic] we know settles in. Yet, this place that is just outside our comfort zone is a beautiful place to be in—it's a place of discovery of new ideas and seeing old ideas anew (7).

In this fashion, South-South literary connectivities may become "epistemic catalysts" (West-Pavlov 2018, 7) and exploring them can even contribute to overcoming an "epistemic blindness" that defines the Global South only through its difference to the North or western cultural and literary traditions (Klengel and Ortiz Wallner 2016, 12).

Mukoma wa Ngugi's reflections are themselves an example of South-South connectivity and knowledge production, as they rely on Édouard Glissant's *Poetics of Relation*. In this poetic essay, and further in his *Introduction to a Poetics of Diversity*, Glissant (1997, 2020) develops a vision of a globalized world determined by transversal movements, transcultural encounters and heterogeneous realities that altogether shape a "chaos-world" (*chaos-monde*) of unforeseen and unsystematic relationalities. Glissant stresses uncontrollable "confluences" and an increasing intermingling of diversities, both of which oppose monolithic world views. This ongoing process of cultural diversification, which he terms "creolization", enables horizontal instead of hierarchical knowledge exchange.

Following Glissant and Mukoma wa Ngugi, therefore, the aim of this volume is to explore "South-South" relations in terms of a widening global communicative network of heterogenous relationalities that involve producers of world literature as well as its readers; it thus will move beyond positioning the perspective of the "Global South" in a new hierarchy of critical scrutiny, by confining "non-western" literatures within territorialized models of (national) literatures and cultures. In this context, Ngũgĩ wa Thiong'o (2012) has introduced the concept of "globalectical reading" that fosters horizontal "interconnections" by "breaking open the prison house of imagination built on theories and outlooks that would seem to signify the content within is classified, open to only a few" (61).

More recently, some studies have begun to reconceptualize world literature from the Global South by showing how "lateral" South-South relations shape the globalized literary world. In the volume *Convivial Worlds: Writing Relation from Africa*, Tina Steiner (2021) has explored "the figurative and literal space of Oceanic Southern and Eastern Africa as a fluid interregional arena of relation" (152) and highlighted "the patterns of human connectedness that [...] translocal convivial practices weave" (148). The literary works of the "Indian Ocean African region" (151) she analyses in her study are thus both products of long-standing South-South relations and producers of convivial imaginaries that include, but are not predicated by, North-South relations:

> The narratives thus draw on a lateral imaginary of a history of South-South circulation of goods, people and ideas between Africa, South Asia and the Arabian peninsula which cannot be subsumed under the colony-metropole axis, even though imperial North-South conquest and postcolonial migratory patterns to the North are prominent in the narratives as well. (151)

Focussing on a different, yet related facet of literary relation and connectivity, Ngũgĩ (2012) has stressed the fact that postcolonial migrant writers, those who cross "languages, nations, countries and continents" (54), also contribute to create an understanding of world literature "on the move". Several chapters of this volume undertake such travels across languages, continents and cultures to highlight world literary movements, examine South-South connections and scrutinize translocal modes of literary creativity. The present volume emphasizes the multiple and often contradictory processes that shape an entangled, global literary world. It aims to describe global literary production and reception from multiple and diverse points of view instead of imposing a unifying set of assumptions.

Thus, suggesting a second shift in critical scrutiny, this collection approaches and rethinks the idea of world literature along the notion of "entanglements": as a field of variously criss-crossing relations of literary activity such as writing, reading, publishing, promoting, performing, or debating literature. At first glance, this framework may seem less critically appealing than the concept of an uneven world clearly structured along capitalist and postcolonial formations. As Siri Hustvedt (2016) has observed in a different context, "clean, hard boundaries have a nice logical feeling and entangled interactions suggest something messier, perhaps even something less rational" (169). Such critical aversion to the messy and seemingly irrational may well explain why many interventions in the world literature debate still seek to establish a model with clear logical criteria by which critical judgement is enabled. Yet our goal is not a normative guideline but a tool that helps us perceive the intricacies of global literary interactions. We may well need concepts that, rather than clinging to hard boundaries, rely on the relational as well as on the rational. The focus on "entanglements" allows this volume to take into account a myriad of relationships beyond the confines of literary canons, cultural containers or national borders, without the need to reduce their complexity immediately to structures that can be described from a global, universalizing perspective. Instead, it enables us to look at how world literature can be (re-)envisioned from a range of Global South perspectives and how these literatures read and (re-) write the world through new transnational, transregional and transcultural imaginaries. With its focus on "entanglements", this volume thus seeks to promote a new conceptual framework and a shift in our methodologies for studying multilateral relationships in, around, and from the Global South.

Reading South-South Relations

In order to broaden our understanding of the multipolar entanglements that shape our globalized world, the following chapters discuss individual case studies that highlight literary relationships and practices across the Global South as well as new fictional and theoretical imaginaries of world literature.

The volume opens with an investigation of the current critical deadlock between competing calls for expanding or restricting the imaginary libraries of world literature. Maren Scheurer's chapter, "Survival of the Fittest, or, What Is a Classic? J. M. Coetzee, Aesthetic Darwinism and World Literature", uses Jorge Luis Borges's and J. M. Coetzee's critical imaging of (in)finite libraries as a starting point to trace the anxieties and hopes with which critics invest the notion of world literature. In his lecture "What Is a Classic?", Coetzee reflects on his own youthful response to the classics and suggests that these prove themselves through survival. He thus offers a potential counterpoint to other versions of aesthetic Darwinism that pervade the debates on world literature from Erich Auerbach and René Étiemble to Pascale Casanova and Franco Moretti. With Coetzee's re-examination of the classic, Scheurer argues that, instead of employing the notion of "survival" as another bulwark against the intrusion of non-European texts into the canon, it can be read as a challenge to the critical environment which produces it—by highlighting that the supposedly timeless classic is itself entangled in a field of literary interactions and re-envisionings. Scheurer's chapter points the way toward a different understanding of world literature, in which voices from the Global South are equal partners in a set of relations rather than rare objects of survival.

Delphine Munos's chapter, "'Tilting Camus Sideways': Intertextual Entanglements between Albert Camus's *L'Étranger* and Kamel Daoud's *Meursault, contre-enquête*", continues this critical investigation of the classic from a postcolonial perspective. Munos reads Kamel Daoud's response to Albert Camus's "classic" *L'Étranger* as much more than an example of "writing back". She argues that, in isolation, neither traditional world literary nor postcolonial approaches can do justice to the conversation between the two texts and follows Stefan Helgesson's (2014) plea for combining the two methodologies. Through this combination, the chapter first sheds new light on the political and historical entanglements that have shaped the conception and reception of *L'Étranger* in its colonial and postcolonial contexts, which establishes Camus's novel as much more grounded in Algeria than traditional postcolonial critiques want to admit. In a second step, the chapter examines how the "web of intertextual entanglements" (62) between Camus and Daoud re-grounds Camus in contemporary Algeria, highlights complexities of the present moment that cannot be captured by postcolonial readings alone, and instead gestures towards a continual production of meaning in the intertextual relation.

With the concept of "literatures without a fixed abode", the subsequent chapter offers a different concept for pursuing these continually moving relations of meaning. Ottmar Ette's "Transareal Cities and the Literatures Without a Fixed Abode in Assia Djebar, Emine Sevgi Özdamar and Cécile Wajsbrot" uses the transareal city space as a starting point for its reading of Djebar's *Les Nuits de Strasbourg*,

Özdamar's *Istanbul-Berlin Trilogy*, and Wajsbrot's *L'Île aux musées*. As early as in the Epic of Gilgamesh, the city is presented as a multiply traversed space that is linked, through travel, to countless regions across the globe. In the three novels, Berlin, Istanbul, and Strasbourg are similarly highlighted as vital sites of exchange in which cultural and literary imageries of the Global North and the Global South interact within a vectorial understanding of urbanity. These spaces emerge from entanglements in which European and Global South literatures are themselves de- and relocated, and in this vein, the chapter offers a re-conceptualization of world literature as "literatures of the world" in order to do justice to the "transareal" and "polylogical" movements of writers and their works across the globe. It highlights the importance of literatures without a fixed abode in our current literary practices, theories, and methodologies, and urges us to consider literary expressions as phenomena that are global, interconnected, and continually in motion.

Mobility remains a focus in Jan Rupp's chapter, "Heterodox Maps of World Literature and South-to-South Dialogue in Caribbean Writing". Rupp investigates the intertwined "routes and roots" in the island imaginary of the Caribbean, which is shaped both by multiple paths of forced and voluntary migrations and by insularity, belonging to the island and to the homelands. The chapter investigates these multiple coordinates of the island imaginary in an effort to bring together a focus on roots with circulatory models of world literature and develop alternative imaginaries to the static North/South model through travel, translation, and world-making. With these goals in mind, Rupp discusses Sam Selvon's *An Island Is a World* as a portrait of Trinidad that looks to the metropolis but also envisions "alternative pathways and centres" through the Indian community. This reading is paralleled with a discussion of Kei Miller and Marlon James's participation in the Jaipur Literature Festival, seeing them as a new generation of transcultural Caribbean writers who exemplify the South-South dialogue in a wider context of Indo-Caribbean writing. In this way, Rupp also highlights the importance of literary practices beyond the "written book" in the constitution of an entangled, global literary space, such as literary readings, festivals, and joint media appearances.

The potential of world literature beyond medial fixtures is also explored in the following chapter, Ana Sobral's and Eduardo Jorge de Oliveira's "Movements, Diasporas, Entanglements: Traces of the Brazil-Angola Slave Trade in Contemporary Voices". For a 2018 cultural event at Zurich's Cabaret Voltaire, Sobral and Oliveira invited the Brazilian poet Ricardo Aleixo and the Angolan rap artist Diamondogg to discuss and perform their work. Sobral's and Oliveira's reading of these texts and their exchanges is thus based on a staged South-South encounter, which highlights and connects contemporary practices in orature from the Global South. They argue that the voice is not only a source of formal organization but also a vehicle to transport the entangled history of the Black Atlantic. Aleixo and Diamondogg vocalize the histories of slavery, trauma and resistance, bringing the past into the present and highlighting the embodied voice as an important counterforce to the Eurocentric priority of written text. The chapter thus reveals historical routes that may enable further enquiry of literary South-South dialogues in the future.

While tracing a similar concern with subaltern voices articulating decolonizing strategies in the postcolonial world, Maggie Bowers, in her chapter "Alternative Modernities, Magical Realism and World Literatures of the Global South", returns us to two canonical Global South texts, Gabriel García Márquez's *One Hundred Years of Solitude* and Ngũgĩ wa Thiong'o's *Wizard of the Crow*. Bowers reads both novels in the tradition of magical realism, a concept which, for her, shares crucial contradictions with the concept of world literature: while both are associated with and often located primarily in the Global South, they have been shaped by critics from the Global North and invested with their projections of Otherness and the subaltern. The chapter explores the two novels as related projects in articulating their own positions to modernity. Following Dilip Parameshwar Gaonkar's (2001) concept of "alternative modernities", Bowers unfolds the messy entanglements that shape their visions of modernity to reveal complex formations that cannot be disentangled into western influences and indigenous traditions or science and magic. She sees them instead as productively merging political and economic pressures, resistance, and creativity. In tracing the indirect South-South dialogue between García Márquez's and Ngũgĩ's novels, the chapter highlights the challenges and creative transformations introduced to notions of "modernity", "world literature", and "magical realism" from the Global South.

A similar re-envisioning of an aesthetics that has traditionally been firmly centred in the Global North—surrealism—is presented in Andrea Gremels's chapter "Re-Envisioning Surrealism from Argentina and Mexico: Julio Cortázar's *Teoría del túnel* and Octavio Paz's *El arco y la lira*". Gremels reads Cortázar's and Paz's poetological essays in opposition to concepts of world literature in which the peripheries react to aesthetic innovations in the centre, such as Casanova's (2004) *The World Republic of Letters*. Surrealism, in particular, is frequently understood as a modernist movement located firmly in Paris and in the hands of André Breton. Countering this understanding, Gremels shows that surrealism evolved within polycentric entanglements of contestation and transformation in Latin America. For Cortázar and Paz, surrealism emerges as an all-embracing world view or as "cosmovision"—a tool in their search for a multiple modernity that moves beyond the western focus on utilitarian reason. However, far from simply appropriating surrealism, their reconceptualization of its aesthetics into an ahistorical ethics of otherness and a voice of nonconformity re-envisions surrealism itself as world literature. As Gremels argues, Cortázar's and Paz's interventions challenge the notion of a literary norm and a world order fixed to a "centre" and instead celebrate the "eccentric" view of a surrealist perspective.

Lucy Gasser also discusses a collaborative effort at re-conceptualizing "world", "world literature", and "World Literature Studies" from the Global South in her chapter "What's in a World? Rerouting World Literature with *Lotus* and the Afro-Asian Writers' Association". Gasser finds impulses for methodological innovation and a critical practice of South-South relations in the exchanges of the Afro-Asian

Writers' Association recorded in its quarterly journal *Lotus*, where writers from the so-called "Third World" re-imagined exactly what kind of world and what kind of world literature they would work towards in discussions that took place beyond the colonial metropolis and western conceptions of literary theory. While some voices reiterate the notion of world literature as a canon of works in which Afro-Asian literature would have to gain recognition, others implicitly articulate and already practice notions of world literature and World Literature Studies on the basis of South-South relations and cultural exchange. In this way, they move outside European conceptions of literature, beyond negative identities such as "non-colonial" or "non-European", and introduce new notions of worldliness.

The final chapter in the volume, Frank Schulze-Engler's "Bwana Goethe and the Remaking of World Literature: Afrasian Imaginaries in M.G. Vassanji's *The Magic of Saida*", similarly turns to Afrasian imaginaries in order to "remake" world literature. Rejecting stratified models of world literature that rely on centre and periphery to describe literature as a global capitalist system as well as a strict differentiation between postcolonial and world literature, which locks postcolonial literatures forever in their victimological relation to the west, Schulze-Engler relies on a "globalectical reading" of world literature (Ngũgĩ 2012) that renounces hierarchical thought and instead focuses on interactions, mutual impact, shared ideas, and self-reflection. Highlighting the transregional connections between Africa and Asia, the chapter approaches Vassanji's novel *The Magic of Saida* as a case in point, which depicts "entangled Afrasian histories" based on centuries of mutual exchange, identities shaped in this interplay and cutting across stable definitions of "African", "Asian", and "Arab". In this way, the literary text offers a self-reflexivity that recognizes its own implicatedness, criticizes unconditional solidarities and instead advocates a multipolar imagination that is capable of envisioning such multiple entanglements. To do justice to the dynamics of an increasingly decentred and multipolar world, Schulze-Engler argues, literary scholarship must adopt this imagination and "follow literature onto the contested and serrated terrain where the social imaginaries of a globalized world are produced, negotiated, and transformed" (295).

Although the volume introduces crucial shifts in world literary debates towards acknowledging the importance and productivity of South-South relations and their complex, wide-ranging entanglements, we consider this intervention to be a starting point. In order to gain a wider, more encompassing understanding of the dynamic exchanges and relations highlighted here, it will be necessary to extend, challenge and transform these reflections by bringing into play further academic disciplines, geographical locations and literary examples. In this regard, the volume does not attempt to offer a final word on an ever-growing world literature debate. Instead, it actively seeks to extend debates and invite viewpoints that envision world literature from the Global South and beyond towards ever wider and richer entanglements.

Bibliography

Achenbach, Ruth, Jan Beek, John Njenga Karugia, Rirhandu Mageza-Barthel, and Frank Schulze-Engler, eds. 2020. *Afrasian Transformations: Transregional Perspectives on Development Cooperation, Social Mobility and Cultural Change.* Leiden: Brill.

Bessière, Jean, and Gerald Gillespie, eds. 2015. *Contextualizing World Literature.* New York: Peter Lang.

Bucheli, Roman. 2021. "Literaturnobelpreis: Die krachende Verabschiedung in die Bedeutungslosigkeit". [The Nobel Prize in Literature: The Thunderous Leave-Taking into Insignificance]. *Neue Zürcher Zeitung*, 7 October. https://www.nzz.ch/feuilleton/literaturnobelpreis-fuer-abdulrazak-gurnah-autor-ohne-leser-ld.1649325.

Casanova, Pascale. 2004. *The World Republic of Letters.* Translated by M.B. DeBevoise (Original: *La République mondiale des Lettres*, 1999). Cambridge, MA: Harvard University Press.

Damrosch, David. 2003. *What Is World Literature?* Princeton, NJ: Princeton University Press.

Damrosch, David, ed. 2014. *World Literature in Theory*. Malden, MA: John Wiley & Sons.

Etherington, Ben, and Jarad Zimbler. 2018. "Introduction." *The Cambridge Companion to World Literature*, edited by Ben Etherington and Jarad Zimbler, 1–19. Cambridge: Cambridge University Press.

Ette, Ottmar. *TransArea: A Literary History of Globalization. TransArea.* Berlin and Boston, MA: De Gruyter, 2016.

Gaonkar, Dilip Parameshwar. 2001. *Alternative Modernities*. Durham, NC: Duke University Press.

Glissant, Édouard. 2020. *Introduction to a Poetics of Diversity*. Translated by Celia Britton (Original: *Introduction à une poétique du divers*). Liverpool: Liverpool University Press.

Glissant, Édouard. 1997. *Poetics of Relation.* Translated by Betsy Wing (Original: *Poétique de la relation*, 1990). Ann Arbor, MI: Michigan University Press.

Helgesson, Stefan. 2014. "Postcolonialism and World Literature." *Interventions* 16 (4): 483–500.

Hiro, Dilip. 2010. *After Empire: The Birth of a Multipolar World*. New York: Nations Books.

Hustvedt, Siri. 2017. *A Woman Looking at Men Looking at Women: Essays on Art, Sex, and the Mind*. London: Sceptre.

Klengel, Susanne, and Alexandra Ortiz Wallner. 2016: "A New Politics and Poetics of Thinking Latin America/India. SUR/SOUTH and a Different Orientalism". *SUR/SOUTH: Poetics and Politics of Thinking Latin-America–India*, edited by Susanne Klengel and Alexandra Ortiz Wallner, 7–26. Madrid and Frankfurt: Iberoamericana and Vervuert.

Kloß, Sinah. 2017. "The Global South as Subversive Practice: Challenges and Potentials of a Heuristic Concept". *The Global South* 11 (2): 1–17. https://doi.org/10.2979/globalsouth.

Lamping, Dieter, and Galin Tihanov, eds. 2019. *Vergleichende Weltliteraturen/Comparative World Literatures: DFG-Symposium 2018*. Berlin: J. B. Metzler.

Maurya, Vibha. 2016. "Cruces Revolucionarios: La recepción de la poesía de Pablo Neruda en India." *Sur/South: Poetics and Politics of Thinking Latin America / India*, edited by Susanne Klengel and Alexandra Ortiz Wallner, 39–57. Madrid and Frankfurt: Iberoamericana und Vervuert.

Moretti, Franco. 2000. "Conjectures on World Literature." *New Left Review* 1: 54–68.

Müller, Gesine, and Mariano Siskind, eds. 2019. *World Literature, Cosmopolitanism, Globality: Beyond, Against, Post, Otherwise.* Berlin and Boston, MA: De Gruyter.

Müller, Gesine, Jorge J. Locane, and Benjamin Loy, ed. 2018. *Re-Mapping World Literature: Writing, Book Markets and Epistemologies between Latin America and the Global South.* Berlin and Boston, MA: De Gruyter.

Ngũgĩ wa Thiong'o. [1973] 1981. "The Links That Bind Us." *Writers in Politics: Essays*, by Ngũgĩ wa Thiong'o, 101–06. London: Heinemann.

Ngũgĩ wa Thiong'o. 2012. *Globalectics.* New York: Columbia University Press.

Nickels, Joel. 2018. *World Literature and the Geographies of Resistance.* Cambridge: Cambridge University Press.

Nobel Prize Outreach 2021. "The Nobel Prize in Literature 2021." NobelPrize.org. Accessed 25 October, 2021. https://www.nobelprize.org/prizes/literature/2021/summary/

Pollatschek, Nele. 2021. "Ist der gut?" [Is he Good?]. *Süddeutsche Zeitung* 237, 13 October: 9.

Prendergast, Christopher, ed. 2004. *Debating World Literature.* London: Verso.

Said, Edward. 1993. *Culture and Imperialism.* New York: Knopf.

Steiner, Tina. 2021. *Convivial Worlds: Writing Relation from Africa.* Milton Park, Abingdon and New York: Routledge.

Sturm-Trigonakis, Elke, ed. 2020. *World Literature and the Postcolonial: Narratives of (Neo) Colonialization in a Globalized World.* Berlin: J. B. Metzler.

Thomson, Mads Rosendahl. 2009. *Mapping World Literature: International Canonization and Transnational Literatures.* London: Continuum.

wa Ngugi, Mukoma. 2012. "Rethinking the Global South." *Journal of Contemporary Thought* 35: 5–10.

Warwick Research Collective. 2015. *Combined and Uneven Development Towards a New Theory of World-Literature.* Liverpool: Liverpool University Press.

West-Pavlov, Russell. 2018. "Toward the Global South: Concept or Chimera, Paradigm or Panacea?" *The Global South and Literature,* edited by Russell West-Pavlov, 1–20. Cambridge: Cambridge University Press.

Yoon, Duncan M. 2015. "'Our Forces Have Redoubled': World Literature, Postcolonialism, and the Afro-Asian Writers' Bureau." *The Cambridge Journal of Postcolonial Literary Inquiry* 2 (2): 233–52.

Young, Robert J.C. 2011. "World Literature and Postcolonialism." *The Routledge Companion to World Literature,* edited by Theo D'haen, David Damrosch, and Djelal Kadir, 213–22. New York: Routledge.

Survival of the Fittest, or, What Is a Classic? J.M. Coetzee, Aesthetic Darwinism and World Literature

Maren Scheurer

Introduction: The Library of World Literature

In his famous story "La biblioteca de Babel" ("The Library of Babel"), Jorge Luis Borges (1998) describes a library-universe which "is composed of an indefinite and perhaps infinite number of hexagonal galleries" (112)[1] and whose "bookshelves contain [. . .] all that is able to be expressed, in every language" (115).[2] When the inhabitants of the library first come to an understanding of the dimensions of their universe, they feel "unbounded joy", for they believe themselves to be in possession of "an intact and secret treasure" (115).[3] However, as soon as they realize that this treasure is too vast and scattered for them to ever be mastered, "the unbridled hopefulness" is succeeded by depression and social upheaval: some librarians ravage the shelves in an attempt to eliminate the "worthless books" (116), while others simply commit suicide.[4]

J.M. Coetzee's aging novelist Elizabeth Costello claims to suffer from a different vision of the library: "Not a library in which all

1 Original: "El universo (que otros llaman la Biblioteca) se compone de un número indefinido, y tal vez infinito, de galerías hexagonales" (Borges 1961, 85).

2 Original: "De esas premisas incontrovertibles dedujo [. . .] que sus anaqueles registran [. . .] todo lo que es dable expresar: en todos los idiomas" (Borges 1961, 89).

3 Original: "Cuando se proclamó que la Biblioteca abarcaba todos los libros, la primera impresión fue de extravagante felicidad. Todos los hombres se sintieron señores de un tesoro intacto y secreto" (Borges 1961, 90).

4 Original: "A la desaforada esperanza, sucedió, como es natural, una depresión excesiva. [. . .] Otros, inversamente, creyeron que lo primordial era eliminar las obras inútiles" (Borges 1961, 91).

conceivable books, past, present and future, coexist but a library from which books that were really conceived, written and published are absent, absent even from the memory of the librarians" (Coetzee 2004, 17–18). Costello knows that any library, even if it is as big as the British Library or the Library of Congress, will eventually have to get rid of some volumes: "As the demand for space grows, the ugly and unread and unwanted will be carted off to some facility or other and tossed into a furnace, and all trace of them will be liquidated from the master catalogue. After which it will be as if they had never existed" (17). Costello apparently doubts the survival of the "unfit", the "ugly and unread and unwanted". She describes a library in which an invisible struggle for existence, linked to the "demand for space", determines the content of the catalogue. Costello's musings do not represent the first time this concern with aesthetic survival has appeared in Coetzee's work. In his 1991 lecture "What Is a Classic?", he comes up with a hesitant, yet simple definition: "the classic is what survives" (Coetzee 2002, 19). In positing that the classic proves itself through its persistence in an environment in which only the fittest survive, Coetzee conceives of the distribution and reception of art in broadly Darwinian terms.

Coetzee's lecture, as well as its precursor, T.S. Eliot's 1944 lecture of the same title, have previously been linked to the debates surrounding world literature by Robert J.C. Young (2011, 214) and by Ankhi Mukherjee (2010, 1035). For better or for worse, the notion of the classic remains important to many contemporary understandings of world literature. A limited selection of classics and masterpieces (Damrosch 2003, 15) is still frequently opposed to a quantitative model of world literature which would comprise the sum of all the world's literatures. The virtual infinity of this model may cause a considerable degree of anxiety, comparable to Borges's *biblioteca*: The impossibility of charting this vast terrain and the desire for guidance has led to many efforts to limit the critical playing field by seeking the "classics" of world literature (Shivani 2012, 54), identifiable through their translatability, transnationality, universality, or aesthetic value. However, such a canon brings with it a different problem, envisioned by Elizabeth Costello: that its libraries will not hold enough, that they discard too much, and for the wrong reasons.

It is no accident that these visions of (in-)finite libraries are connected to visions of world literature. B. Venkat Mani (2017), in his book *Recoding World Literature*, which incidentally also begins with a reference to Borges, argues that libraries "are not mere storehouses of information":

> They are places where texts from many places around the world can be gathered, catalogued, and known, and as such they present themselves as images of the world. [...] Books and libraries operate on the probability of imagining the world, as a whole or in parts. They offer the possibility of encoding the universe and the world—including divisions, fragmentations, differentiations—making the world and the universe legible, interpretable, decodable, and re-codable. As much as literature itself encodes the world with aural and verbal signs and promotes the pursuance of mimesis and representation—aesthetic, epistemic, political—libraries present themselves as prolific, substantial, and expansive (if not entirely all-encompassing) *texts* that rely on the collective fiction of knowledge about the world. (11; original emphasis)

As such, the visions of the world that libraries present need to be managed. Libraries are not "a neutral space" but deeply enmeshed in politics and "historical contingencies" (16). Renegotiating the library of world literature thus also means renegotiating the vision of the world it presents, but this renegotiation itself cannot be disassociated from the world in which it is attempted. No wonder that the conception of such a library produces methodological and political concerns, whether it is limited to the classics of world literature or whether a wider purview is aimed for, a catalogue of the literatures of the world.

In what follows, I will not reopen the debate of *whether* we actually need the classic but ask, instead, *why* we continue to return to it. The question is particularly pressing considering the embattled position of Global South literatures within the realms of world literature and the classic. It is perhaps no accident that Borges and Coetzee, both modern "classics" writing from Argentina and South Africa and Australia, respectively, have formulated related visions of nightmarish libraries as an expression of that embattlement. In my inquiry of the critical debates around world literature, I will take my cues from Coetzee's intuitions: Costello's "library anxiety" and the survival of the classic. In a first step, I examine the critic's fear of the vast library of world literature, with close readings of Erich Auerbach's and René Étiemble's foundational contributions to the debate. These readings suggest that, faced with enormous responsibilities and impossible tasks, critics encounter their own limitations in their confrontation with world literature. The survival metaphor drives my second line of inquiry which identifies the broad outlines of what I call "Aesthetic Darwinism" in several key texts on world literature. Franco Moretti, in particular, draws up a model of the literary world which relies heavily on a Darwinian imaginary; a technique which relieves him, I argue, of the anxiety that haunts other critics, albeit with problematic consequences. As a final step, I will return to the motif of aesthetic survival in Coetzee's lecture. By ultimately reversing the Darwinian logic, Coetzee insists on the agency and responsibility of the critical environment in the formation of the classic, reminding us that we cannot—and perhaps should not—get rid of anxiety and uncertainty as long as we roam the libraries of (world) literature.

Library Anxiety: World Literature and Comparative Literature

Although a huge number of recent publications on world literature are enthusiastic, even celebratory in tone, the Borgesian anxiety lingers on. A significant number of texts trying to chart the world's literary production feature passages which betray doubt, anxiety, helplessness, or concern. David Damrosch (2003), for example, notes that 19th-century "devotees of the classics were distressed" and contemporary readers "have felt a comparable alarm" as their canons opened to an ever-wider range of literary works (16). In a similar vein, Ngũgĩ wa Thiong'o (2012) observes that,

> confronted with [... the] vastness [of world literature], it is easy for organizers of literary knowledge to stop in fright and stay within a national boundary, taking comfort in the certainty of the structures already tried and passed on as tradition. (55–56)

For Angelika Corbineau-Hoffmann (2013), the ever-growing corpus of all literatures with its "frightening dimensions" (24)[5] in a continually expanding world presents the critic with a "Herculean task" (23),[6] and although she is wary of the Eurocentric tradition of Comparative Literature, taking refuge in a canon which sets up qualitative boundaries to world literature sounds increasingly like the safer option. The agreement over a foundation of worthwhile texts is, she argues, a precondition for communication among readers; in the widening of the terrain envisioned by quantitative perspectives on world literature, she fears that "every orientation is lost. Instead of a literary world map all we get is the indecipherable sketch of a labyrinth of texts, in which readers roam about helplessly" (26).[7] We are, in other words, back in Borges's library.

To get a better sense of where that anxiety is coming from, I examine two "classic" texts from Comparative Literature, a discipline which, with the rise of world literature, has often feared for its own survival (Damrosch and Spivak 2011, 456; Warwick Research Collective 2015, 1). I will begin with Auerbach's 1952 essay "Philologie der Weltliteratur" ("Philology and *Weltliteratur*")—arguably one of the first and most influential post-war engagements with world literature in comparative studies. As a companion piece expressing surprisingly similar anxieties, I will then turn to Étiemble's 1974 essay "Faut-il réviser la notion de *Weltliteratur*?" ("Should We Rethink the Notion of World Literature?"), one of the first and most forceful proposals for a quantitative approach to world literature.

---

5 Original: "Doch auch diese [die 'schöne' Literatur] nimmt mit fortschreitender Produktion beängstigende Dimensionen an" (Corbineau-Hoffmann 2013, 24). All translations from this text are mine.

6 Original: "Ein solches Textkorpus zu erfassen wäre nämlich eine Herkulesarbeit" (Corbineau-Hoffmann 2013, 23).

7 Original: "'Weltliteratur' [. . .] erweitert aber deren Terrain derart, dass jede Orientierung verloren geht. Statt einer literarischen Weltkarte besitzen wir nur die nicht zu entziffernde Skizze eines Labyrinths von Texten, in dem der Leser hilflos herumirrt" (Corbineau-Hoffmann 2013, 26).

Auerbach's essay is characterized by a sense of urgency. Fearing that the diversity of the world's languages and cultures will soon be eroded by European-American or Soviet-Russian standardization, Auerbach (1969) urges us to take stock of our literary heritage:

> Should mankind succeed in withstanding the shock of so mighty and rapid a process of concentration—for which the spiritual preparation has been poor—then man will have to accustom himself to existence in a standardized world, to a single literary culture, only a few literary languages, and perhaps even a single literary language. And herewith the notion of *Weltliteratur* would be at once realized and destroyed. (3)[8]

Goethe's vision of world literature—less a canon of texts than a process in which different literary traditions come together and enter a world-wide dialogue with each other—would lose its dialogicity and multiplicity in the very unification of the literary world. Auerbach's vocabulary indicates his distress: The "*fateful* coalescence of cultures for those people who are in the midst of the *terminal* phase of fruitful multiplicity" is "*inevitable*", and measures need to be taken so that "the full range of the spiritual movements of the last thousand years will not *atrophy* within them" (7; emphasis added).[9] If anything is to happen to the Borgesian library in Auerbach's vision of globalization,

8 Original: "Sollte es der Menschheit gelingen, sich durch die Erschütterungen hindurchzuretten, die ein so gewaltiger, so reißend schneller und innerlich so schlecht vorbereiteter Konzentrationsprozeß mit sich bringt, so wird man sich an den Gedanken gewöhnen müssen, daß auf einer einheitlich organisierten Erde nur eine einzige literarische Kultur, ja selbst in vergleichsweise kurzer Zeit nur wenige literarische Sprachen, bald vielleicht nur eine, als lebend übrigbleiben. Und damit wäre der Gedanke der Weltliteratur zugleich verwirklicht und zerstört" (Auerbach 1952, 39).

9 Original: "Die hier vertretene Vorstellung von Weltliteratur [. . .] nimmt die sich vollziehende Standardisierung der Erdkultur als *unentrinnbar*. Den im *Endstadium* einer fruchtbaren Mannigfaltigkeit begriffenen Völkern will sie das Bewußtsein ihres *schicksalsvollen* Zusammenwachsens präzisieren und erhalten, [. . .] um auf diese Art den Reichtum und die Tiefe der Geistesbewegungen während der letzten Jahrtausende in ihnen nicht *verkümmern* zu lassen" (Auerbach 1952, 42, emphasis added).

it is that the varieties of idioms will get lost—the library will become standardized, will be robbed of its multiplicity.

I won't dwell here on Auerbach's arguably questionable concept of globalization as standardization and turn to a much more puzzling feature of his argument: crucially—and paradoxically—Auerbach's essay is characterized by a double anxiety. At the same time that it warns us against standardization—and hence a loss of the richness and variety of the library of world literature—it is also afraid of the opposite of that standardization, of the very richness the tradition of world literature has already acquired. In the face of the threat of "impoverishment" (5),[10] the literary historian is called upon to preserve our knowledge of the varied traditions that have come upon us, and the task of collecting and making sense of the vast material from literary history must be tackled as long as there are still people out there who can do so. Auerbach believes that to accomplish this task, at least a few critics must "command that material [of *Weltliteratur*]—or at least a major part of it". However, in light of the "superabundance of materials, of methods and of points of view", this has already become "virtually impossible":

> We possess literatures ranging over six thousand years, from all parts of the world, in perhaps fifty literary languages. Many cultures known to us today were unknown a hundred years ago; many of the ones already known to us in the past were known only partially. (8)[11]

10 Original: "Verarmung" (Auerbach 1952, 41).

11 Original: "Damit die Aufgabe der Durchdringung und Gestaltung erfüllt wird, muß es wenigstens noch einige geben, die das Gesamte der Weltliteratur oder doch wenigstens große Teile derselben aus eigener Erfahrung und Forschung beherrschen. Das aber ist, wegen der Überfülle des Materials, der Methoden und der Anschauungsweisen beinahe unmöglich geworden. Wir besitzen Material aus sechs Jahrtausenden, aus allen Teilen der Erde, in vielleicht fünfzig Literatursprachen. Viele der Kulturen, von denen wir jetzt Kenntnis haben, waren vor hundert Jahren noch unentdeckt, von anderen kannte man nur einen Bruchteil der heute vorliegenden Zeugnisse" (Auerbach 1952, 43).

Thus, Auerbach worries that philologists may no longer be equipped to synthesize their knowledge of the world's literatures: "A single lifetime seems too short to create even the preliminaries" (11).[12] Implied in this avowal of impotence are numerous related issues of philological expertise: historical knowledge and understanding, linguistic competence, theoretical qualification, as well as a wide and thorough reading practice—all of which have become more difficult with the growing number of literary resources. Although Auerbach spends the rest of his essay sketching alternative methodologies, the underlying dispiriting insight remains: the sheer bulk of available literature can no longer be managed by the traditional philologist, who must look for different means of managing and justifying his or her work. Auerbach calls for "synthesis" under a specific "point of departure" rather than "encylopedic collecting" (12–14);[13] for him, at least, the solution to the anxiety cannot be a mere chart of the vast but shrinking library.

At least since the "canon wars" (Bachmann-Medick 2001, 363), another anxiety has been added to the project of world literature: if it sticks comfortably to the safety of the established canon, it is prone to exclude the writing of women, of minorities, and of the Global South. Corbineau-Hoffmann (2013) sees older conceptions of world literature "under the suspicion" of considering only a fraction of the world's cultures (28)[14] and admits that the canon needs to be expanded. But the possibility of an infinite number of such expansions

---

12 Original: "Ein Leben scheint zu kurz, um auch nur die Vorbedingungen dafür zu schaffen" (Auerbach 1952, 45).

13 Original: "Wir sind also auf das Individuum zurückverwiesen: wie kann es zur Synthese gelangen? Jedenfalls nicht, so scheint mir, auf dem Wege des enzyklopädischen Sammelns. [...] [F]ür die Durchführung einer großen synthetischen Absicht ist zunächst ein Ansatz zu finden" (Auerbach 1952, 46-47).

14 Original: "Verdächtigt, nur einen Ausschnitt der Kultur zu berücksichtigen, nämlich die aus Europa stammende Kultur des weißen Mannes, erfuhr der traditionelle Begriff von Weltliteratur eine entschiedene Erweiterung" (Corbineau-Hoffmann 2013, 28).

once again raises the spectre of the quantitative version of world literature in which "the demarcation of boundaries becomes impossible" (28).[15]

This quantitative vision is usually associated with René Étiemble's 1974 intervention, "Faut-il réviser la notion de *Weltliteratur*?" Étiemble was one of the earliest critics of Comparative Literature's focus on European literature, and his essay is a forceful testament to that critique. Nevertheless, it is striking that Étiemble's plea ends with the same general impression with which Auerbach's began:

> We are at one and the same time filled with information and overwhelmed by its excess. To the point even that at precisely the moment at which world literature finally becomes possible it becomes at the same time almost impossible. Of course, I hope that everyone of us feels under obligation to the impossible. (Étiemble 2014, 95)[16]

As we will see, Étiemble criticizes the limitations imposed on world literature, but, like Auerbach, he is also worried about over-expansion. He notes that "this *Weltliteratur*", by which he means a "bourgeois" notion of world literature as the most valued literature of one's own cultural realm,

> has illiberally participated in the denigration or even the systematic destruction of the African, Indian, Amerindian, Madagascan, Indonesian, Vietnamese and other literatures [. . .]. The European priests, soldiers, and merchants have in effect replaced Goethe's

15 Original: "Etwas anderes wäre es nur, Kanonbildung als solche für fragwürdig zu halten mit der konkreten Folge, im Spektrum der möglichen Lektüren überhaupt keine Grenzziehungen mehr vornehmen zu können" (Corbineau-Hoffmann 2013, 28).

16 Original: "Nous sommes à la fois comblés d'informations, et débordés par l'excès des informations. De sorte qu'au moment précis où la *Weltliteratur* devient enfin possible, elle devient du même coup quasiment impossible. A l'impossible, il est vrai, chacun de nous, je l'espère, se sent tenu" (Étiemble 1974, 32).

> generous conception with one in which literature is divided between that of the masters and that of the slaves. (86–87)[17]

Étiemble's well-known resolution to this destructive tendency within world literature is its revision: "Let us proclaim that literature from now on can only mean the totality of all literatures, whether alive or dead, of which there remain written, or even only oral, traces, without further discrimination as to language, politics or religion" (88).[18] So we might conclude that Étiemble is rather in favour of the total library, and his claim, his "obligation to the impossible", stands as a bold move in the face of the anxieties this total library produces.

Nevertheless, Étiemble openly admits to suffering from these very same anxieties:

> I am immediately seized by a kind of panic terror, which reminds me of the proverb "grasp all, lose all." What would such theoretical openness of spirit to all literatures, whether present or past, bring us given that any human mind, however capacious we may imagine it, is limited by the average length of our lives? (88)

He tries to appease his worries with the acknowledgement that even the complete knowledge of one national literature would be impossible for a single individual and that everyone "can and hence must construct his own personal library of world literature" (88).[19] Is the

17 Original: "D'autre part, cette *Weltliteratur* qui fut peut-être un produit de la conscience bourgeoise à l'ère du libre-échangisme, comment oublierais-je qu'en effet elle prit aisément son parti de l'abaissement ou de la destruction systématique des littératures africaines, indiennes, amérindiennes, malgache, indonésienne, viêtnamienne et autres. [. . .] A une conception généreuse, celle de Goethe, les prêtres, les soudards, les marchands européens ont substitué une situation de fait où la littérature se scindait entre littératures de maîtres et littératures d'esclaves" (Étiemble 1974, 14–15).

18 Original: "proclamons que la littérature ne peut être désormais que l'ensemble de toutes les littératures, vivantes ou mortes, dont nous avons gardé des traces écrites, ou seulement orales, et ce, sans discrimination langagière, politique ou religieuse" (Étiemble 1974, 18).

19 Original: "Remplaçant ainsi la *Weltliteratur* du [. . .] la littérature tout court, sitôt que j'en prends conscience, m'impose hélas une façon de terreur panique, que renforce en moi le proverbe *qui trop embrasse mal étreint.* De quel profit cette ouverture théorique de l'esprit à toutes les littératures,

problem then solved by a personal approach, an individually constructed library? Apparently not, for the essay goes on to scour world literature reading lists produced in France and Germany in the 20th century and finds them sorely lacking, not just in their attention to non-European literatures but also in their discrimination regarding European literature. Étiemble has nothing but contempt for this Eurocentrism, as becomes obvious when he acknowledges that many of these texts will have to be read in translation:

> In fact, the good use to which each of us will put literature will depend on the progress made in an art usually looked down upon. This also means that whoever wants to really educate himself in literature will have to read Saikaku in translation rather than Péladan in the original, Ilango Idagal in translation rather than Françoise Sagan in the original, Hallaj in translation rather than Géraldy in the original, Kabir in translation rather than Anna de Noailles in the original. (93)[20]

Here, he opposes great voices of Japanese, Tamil, Persian, and Indian literature with—arguably—minor voices in French literature, which yet replaced the former ones in the European canons he studied. An important intervention in favour of the literatures of the Global South—but what becomes slowly obvious here is that Étiemble is not, in fact, arguing for the total library after all; instead, the repeated "rather than" suggests that he wants the library to be revised and restocked. A final thought experiment he invites his readers to join underlines that Étiemble is no less prone to library anxiety than the other critical voices we have heard so far:

---

présentes ou passées, puisque l'esprit humain, si gourmand qu'on le rêve, est borné par la durée moyenne de notre vie? [...] Chacun d'entre nous [...] peut et par conséquent doit se construire sa bibliothèque personnelle de *Weltliteratur*" (Étiemble 1974, 18; original emphasis).

20 Original: "Le bon usage de chacun de nous fera de la littérature dépendra en vérité des progrès d'un art méprisé. C'est dire d'autre part que celui qui veut se former à la littérature devra lire plutôt Saikaku en traduction que Péladan dans le texte, Ilango Adigal en traduction que Françoise Sagan dans le texte, Hallaj en traduction que Géraldy dans le texte, Kabir en traduction qu'Anna de Noailles dans le texte" (Étiemble 1974, 27).

> Indeed, do the sum yourself: give yourself fifty years of life without one day of illness or rest, or altogether 18,262 days. Rigorously taking into account periods of sleep, meals, the obligations and the pleasures of life and of your profession, estimate the time left to you for reading masterpieces with the sole purpose of finding out what precisely is literature. (93)[21]

Presuming that one might be able to master one book a day—with shorter texts compensating for longer ones—Étiemble concludes:

> Now, when measured against the total number of very beautiful books that exist in the world, what are 18,262 titles? Sheer poverty. [. . .] This means that instead of wasting one's time with reading a thousand bad books of which the whole world talks, one will be able to choose from the tens of thousands of great works that are only awaiting our good-will. (93–94)[22]

Clearly, an endless number of texts is not desirable for Étiemble either. A selection or limitation needs to be agreed upon, even if he still asks that in our pursuit of "*knowledge*" about literature "our only limits should be comprehensiveness and truth" (95; original emphasis).[23] A value judgment underlies Étiemble's plea, even as he argues for an expansion of the operating range of the library of world literature, and this value judgment is driven by the "panic terror" that we are not equipped to deal with the wealth of material we are presented with once we leave the narrow confines of the classics of European literature.

---

21 Original: "Faites en effet le calcul que voici: donnez-vous cinquante ans de vie, sans un jour de maladie ou de repos, soit 18 262 jours. Compte rigoureusement tenu du sommeil, des repas, des obligations et des plaisirs de la vie, du métier, estimez le temps qui vous reste pour lire des chefs-d'œuvre dans le seul dessein d'entrevoir ce que c'est au juste que la littérature" (Étiemble 1974, 27–28).

22 Original: "Par rapport au nombre des très beaux livres qui existent, qu'est-ce que 18 262 titres? Une misère. [. . .] Cela signifie qu'au lieu de gaspiller son temps à lire mille mauvais livres dont tout le monde parle, on saura choisir parmi les dizaines de milliers de grandes œuvres qui n'attendent que notre bonne volonté" (Étiemble 1974, 28).

23 Original: "la *connaissance* qu'il convient d'en compiler [. . .]. Là, point d'autres bornes que celles de la plénitude et de la vérité" (Étiemble 1974, 31; original emphasis).

Looking at Auerbach's and Étiemble's difficulties in coming to grips with the challenges of the field, one might, with Damrosch (2011), summarize that the comparatist's anxieties come from the admonition that studying and teaching world literature may be "methodologically naïve, culturally deracinated, philologically compromised, and ideologically suspect" (461). Sticking to a proven set of classics, even if those classics are no longer derived from the European tradition exclusively, is a relief from the multitude of responsibilities the critic would take on if she were to venture into the infinite labyrinths of world literature.

Survival of the Fittest: Aesthetic Darwinism and World Literature

As the previous discussion has shown, however, there is no way around the anxiety: with or without a canon of classics, the critic always treads uncertain ground. Strolling through the stacks of the world's library would be less frightening with a unifying framework at hand, a framework which at the same time avoids the pitfalls of arbitrary reading and the suspicions of elitist canon-building. In this context, it is noteworthy that recent models of world literature have frequently relied on Charles Darwin's evolutionary theory and terminology. Damrosch (2013), for instance, ascribes the persistence and survival of classic works to "their adaptability to new times and even new media" (160). In this light, Damrosch's (2003) definition that world literature "encompass[es] all literary works that circulate beyond their culture of origin" (4) reads like a determination of "reproductive success" via geographical distribution. In *The World Republic of Letters*, Pascale Casanova (2004), who endeavours to study the laws of "a world of rivalry, struggle, and inequality" (4), also relies on what Anis Shivani (2012) calls a "cynical Darwinian dynamic" (59). The most outright employment of Darwinism in critical writings on world literature can be found in Franco Moretti's work. Indeed, Susan Stanford Friedman (2012) claims that Moretti, just like Casanova, draws part of his rhetorics from Social Darwinism (502). Following her critique, I will here revisit Moretti's rhetorics in two representative articles and spell out what I prefer to call Aesthetic Darwinism: the recourse to Darwinian metaphors to describe aesthetic phenomena.

In contrast to many other critics, Moretti seems to be excited rather than frightened by the prospect of studying the entire literary world. Apparently, he has found a way to dodge the problems that haunt traditional literary scholarship. In "Conjectures on World Literature" (2000a), he calls for a revision of conventional methodologies: "the sheer enormity of the task makes it clear that world literature cannot be literature, bigger; what we are already doing, just more of it" (55). Moretti's suggestion for a solution, "distant reading", is linked to a desire to leave behind the narrow canon of the classics (57). With the help of other readers, scanning texts, and digital methods, Moretti extends his work not just to a few limited *chef d'oeuvres* but also to a large number of other, less canonical, even forgotten, works. In other words, he defies Étiemble's 18,262 maximum lifetime titles by redefining what "reading" means. In this way, Moretti intends to "mak[e] visible all the forgotten books that have been lost on the countless dead branches of literary history, [. . .] challeng[ing] the elite culture of the literary field by confronting its well-organized and strongly-defended gated community with the mass culture of excluded books" (Kilian 2016, 9). In this fashion, Moretti also seems to defy Étiemble's normative distinction between "masterpieces" and "bad books", from whatever tradition they might arise.

The example with which he illustrates his claim in "Conjectures", however, is so steeped in a Darwinian logic that it ultimately fails to move beyond a hierarchization of texts. Moretti (2000a) traces a specific "*law of literary evolution*" to explain the rise of the modern novel: "in cultures that belong to the periphery of the literary system [. . .], the modern novel first arises not as an autonomous development but as a compromise between a western formal influence (usually French or English) and local materials" (58; original emphasis). So, the Japanese novel, for example, constitutes itself out of "Japanese social experience" and "the abstract formal patterns of Western novel construction" (58), which suggests that a dominant formal pattern spreads by displacing other formal patterns and all the while adapting to the local environment. Moretti (2003) does indeed assume that form works like DNA, "the repeatable element of literature", and is "likely to play a role in the replication and long-term survival of a literary genre" (142). In tracing this development of the adaptation of the western novel in the "peripheries" of Europe and the Global South, Moretti (2000a) also encounters "a system of *variations*": a wide spectrum of different varieties of literary forms which "struggle for symbolic hegemony" against the pressures of a dominant "Anglo-French core" of culture (64; original emphasis). In Moretti's world, "powerful literatures mak[e] life hard for the others" (65). There is no attempt to hide the fact that this language is borrowed from evolutionary theory: the "struggle for existence" is equally palpable as Darwin's concern with varieties and variability, which pervades *On the Origin of Species*. Indeed, in a later review of his work with evolutionary theory, Moretti (2003) explains: "It is easy to see why evolution is a good model for literary history: it is a theory that explains the extraordinary variety and complexity of existing forms on the basis of a historical process" (123).

In "The Slaughterhouse of Literature" (2000b), Moretti's readily avowed Darwinian outlook[24] is even more pronounced. Observing that the "majority of books disappear forever" (207), Moretti attributes the "slaughter of literature" to readers: "who read novel A (but not B [. . .]) and so keep A 'alive' into the next generation [. . .]. Readers, not professors, make canons" (209), or, in more abstract terms, "the market selects the canon" (210). Moretti even poses that the formal innovations which trigger a reader's selection are found "by chance" (215). A perfect Darwinian model: random variations are subjected to a process of cultural selection, which, generation after generation, determines the survival of those forms which are best

24 Moretti (2003) himself acknowledges the use of evolutionary theory in his book *Modern Epic* and the articles "The Slaughterhouse of Literature" and "Graphs, Maps, Trees" (123).

adapted to the requirements of a market-driven environment. Interestingly, Moretti is very keen on deemphasizing the creative and variable elements of this process, as if he were dealing not with cultural but natural selection, not with a cultural construct, but with natural law. Due to the "rigidity of literary evolution", Moretti argues, for instance, that a writer cannot move beyond the form in which he has learned to write (222). The result is "a culture which is as unyielding as DNA" (222). Leaving aside for a moment the fact that DNA does not provide an individual with an ironclad blueprint, the advantage of this metaphorical outline of cultural evolution is obvious: Moretti constructs a completely determined culture in which aesthetic varieties settle the question of "strength" or "value" in their own struggles on the market and in which new forms are a matter of chance, not of choice or genius. Literary forms no longer need to be evaluated on the tricky and dubious basis of aesthetic judgement but can be considered in terms of their potential for survival, which can be measured in two ways: by determining which texts "continue to be read" and which texts successfully migrate and adapt to other spheres of influence (Prendergast 2005, 49). Such an evolutionarily determined culture can supposedly be studied with scientific methods that promise certainties rather than ever new precarious interpretations.

Critics have already pointed out numerous problems with Moretti's use of biological metaphors. Christopher Prendergast (2005) has identified a tendency towards circularity in Moretti's arguments, a jumping to conclusions without real evidence (50), and inconsistencies in his analogy, such as the different time scales of cultural and biological evolution (57) or the lack of proper "speciation" in the ever-hybrid forms we encounter in culture (58). What sounds like scientific reasoning is, in fact, reasoning by analogy (Huggan 2011, 495). Moretti risks "lapsing into a form of social Darwinism" which, Graham Huggan argues, is "as dangerous in application as it is unfaithful to the evolutionary teachings of Darwin himself" (496). Patrick Kilian has also rightly pointed out that "the evolutionary model fails to depict the hidden power structures in the process of canonmaking by envisioning the cultural selection as exclusively regulated by the economic laws of the literary market" (9). By thus superimposing "the biological on the economic", Moretti is not actually paying tribute to what is lost, as Prendergast (2005) argues; instead, "Moretti wants to explain why it is doomed to being lost", which runs the risk of writing "a version of victors' history" (60–61). And even if, as Wai Chee Dimock (2006) asks, we agree that what we need is "a distributive map, reflecting the circulation and evolution of literary forms"—"a developmental database"—is not "the literary field [...] still incomplete, its kinship network only partly actualized, with many new members still to be added"? Should we look at "comparative morphology" not "as a thinning process, one that leads to a formalizable law" but as "a thickening process, one that keeps a full, cumulative, and not necessarily unified record" (90–91)? I do not want to go any further into these justified objections or point out further contradictions and misunderstandings of Darwin's theory, although there are plenty. Instead, I am intrigued by the metaphorical dynamics thus introduced into the debate. Why does Moretti's evolutionary analogy, despite its obvious shortcomings, remain attractive to scholars? And if the Darwinian models were indeed the "metaphors we live by" (Lakoff and Johnson 2003), what would be the consequences for the critic and for literary history?

As exemplified by Elizabeth Costello's dread of the Darwinian library—another slaughterhouse of literature—the evolutionary metaphor could in itself be frightening; and even if one does not think about the possibility of extinction, the importance of coincidence in Darwin's theory was and still is enough to unsettle his readers. However, as Gillian Beer (2009) has pointed out, Darwin's "plot" has several, quasi-mythological attractions: the "all-inclusiveness of its explanation", "its inherent purposiveness", and its welcoming of "difference, plenitude, [and] multifariousness" (12). Without suggesting a single (and thus too simple) narrative, a Darwinian paradigm allows us to think of literary history as a series of necessary aesthetic and social developments that ultimately serve the progress of literary form. If the market determines the cultural product, then we need not worry about the implications produced by the developments we study. In response to Prendergast's critique, Moretti (2003) has in fact made precisely this claim:

> I set out to explain the logic behind literary survival and oblivion; I studied a specific historical episode; and then I described what I found: namely, that the texts that survived were formally and symbolically more suited to their environment than their competitors. Since I don't believe that the market produces the best of all possible literatures [. . .] I would have been *delighted* to find complex, meaningful detective stories unfairly sacrificed to Holmes's success. But—I have not found them. Nor has Prendergast. Nor has anyone else. And in the total absence of contrary evidence, why on earth should I drop a perfectly plausible explanation? Because it sounds politically *wrong*? (145; original emphasis)

For Moretti, his findings are completely independent from his own agency; the Darwinian model allows him to assume that the literary evolution he studies follows rules that can be deduced from the evidence we find in the present: Sherlock Holmes is the better detective story because it survived; and we know it was best because we cannot find any proof of the contrary. In other words, the library of world literature has its own, complex rules which determine the content of its shelves; the critic, as Darwin before him, is free to collect samples and study the multitudinous relationships between its volumes, but he is relieved from other anxiety-inducing tasks, such as deliberating over the aesthetic and political choices involved in equipping the library, and he need not fear that the library might grow beyond its present dimensions: for the "polity of nature", as Darwin (2008) insisted, provides room for a constant level of diversity only (84). Although this narrative may be enticing, Coetzee's different employment of Aesthetic Darwinism suggests that we are taking the easy way out if we leave the struggle for existence to a market which benefits the fittest.

Testing the Timeless: The Classic and the Critic

J.M. Coetzee's work is frequently cited as an example of world literature in the making. Based in South Africa and Australia, the Nobel laureate's novels are deemed to be dialogic, reflective, and "born-translated" (Walkowitz 2009, 569). They interrogate the classics of European literature[25]—Defoe, Dostoyevsky, Kafka—and seem to be written for translation and global circulation. Coetzee is, however, not only deeply suspicious of his own status as a contemporary classic,[26] he is also suspicious of the classic in general.

Coetzee begins his lecture "What Is a Classic?" with a close analysis of T.S. Eliot's lecture of the same name. Eliot delivered his address before the Virgil Society in October 1944, so it is clearly to be read in the context of World War II. For Eliot (1965), the classic must have achieved a certain maturity—of mind, manners, and language (14)—and in this perfection, the classic tends to exhaust "not a form only, but the language of his time; and when he is a wholly classic poet, the language of his time will be the language in its perfection" (24). But the classic is also defined by "exhibiting an amplitude, a catholicity" (18), by which Eliot does not necessarily mean a certain kind of religious creed, but certainly a "religious sensibility", which he sees as opposed to "provinciality" (18). In other words, the classic possesses "*comprehensiveness*":

> The classic must, within its formal limitations, express the maximum possible of the whole range of feeling which represents the character of the people who speak that language. It will represent this at its best, and it will also have the widest appeal: among the people to which it belongs, it will find its response among all classes and conditions of men. When a work of literature has, beyond this comprehensiveness in relation to its own language, an equal significance in relation to a number of foreign literatures, we may say that it has also universality. (27; original emphasis)

---

25 Although his novels are a form of writing back to the canon, Coetzee has been criticized for the "Eurocentrism" implied in turning exclusively to the western tradition of literature. Tonje Vold (2011) notes that, even in writing back, Coetzee's works "have often worked to confirm the high canon" (49). Such a reading, however, neglects the fact that Coetzee does not simply confirm the positions of Defoe or Dostoyevsky but destabilizes their authorial position and introduces other voices into a dialogue with the canon.

26 "I don't have much faith that my work will endure", he confesses to Paul Auster (Coetzee and Auster 2013, 134).

Eliot's logic sounds familiar: the classic possesses the qualities to survive not only in its original environment but also in foreign climates. His notion relies too much on inherent aesthetic quality and universality (rather than chance and adaptability) to be Darwinian, but it shares the concern for survival with the positions we have examined so far. For Eliot, however, the playing field is extremely limited. In fact, there can be no other true classic than Virgil: "No modern language can hope to produce a classic, in the sense in which I have called Virgil a classic. Our classic, the classic of all Europe, is Virgil" (31). Maturity and universality have long since become problematic as aesthetic values, and we might in turn dismiss Eliot's vision of the classic as utterly provincial: his wholly Eurocentric point of view seems to leave no room to consider other traditions than the ones he is familiar with.

Coetzee, however, chooses a different and possibly more productive route. He deftly analyses Eliot's attempt to impose Virgil as the "dominant voice" of Europe (Coetzee 2002, 2) and to claim "a cultural-historical unity for Western European Christendom" (6) in light of the American writer's own personal and historical position. This reading exposes Eliot's project as

> the essentially magical enterprise of a man trying to redefine the world around himself—rather than confronting the reality of his not-so-grand position as a man whose narrowly academic, Eurocentric education had prepared him for little else but life as a mandarin in one of the New England ivory towers. (8–9)

In short, Coetzee sheds light on Eliot's anxiety as a poet-critic in a rapidly changing world and on Eliot's attempt to dispel this anxiety by aligning himself with the classic.

Coetzee, however, is far from accepting this analysis as a final verdict on Eliot's project. In fact, by highlighting Eliot's "colonial fate" (Coetzee 2002, 8) as an American desperate to redefine himself as English, Coetzee identifies himself with Eliot's need for cultural redefinition and reassurance. This forces him to reconsider his own first experience of the classic, a chance encounter with Johann Sebastian Bach's *Well-Tempered Clavier* at the age of 15:

> Is there some non-vacuous sense in which I can say that the spirit of Bach was speaking to me across the ages, across the seas, putting before me certain ideals; or was what was really going on at that moment that I was symbolically electing high European culture, and command of the codes of that culture, as a route that would take me out of my class position in white South African society [...]? In other words, was the experience what I understood it to be—a disinterested and in a sense impersonal aesthetic experience—or was it really the masked expression of a material interest? (10–11)

I have quoted this section at length not just because it provides a preliminary definition of the classic—a work of art which speaks across the ages[27]—but also because it encapsulates Coetzee's own anxiety that the classic, instead of communicating something, simply reflects his personal, social, and professional insecurities. As Coetzee explores in even more depth in his autofictional novels *Boyhood* and *Youth*, his fascination with the classic is an expression of his contradictory identity as a South African: part of the elite as a white citizen of the apartheid state, but isolated by his English language from the Afrikaans community and frowned upon by British high culture because of his origins in a Global South "colony".

To jump ahead: Coetzee comes to the conclusion that there is something about the classic which "speaks" across the ages, although not "unproblematically" so: the classic is not timeless but "historically constituted" (Coetzee 2002, 12). Bach, to stick with Coetzee's example, was not an instant classic and far from popular during or immediately after his lifetime. It was Felix Mendelssohn's 1829 Romantic re-performance of the *St. Matthew Passion* which lifted Bach from public obscurity. However, Coetzee emphasizes that Bach had never been obscure in specialist circles, where his music continued to be studied and practiced (16–17). Within the musical profession,

27 Coetzee (2008) reiterates that definition of the classic in his later novel *Diary of a Bad Year*, albeit with much more irony than before: "Another of the meanings of 'the classic': to be on the shelf waiting to be taken down for the thousandth, the millionth time. The classic: the perduring. No wonder publishers are so eager to claim classic status for their authors!" (190).

then, Bach has continually been tested, which leads Coetzee to re-approach the classics question: "Dare I suggest that the classic in music is what emerges intact from this process of day-by-day testing?" (18). Mukherjee (2010) has shown that by claiming that the "classic defines itself by surviving" (19), Coetzee actually eliminates the possibility of defining the classic (1034). For him, the classic is not something that has an essential "quality" or "value in itself"; it relies, instead, on a never-ending process: its continued survival within its critical environment (Coetzee 2002, 18–19). The testing ground for the classic is not located in a wider social context—readers or the market—but in a narrow professional one.

Where does that leave literature and literary criticism? Coetzee (2002) suggests that

> criticism is that which is duty-bound to interrogate the classic. Thus the fear that the classic will not survive the de-centring acts of criticism may be turned on its head: rather than being the foe of the classic, criticism, and indeed criticism of the most sceptical kind, may be what the classic uses to define itself and ensure its survival. (19)

Coetzee's initial analysis appears to be similar to the previously discussed versions of Aesthetic Darwinism: the work of art must struggle to survive in a hostile environment. If the classic thus emerged as a necessity of an evolutionary process in which the fittest forms survive critical testing, there would be no need to anxiously question the classic or the canon. However, Coetzee's argument forces us to reconsider the determinism inherent in such a mode of thinking. The classic does not survive *against* the pressures of the environment but *because of it*. Thus, Coetzee (2002) insists on the agency and the responsibility of the critics who shape this environment. Although he calls for a "certain confidence" in the critical tradition "that it will not devote labour and attention [. . .] to pieces of [art] whose life-functions have terminated" (18), this is just another way of saying that safety is not to be had. Moretti's comfortable insistence on the evidence of the evolutionary process is thus unsettled and the certainties the critic gained through a reliance on Darwinism fade away. In fact, Coetzee's lecture demonstrates that criticism must create uncertainties: analyzing the history and the contexts of Eliot's lecture, Coetzee cannot help but question his own position as a critic and as a connoisseur of music. Such questioning forces him to confront the irresolvable entanglements produced by his situatedness in the Global South and his involvement in the European tradition as a means of transcending the perceived limitations of his South African identity. The classic never simply poses an alternative between a disinterested aesthetic experience or a material interest: historically constituted, critically tested, individually discovered, it is always both past and present, impersonal and personal, private and political.

Conclusion: Surviving Anxiety

At this point, and by way of conclusion, I would like to return briefly to Coetzee's novel *Elizabeth Costello* and the two visions of the library with which I began this chapter. This novel, which may be described as a series of speeches and critical debates, is a perfect example of Coetzee's recursive and self-critical dialogic technique: Elizabeth Costello's speeches are always counterbalanced with other speeches, critical statements are always destabilized by other characters' or the narrator's comments, and supposed certainties are always followed by explicit or implicit questions. This, I believe, is Coetzee's most detailed portrait of the critical environment he only alludes to in his lecture. It is generated by uncertainties, by impossible tasks, as well as by contradictory opinions, influences, and theoretical positions. Anxiety and discomfort are the conditions of this environment, and they must not be resolved. If it is at all possible to describe Coetzee's theory of the classic in terms of "Aesthetic Darwinism", it is so in the spirit of the most self-aware passages in *The Origin of Species*, which acknowledge that nature holds such "ever-increasing circles of complexity" that it could not ultimately be understood (Darwin 2008, 58) other than by "metaphorical" or speculative means (51). Turning critics into scientists and equipping them with scientific vocabulary may be a way of evading the uncertainty, but it is, as Coetzee reminds us, not its remedy. If even the classic depends on criticism for its survival, we must not stop submitting the classic and ourselves to testing, which, by definition, is a process without certain results. Whatever anxieties the critic may harbour—an uneasiness with translations, doubts about the intrusion or exclusion of Global South texts from the canon, methodological or ideological perplexity—they are part of the critical environment which shapes the classic and infinite versions of world literature. The questions that we must put to ourselves are: What are we using the classic for and what are we using world literature for? Do we have to dissolve our uncertainties and shed the metaphors of anxiety or can we find ways of using that very anxiety as a tool to increase our awareness of the "circles of complexity"? Can we use Coetzee's critique as a starting point to reflect on our own entanglements, as critics, in the global literary world?

At the end of the speech that I have quoted earlier, Elizabeth Costello herself revises her fear of the Darwinian library and argues that there "must be some limit to the burden of remembering" (Coetzee 2004, 20), and thus some limit to the library. In contrast, Borges's (1961) narrator finds comfort in the "elegant hope" that the infinite disorder of the library will ultimately be perceived as order (118).[28] Whichever version of the library we fear most, the slaughterhouse of literature or the "biblioteca de Babel", chances are that the nightmare holds its own comforts.

Bibliography

Auerbach, Erich. 1952. "Philologie der Weltliteratur." In *Weltliteratur: Festgabe für Fritz Strich zum 70. Geburtstag*, edited by Walter Muschg and Emil Staiger, 39–50. Bern: Francke.

Auerbach, Erich. 1969. "Philology and *Weltliteratur*." Translated by Edward and Maire Said. *The Centennial Review* 13 (1): 1–17.

28 Original: "Si un eterno viajero la atravesara en cualquier dirección, comprobaría al cabo de los siglos que los mismos volúmenes se repiten en el mismo desorden (que, repetido, sería un orden: el Orden). Mi soledad se alegra con esa elegante esperanza" (Borges 1961, 95).

Bachmann-Medick, Doris. 2001. "Is There a Literary History of World Literature?" *REAL: Yearbook of Research in English and American Literature* 17: 359–72.

Beer, Gillian. 2009. *Darwin's Plots: Evolutionary Narrative in Darwin, George Eliot and Nineteenth-Century Fiction*. Cambridge: Cambridge University Press.

Borges, Jorge Luis. 1961. "La biblioteca de Babel." In *Ficciones*, 85–95. Buenos Aires: Emecé Editores.

Borges, Jorge Luis. 1998. "The Library of Babel." In *Collected Fictions*, translated by Andrew Hurley, 112–18. New York: Penguin.

Casanova, Pascale. 2004. *The World Republic of Letters*. Translated by M.B. DeBevoise (Original: *La République mondiale des Lettres*, 1999). Cambridge, MA: Harvard University Press.

Coetzee, J.M. 1998. *Boyhood: Scenes from Provincial Life*. London: Vintage.

Coetzee, J.M. 2002. "What Is a Classic?" In *Stranger Shores: Essays 1986–1999*, 1–19. London: Vintage.

Coetzee, J.M. 2003. *Youth*. London: Vintage.

Coetzee, J.M. 2004. *Elizabeth Costello*. London: Vintage.

Coetzee, J.M. 2008. *Diary of a Bad Year*. London: Vintage.

Coetzee, J.M., and Paul Auster. 2013. *Here and Now. Letters: 2008–2011*. London: Faber and Faber.

Corbineau-Hoffmann, Angelika. 2013. *Einführung in die Komparatistik* [Introduction to Comparative Literature]. Berlin: Erich Schmidt Verlag.

Damrosch, David. 2003. *What Is World Literature?* Princeton, NJ: Princeton University Press.

Damrosch, David. 2013. "World Literature in a Postliterary Age." *Modern Language Quarterly* 74 (2): 151–70.

Damrosch, David, and Gayatri Chakravorty Spivak. 2011. "Comparative Literature/World Literature: A Discussion with Gayatri Chakravorty Spivak and David Damrosch." *Comparative Literature Studies* 48 (4): 455–85.

Darwin, Charles. 2008. *On the Origin of Species*. Oxford: Oxford University Press.

Dimock, Wai Chee. 2006. "Genre as World System: Epic and Novel on Four Continents." *Narrative* 14 (1): 85–101.

Eliot, T.S. 1965. *What Is a Classic? An Address Delivered Before the Virgil Society on the 16th of October 1944.* London: Faber & Faber.

Étiemble, René. 1974. "Faut-il réviser la notion de *Weltliteratur*?" *Essais de littérature (vraiment) générale*, by René Étiemble, 13–35. Paris: Gallimard.

Étiemble, René. 2014. "Should We Rethink the Notion of World Literature?" In *World Literature in Theory*, edited by David Damrosch, 85–98. Hoboken, NJ: Wiley.

Friedman, Susan Stanford. 2012. "World Modernisms, World Literature, and Comparativity." In *The Oxford Handbook of Global Modernisms*, edited by Mark Wollaeger with Matt Eatough, 499–525. Oxford: Oxford University Press.

Huggan, Graham. 2011. "The Trouble with World Literature." In *A Companion to Comparative Literature*, edited by Ali Behdad and Dominic Thomas, 490–506. Oxford: Wiley-Blackwell.

Kilian, Patrick. 2016. "Of Trees and Genealogies: A Foucauldian Commentary on Franco Moretti." *Le Foucaldien* 2 (1): 1–10.

Lakoff, George, and Mark Johnson. 2003. *Metaphors We Live By*. Chicago, IL: University of Chicago Press.

Mani, B. Venkat. 2017. *Recoding World Literature: Libraries, Print Culture, and Germany's Pact with Books.* New York: Fordham University Press.

Moretti, Franco. 2000a. "Conjectures on World Literature." *New Left Review* 1: 54–68.

Moretti, Franco. 2000b. "The Slaughterhouse of Literature." *Modern Language Quarterly* 61 (1): 207–27.

Moretti, Franco. 2003. *Distant Reading*. London: Verso.

Mukherjee, Ankhi. 2010. "'What Is a Classic?': International Literary Criticism and the Classic Question." *PMLA* 125 (4): 1026–42.

Ngũgĩ wa Thiong'o. 2012. *Globalectics.* New York: Columbia University Press.

Prendergast, Christopher. 2005. "Evolution and Literary History: A Response to Franco Moretti." *New Left Review* 34: 40–62.

Shivani, Anis. 2012. "What Is World Literature?" *Boulevard* 27 (3): 53–63.

Vold, Tonje. 2011. "How to 'Rise Above Mere Nationality': Coetzee's Novels *Youth* and *Slow Man* in the World Republic of Letters." *Twentieth-Century Literature* 57 (1): 34–53.

Walkowitz, Rebecca L. 2009. "Comparison Literature." *New Literary History* 40: 567–82.

Warwick Research Collective. 2015. *Combined and Uneven Development: Towards a New Theory of World-Literature.* Liverpool: Liverpool University Press.

Young, Robert J.C. 2011. "World Literature and Postcolonialism." *The Routledge Companion to World Literature*, edited by Theo D'haen, David Damrosch, and Djelal Kadir, 213–22. New York: Routledge.

"Tilting Camus Sideways": Intertextual Entanglements between Albert Camus's *L'Étranger* and Kamel Daoud's *Meursault, contre-enquête*

Delphine Munos

In a now-classic attempt at defining which texts might qualify as world literature, David Damrosch (2003) posits two main conditions; firstly, that such a text be "read *as* literature"; secondly, that it "circulat[e] out into a broader world beyond its linguistic and cultural point of origin" (6; original emphasis). Undoubtedly, Albert Camus's novel *L'Étranger* (*The Stranger*, 1942) does more than just tick the boxes of Damrosch's definition: it has entered world literature with a bang. Since its inception, the novel has indeed been translated into 60 languages[1] and sold more than six million copies (Kaplan 2016a), which makes it clear that the reception and impact of Camus's novel should be assessed not only on a national, but a transcontinental scale. In the prologue to a book retracing how *L'Étranger* came to life—indeed how Camus "discovered the novel within himself"—Alice Kaplan (2016a) aptly remarks that "reading *The Stranger* is a rite of passage. People from all over the world connect the book to their coming of age, to grappling with the toughest questions of existence" (1). Exemplifying Ankhi Mukherjee's (2014) remark that "a classic is that which

1 Relying on the Gallimard files, Adele King (1992) remarks that "translations of *L'Étranger* exist [. . .] in the following editions: Afrikaans, Albanian, American, Assamese, Basque, Bengali, Bulgarian, Catalan, Czech, Danish, Dutch, English, Finnish, Franco-Chinese, German, Hebrew, Hindi, Hungarian, Icelandic, Indonesian, Italian, Japanese, Kannada, Macedonian, Malayalam, Malaysian, Maltese, Norwegian, Polish, Portuguese, Punjabi, Rumanian, Russian, Serbo-Croat, Slovene, Spanish, Swedish, Tamil, Telegu, Welsh". Drawing on Edouard Glissant, King even mentions a Martinican writer translating novels into Creole, which he self-publishes in typewritten versions, among them *Mun andewo-a,* a Creole version of *L'Étranger* (2).

survives ideological determination as well as sceptical questioning" (39), Kaplan adds: "you can construct a pretty accurate history of twentieth-century literary criticism by following the successive waves of analysis of *The Stranger*: existentialism, new criticism, deconstruction, feminism, postcolonial studies" (2).

Today, it is worth noting that certain "waves of analysis" stick more than others, making it impossible for most critics—especially those from the Global South—to envisage Camus's classic in isolation from postcolonial readings of it. Looking back on his own "rite of passage", that is, his life-changing experience of reading the English translation of *L'Étranger* in Madras, India, at age 17, Rajagopalan Radhakrishnan (2017) cannot help cringing at the thought that his teenage self was irremediably seduced by the philosophical acuity of the book even as he blatantly ignored, at the time, the colonial undertones at play in Camus's anonymization of the Arab victim. "Here I was", Radhakrishnan reminisces, "a postcolonial teenager" who was "profoundly critical of his 'given' Hindu Brahmin, ritualistic, fundamentalist casteist, patriarchal, misogynistic, Islamophobic filiation"—and "I was in solidarity with the philosophical subjectivity of the *pied-noir*", while being "totally out of tune with the forced anonymity of the scapegoat Algerian Arab. How ugly and disgusting!" (441).

Radhakrishnan's tongue-in-cheek anecdote suggests that classics which are taken to be representative of world literature not only "circulate out into the broader world", to refer again to Damrosch's definition; they also remain firmly embedded in local contexts, and what is more, they continually travel towards meaning, being interpreted and re-interpreted by scholars working from different schools of criticism. After all, as Edward Said (1983) points out in a different context, texts can also be likened to objects "whose interpretation *has already commenced*"—objects, he adds, whose "circumstantiality" and "worldliness" work in tandem, in that the former category constrains their interpretation while the latter gradually burns, so to speak, layers of interpretation into them (39; original emphasis). In other words, if, on the one hand, "texts are always enmeshed in circumstance, time, place, and society—in short, they are in the world" (35), on the other, "they place themselves [...] by soliciting the world's attention", all of which "places restraints upon what can be done with them interpretatively" (Said 1983, 40).

Said's idea that texts constrain their interpretation at the same time as being constrained by it, certainly finds an echo in Stefan Helgesson's (2014) resolve to understand literature both as a "situated" and "circulational" phenomenon, in an attempt to take into consideration the disciplinary fields of both postcolonialism and world literature. After all, while postcolonialism privileges the colonial link and tends to subordinate literary form to political-historical issues, conversely, world literature, by and large, "disconnects literature from its Euro-colonial historicity" (485), which hardly takes on board the fact that "the very act of reading a text 'as literature' is shaped historically" (486). For Helgesson, rather than perceiving postcolonialism and world literature as opponents in "the current 'upscaling' of the humanities to a global level" (484), there would be much to gain in combining the (more literary- and circulational-minded) field of world literature with the (more politically- and situation-oriented) framework of postcolonialism. He also notes that such a complementary approach appears to be particularly fruitful when looking at texts by writers originating from colonies and postcolonies. Indeed, such an approach simultaneously takes on board the poetics of these individual writers, the circulation of their work across continents and languages and, last but not least, their situatedness and the "local irreducibility" (489) of their work in a literary market heavily biased towards audiences based in the Global North. Helgesson is well aware that his endeavour to utilize the best methodological tools offered by postcolonialism and world literature might sound a little idealistic and pertinent to a handful of case studies only. However, for the critic, such a combined approach "may account for literature both as grounded in local, conflictual histories and as a circulational phenomenon that moves across languages and literary fields" (484).

Helgesson's plea for combining postcolonial and world literary methodologies constitutes the main source of inspiration for the present discussion of the circumstantial and worldly intertextual entanglements at play between Camus's *L'Étranger* and Kamel Daoud's *Meursault, contre-enquête* (2013; *The Meursault Investigation*, 2015), a novel which is often marketed as a retelling of Camus's classic. But before teasing out the ways in which a combined world literature/postcolonial approach might be equally pertinent to reading Daoud via Camus and to rereading Camus via Daoud in the contemporary moment, I would like to point out that my decision to go for the term "intertextual entanglements"—instead of, say, intertextuality *tout court*—owes to a specific resolve to show that Daoud's novel goes far beyond any traditionally binary-reversing, or "mainstream" postcolonial (Huggan 2015, 131) agenda of "writing back to the centre". Clearly, Daoud takes postcolonial readings of Camus's *L'Étranger* seriously, in that, as many critics have pointed out, the Algerian writer dutifully fills in the gaps of Camus's classic, finally granting a name and identity to the murdered Arab. However, this classic act of postcolonial redress also coexists with further literary moves, including the conflation of Meursault and Camus as well as the use of a dialogical form similar to the one deployed by Camus in *La Chute* (1956; *The Fall*, 1957), all of which, as I will show, extends an invitation to reassess the entangled "circumstantiality" and "worldliness" of Camus's classic. In a different postcolonial context, that of South Africa, Sarah Nuttall (2009) suggestively defines entanglement as a "condition of being twisted together or entwined, involved with" (1). An entanglement, she adds, is a term "speak[ing] of an intimacy gained even if it was resisted, or ignored, or uninvited"—one that "gestures towards a set of relationships that is complicated, ensnaring, in a tangle, but which also implies a human foldedness" (1). So, in what follows, I will contend that, in addition to revealing the anachronistic character of the postcolonial take in the contemporary moment, *Meursault, contre-enquête*'s web of intertextual entanglements with *L'Étranger* and *La Chute* re-grounds Camus's classic in contemporary Algeria and highlights the dual necessity of situating and "re-worlding" it.

While Franco Moretti (2000) famously notes that world literature is meant to be "a thorn in the side, a permanent intellectual challenge to national literatures" (68), other "world literary dominants" (Helgesson and Vermeulen 2016, 5) such as Damrosch call attention to the ways in which texts becoming world literature are still "bearing the marks of their national origin" (Damrosch 2003, 513). Damrosch hastens to add, however, that the "traces [of these texts' national origins] are increasingly diffused and become ever more sharply refracted as a work travels farther from home" (514). Still, for Damrosch, "works become world literature by being received into the space of a foreign culture, a space defined in many ways by the host culture's national tradition and the present needs of its own writers" (514). Bringing to mind Helgesson's and Vermeulen's apt suggestion (2016) that Damrosch complicates "the seminal question 'what is world literature'" by the "less well-known question "*where* is world literature" (2; original emphasis), Damrosch (2003) himself evokes the figure of the ellipse to make sense of "the ongoing, vital presence of the national within the life of world literature":

> World literature is [. . .] as much about the host culture's values and needs as it is about a work's source culture; hence it is a double refraction, one that can be described through the figure of the ellipse, with the source and host cultures providing the two foci that generate the elliptical space within which a work lives as world literature, connected to both cultures, circumscribed by neither alone. (514)

Damrosch is well aware that his point about the "double refraction" at play in the creation of world literature is over-simplistic in that it fails to take on board ellipses where the first focus—the one associated with the "home culture"—is firmly rooted in one period and one national culture, whereas the second focus—the one associated with the "host culture"—needs to be broadened "beyond one or two periods or national traditions" (514). But I would like to suggest that the opposite is equally true. Indeed Damrosch's musings on the difficulty of ever doing justice to the multiplicity of the second foci—those bearing witness to the multiple national contexts of reception of any given text—ignores the fact that, for colonial and postcolonial writers, the first focus, too, should be widened beyond one single space and national tradition. For instance, as I will show below, the shifting "framing" of Camus—initially as a *French* writer, then as a *French Algerian*, even an *Algerian* writer, or, more recently, as "neither Algerian, nor French" (Breen 2019, 210)—offers a fine instance of the ways in which the space of a "home culture" can also be multiple and unstable across time. In other words, the fact that the reception of *L'Étranger* has also been impacted by shifting representations of the national/colonial identity of its author reveals that "the life of world literature" is invigorated, not only by "the ongoing, vital presence of the national", but also by "the ongoing, vital life of the colonial", to adopt and recycle yet again Damrosch's words. In fact, the entanglement of both the colonial and the national in the "ongoing life" of both Camus's work and his authorial persona will be of key importance when looking at Daoud's recent hijacking (and re-purposing) of *L'Étranger* in the contemporary moment.

For now, let's just say that *Meursault, contre-enquête* is part and parcel of what Madeleine Dobie (2016) has called the new "Camus library" generated by our "Camus moment" (n.p.), a moment that the US critic traces back to the 50th anniversary in 2010 of Camus's death and the 100th anniversary in 2013 of his birth—which is the same year, coincidentally, that Daoud's book, originally written in French, was released in Algeria. For Dobie (2016), this "Camus moment" hinges to a significant extent on a revamping of Camus's image, from that of a "quintessentially French" writer—indeed from an emblem of "resistance, existentialism, and coffee and cigarettes on the terrace of the *Café de Flore*" (n.p.)—to a writer whose birth in colonial Algeria can no longer constitute a mere "footnote to this story" (n.p.). What Dobie makes clear is that, today, whenever the "new Camus" is either celebrated or vilified in the contexts of Algeria, France, and the Anglo-American world, what takes centre-stage is Camus's visceral engagement with the land of his birth as well as his message of non-violence during the Algerian War of Independence (1954–62), a message that had hitherto been deemed irrelevant and/or was oversimplified by historians and literary scholars alike.

A few biographical facts are in order here. Camus was born in Mondovi (present-day Dréan), Algeria, in 1913, into what was called, at the time, the "European" or "French Algerian" community of colonial Algeria. It is worth mentioning that the usual conflation of "French Algerian" (*Français d'Algérie*) and "European" is problematic, in that the former category tends to erase the diverse origins and histories of a group who started being naturalized as French from the 1840s onwards. Historians such as Frederick Cooper (2003) and Todd Shepard (2006) have remarked that only one-fifth of the members of the European community in colonial Algeria originally hailed from France. In fact, the majority of that group came from places as diverse as Malta, Spain, Italy, Corsica, Germany, Greece, and other European countries. What happened is that this group automatically became French from 1889 onwards (Hubbell 2015, 11), as the French colonial authority wanted to secure allegiance on the part of white settlers and their descendants. Camus is a fine instance of a so-called "French Algerian" writer whose origins are in fact more hybrid than it might seem at first sight, because he was of mixed French and Spanish ancestry. Although he is often called a *pied-noir* writer, too, this adjective carries historical associations that do not befit the writer's personal trajectory. Indeed, as Amy L. Hubbell (2015) explains, "it was on their so-called return to France that the *Français d'Algérie* earned the nickname Pieds-Noirs" (9). And Hubbell adds, "while it is often assumed that the *Français d'Algérie* were returning to their homeland, most had never been to France, and a significant percentage were not of French heritage but were naturalized citizens" (9). In fact, contrary to the one million Algeria-born *pieds-noirs* who were "repatriated" to mainland France in the early 1960s, that is, towards the end of the Algerian War of Independence, Camus started living in mainland France in the 1940s, at the outbreak of World War II. *L'Étranger* was in fact released in occupied Paris in 1942, shortly after Camus relocated there.

The plot of the novel is well-known. In the first part of the novel, Meursault, a French Algerian bureaucrat, loses his mother, travels to her funeral, and appears to be unaffected by her death, so much so that he goes to the beach and takes his girlfriend Marie to the movies on the day after his mother's funeral. Shortly after that, the character murders an unnamed Arab on a beach in Algiers for no real motive. In the second part of Camus's classic, Meursault awaits a death sentence following a nonsensical trial which centres less on his murder of a man than on his past inability to display grief at his mother's funeral. Commenting on *L'Étranger* upon its publication, Jean-Paul Sartre (1947) promoted the novel as an exemplar of the philosophy of the Absurd—a reading which seems to have been extremely influential, in France and abroad. Dominique Combe (2013) thus points out that, until the early 1990s, a period marking the start of the institutionalization of postcolonialism in Anglo-American universities, the transnational reception of Camus's work did not significantly differ from its reception in France, with influential monographs on Camus such as that by US scholar Germaine Brée (1959) foregrounding the writer's brand of universalist humanism only.

As Combe (2013) points out, the reception of *L'Étranger* took a decisive turn with the publication of Edward Said's *Culture and Imperialism* in 1993 (2–4). In this book, Said (1994), who is often considered to be one of the founding fathers of postcolonial theory, takes the novel as evidence that Camus's writing is "informed by an extraordinary belated, in some ways incapacitated colonial sensibility" (213). The main thrust of Said's argument is to posit Camus's absolute Frenchness—indeed "his entirely French upbringing in Algeria" and "his true French antecedents" (216)—so as to establish a continuity between Camus and the French colonial enterprise. For Said, readers readily associate Camus's novels with "French novels about France" (212) for the very reason that, in most of these texts, the "choice of an Algerian locale seems purely incidental to the pressing moral issues at hand" (212). In any case, if there is a real motive that might explain Camus's decision to locate *L'Étranger* in Algeria even as its "main reference [. . .] has always been construed as France generally, and more particularly, France under the Nazi Occupation"; Said adds, "the choice is not innocent" (211). It can only be, as the critic argues after Conor Cruise O'Brien, that "much in the tales (e.g.

Meursault's trial) is either a surreptitious or unconscious justification of French rule or an ideological attempt to prettify it" (211). Taking Camus to task for the anonymity of his few Arab characters, in particular for denying the murdered Arab in *L'Étranger* a name and a story, Said concludes that Camus's first novel is "a novel about the deaths of Arabs, deaths that highlight and silently inform the French characters' difficulties of conscience or reflection" (219).

Looking back on Said's influential "contrapuntal" reading of *L'Étranger* from the perspective of 2013, a year that might have marked the height of Dobie's "Camus moment" but that saw intense conflicts over the memorialization of Camus in France,[2] the French historians Benjamin Stora and Jean-Baptiste Péretié (2013) point out that Said's unsparing portrait of Camus as a closet colonialist would have certainly been more nuanced if *Le Premier Homme* (1994; *The First Man*, 1995), Camus's unfinished novel, had already been released at the time (83). In this largely autobiographical novel which was posthumously published in 1994—that is, more than three decades after Camus's death in 1960 but only one year after the release of Said's *Culture and Imperialism*—Camus alludes to his family's poverty and lowly position in the colonial hierarchy through the protagonist Jacques Cormery, a working-class French Algerian orphan who represents Camus's alter-ego. Significantly, Jacques contrasts his feeling of Frenchness with the one expressed by Didier, an upper-class schoolmate whose family is rich enough to own a holiday home in the metropole. For Didier, who represents the ruling class of *colons*, the *patrie* is clearly identified with France. For Jacques, however, who has never travelled to France and lives in poverty in Algiers, "this notion

2 In 2012, the project of a major Camus exhibition in Aix-en-Provence for the Marseille-Provence European Capital of Culture 2013 programme stalled, following the brutal eviction of its curator, the leading French historian of contemporary Algeria, Benjamin Stora, by arch-conservative Aix-en-Provence mayor Maryse Joissains-Masini, and the consequent underhanded appointment of middlebrow philosopher Michel Onfray, before the latter's final decision to back off from what he called "la pétaudière" (the madhouse). See Simon (2012).

of country [has] no meaning" (Camus 1995, 146).[3] Likened by him to a "God" (147) who is "the sovereign dispenser of good things and bad" and can "do anything with the people's destiny" (147), Jacques feels that his Frenchness is all but an "abstraction", that he is, in fact, a "citize[n] in theory of a nebulous nation" (147).[4] Through the opposition between Jacques and Didier in *Le Premier Homme*, Camus shows that the French Algerian community is not homogeneous, and that the community's self-identification with France—which is far from being self-evident[5]—is also determined by class. Arguably, Jacques's (working-class) sense of himself as a "citizen[n] in theory" of a "nebulous" French nation retroactively throws into relief Meursault's own problematic identification with mainland France in *L'Étranger*, ranging from his dislike of Paris—"It's dirty [. . .]. There are pigeons and dark courtyards. Everyone looks pale" (Camus 2013b, 39)[6]—to his wary attitude towards representatives of metropolitan authority such as the magistrate and prison chaplain who challenge his atheism in the second part of the book.

Probably because, today, Meursault is likely to be read alongside Jacques Cormery, that is, a character who problematizes the assumption that the French Algerian community unanimously embraces France as a steady pole of identification, recent readings of *L'Étranger* have shifted the focus from the first to the second part of

3 Original: "cette notion de patrie [est] vide de sens" (226).

4 Original: "[un] citoye[n] théoriqu[e] d'une nation imprécise" (227).

5 Algerian-born Jacques Derrida (1995) comments on the "very marked social gap between the figure of the French of France and the French of Algeria" in his interview "There is No *One* Narcissism" (204). For the Jewish philosopher, "the Frenchman of France was an other [. . .] who was, to be sure, higher on the ladder"; similarly, the language of the Frenchman of France was "the language of the other" (204). Derrida's sense of the French language as the "language of the other" both for French Algerians and for members of the Jewish community of French Algeria certainly shines a light onto Derrida's (1998) famous remark, "I only have one language; it's not mine" in *Monolingualism of the Other; or: The Prosthesis of Origin* (1).

6 Original: "C'est sale. Il y a des pigeons et des cours noires. Les gens ont la peau blanche" (70).

the book, interpreting Meursault's nonsensical trial as a means of exposing the cracks in the character's allegiance to France. Aptly remarking that the French jury ignores Meursault's murder of the Arab and focuses instead on his apparent lack of grief during his mother's funeral and on his refusal to turn to Christianity to atone for his crimes, David Carroll (2007) contends, for instance, that Meursault's trial takes place to "put [the character's] right to French identity into question" (32). In his book, suggestively entitled *Albert Camus the Algerian*—a nod to one of Camus's notes in the Annex section to *Le Premier Homme*[7]—the US critic goes as far as to claim that Meursault's rejection of Christianity during his trial signals his refusal of "the possibility of being assimilated (back) into French society" (33). Carroll's 2007 reading of *L'Étranger* is persuasive, all the more so when considering that even though the novel was released in occupied Paris, Camus researched the main part of the text in Algeria from 1937 to 1940, which are two dates of key importance in relation to shifts in French Algeria's politics of Frenchness. Indeed, while 1937 marked the Popular Front's Blum-Viollette proposal to extend French citizenship to Muslims of Algeria (a proposal which was supported by Camus but was abandoned after the mass resignation of French Algerian mayors), 1940 saw the abrogation of the 1870 *Crémieux* Decree by Vichy France, which resulted in the loss of French citizenship for Algerian Jews until 1943.[8] Suggesting that Meursault condemns himself to be an outsider to French society because, during his trial, he refuses to comply with socio-cultural and Christian religious norms around which the notion of Frenchness is constructed, Carroll contends that Saidian readings of *L'Étranger* miss the mark, as the novel can be seen to critique the politics of Frenchness in colonial Algeria. Indeed, for Carroll, "to judge and indict Camus for his 'colonialist ideology' is not to read him; it is not to treat his literary texts in terms of

---

7 Cf. "what they didn't like in him was the Algerian" (Camus 1995, 219). Original: "ce qu'ils n'aimaient pas en lui, c'était l'Algérien" (Camus 1994, 362).

8 See Shepard (2006, 20–39) for more on this.

the specific questions they actually raise, the contradictions they confront, and the dilemmas they express" (15).

Returning to the ways in which the reception of *L'Étranger* has evolved through time, Stora and Péretié (2013) evoke the difficult memorialization of Camus in contemporary Algeria and today's France, a country where the taboos surrounding the Algerian War have been so extreme that it took the French government until 1999 to officially acknowledge that there had been such a thing as a *war* having been fought in Algeria between 1954 and 1962.[9] For Stora and Péretié, such a difficult memorialization of Camus on both sides of the Mediterranean owes much to the writer's ambiguous stance during the Algerian War, as he neither endorsed full independence nor the colonial status quo while opposing both the ultra-right faction *Organisation Armée Secrète* (OAS) and the nationalist *Front de Libération Nationale* (FLN). As already noted, in their book *Camus brûlant* (*Burning Camus*), Stora and Péretié highlight how crucial *Le Premier Homme* is to any nuanced understanding of Camus's positionality. Indeed, for the historians, the writer gives more visibility to Arab characters in his posthumous novel than in the rest of his fictional output. What's

9 Before 1999, French officials used the euphemism "the events" to address France's involvement in Algeria during the years 1954-1962. It took the French government until 1999 to recognize the role of the French police in the 1961 October Massacre, which took place in Paris during the Algerian War, as hundreds of demonstrators who were in favour of Algerian independence were thrown into the river Seine by the French police, led at the time by Nazi collaborator Maurice Papon. Still, in 2005, the Chirac government performed some serious backpedalling when it demanded that teachers in schools all over the country emphasize the positive role of French colonization, especially in North Africa, before the law on the memory of colonialism was finally repealed by President Chirac in 2006 (see Gurrey 2005). It was only in September 2018, too, that French president Macron finally declared, firstly, that the use of torture by the French army had been systemic during the Algerian War (something which had been hitherto denied), and secondly, that pro-independence French Algerian dissidents such as Maurice Audin had been kidnapped and killed by French paratroopers during the late 1950s in Algeria (see Chrisafis 2018).

more, *Le Premier Homme* foregrounds what the historians call "a fraternity of the poor" (Stora and Péretié 2013, 83; my translation) between Arabs and French Algerians of the working class. In any case, it would be misleading to privilege Camus's novelistic output and *not* read his writings across genres. Stora and Péretié (2013) indeed venture that for Camus, "the space of the novel is not the privileged place for political commitment" (83; my translation). Re-contextualizing Camus's complex stance on the "Algerian question" via his journalistic pieces, Stora and Péretié certainly illuminate aspects of Camus and his work which refreshingly go beyond the colonizer/colonized binary upon which Said's "contrapuntal" argument rests.

What Camus's journalism on Algeria reveals is that his infamous opposition to the creation of the Algerian nation state during the war of liberation was never, in fact, the whole story. For instance, in the wake of the 1945 Sétif and Guelma riots against French rule, which are now deemed to have constituted the undeclared beginning of the Algerian War, Camus published in the Resistance newspaper *Combat* "Crise en Algérie" ("Crisis in Algeria"). In this series of eight articles, Camus begged for political reforms to oppose the injustices of colonialism while contextualizing the Sétif massacres[10] in light of the appalling economic situation of the Arab and Berber populations in French Algeria. A key journalistic piece is also the essay "Algérie 1958", in which the writer explains his position in favour of a federated Algeria where Berbers, Arabs, Jews, and Europeans could live together. Still, when Camus's journalistic pieces were initially published in France in 1958, the volume *Actuelles III: Chroniques Algériennes* was met with widespread critical silence. Possibly, by 1958, the escalation of violence on both sides in Algeria had made Camus's "neither/nor" position irrelevant, and the publication of the volume did not manage to dispel (or just complicate) the deleterious

10 Dubbed "the other 8 May 1945" (see, for instance, Jeune Afrique 2015), the Sétif massacres (in which 100 French Algerians were killed or atrociously mutilated and thousands of Arab Algerians were massacred by French authorities in retaliation) hardly received any coverage in the mainland French press.

effect of his infamous remark while attending a press conference in Stockholm in 1957 on the occasion of his Nobel Prize.[11] Needless to say, the much-belated translation into English of *Actuelles III* in 2013 (entitled *Algerian Chronicles*) not only gave "a new life" (Kaplan 2013, 9) and a new audience to Camus's journalism; it has also allowed the volume to be received at all. And so, if Stora and Péretié are right in seeing in *Actuelles III* a body of work that grounds Camus in Algeria, it is remarkable that such situatedness could only appear by way of translation—that is, by way of a worldly detour.

In many ways, Daoud's novel also operates a worldly detour to ground Camus in Algeria, though it does so by way of intertextual entanglements. As I will show below, *Meursault, contre-enquête* indeed feigns to embrace, at first, the binary-reversing formula of the postcolonial redress novel but ends up revealing instead how Camus's work can be intertextually "tilted [. . .] sideways"[12] (Daoud 2015, 132) so that it exhibits a profound entanglement with contemporary postcolonial Algeria—that is, to return to Nuttall's (2009) understanding of it, "a sense of intimacy gained even if it was resisted, or ignored, or uninvited" (1). Significantly, the opening of Daoud's novel resonates with Saidian echoes, as Harun, the protagonist and first-person narrator, meets a stranger in a bar in today's Oran and starts telling him the

11 Before the advent of the "new Camus", the writer's ambiguous stance during the Algerian War was, by and large, often encapsulated by one sentence only. This was his famous reply to an Algerian student arguing the cause of the FLN during the Stockholm press conference, which was reported (and misquoted) in *Le Monde* at the time, before it was further reduced to a formula highlighting the writer's privileging of his mother over justice. As Kaplan (2013) explains, the Stockholm "tragicomedy of misquotations" resulted in constructing Camus as "a sentimental egotist" (18). Indeed Camus's original reply to the Algerian student, "If [planting bombs in the tramways of Algiers] is justice, then I prefer my mother" ("Si c'est cela [lancer des bombes dans les tramways d'Alger] la justice, je préfère ma mère") was reported in *Le Monde* as "I believe in justice, but I will defend my mother before justice" ("Je crois à la justice, mais je défendrai ma mère avant la justice"), which was later on reduced to "Between justice and my mother, I choose my mother" ("Entre la justice et ma mère, je préfère ma mère"). See Stora and Péretié (2013) for more on this.

12 Original: "en le faisant pencher de côté" (142).

story of Musa, his murdered brother. As Harun drunkenly rages against the circumstances of his brother's death and its absence of memorialization, readers are instantly reminded of Said's framing of Camus as a closet colonialist, and more specifically, of the critic's contention that *L'Étranger* is "a novel about the deaths of Arabs, deaths that highlight and silently inform the French characters' difficulties of conscience or reflection" (Said 1994, 219). Indeed, Harun reveals that the murder of his brother on a beach in Algiers in 1942 was related in a famous novel that anonymized his brother and gave pride of place to the feeling of existential solitude of Meursault, the "writer-killer" (Daoud 2015, 54).

In his review of *Meursault, contre-enquête,* Adam Shatz (2015) remarks that, in Algeria, nationalist critics "have long spoken about *The Stranger* as if the murder it described had actually happened and Camus [. . .] had committed it" (n.p.). As if taking these critics at their word, in his novel, Daoud actualizes the interpretative fallacy that Meursault's murder "actually happened" and seemingly replaces Camus with Meursault. In fact, the suggestion that Harun's story is a twisted retelling of *L'Étranger* is emphasized in the very first sentence of *Meursault, contre-enquête,* which rewrites the famous opening of Camus's classic, namely "My mother died today" (Camus 2013b, 3), while turning it on its head, as the narrator somehow ambivalently declares that "Mama's still alive today" (Daoud 2015, 1).[13] Incensed as he is that his brother was only remembered as "a brief Arab, technically ephemeral" (3),[14] that "even after Independence", no one "ever tried to find out who [his brother's] name was, or where he lived, or what family he came from, or whether he had children" (4), Musa dumps his story on a listener whose name is never mentioned but who is randomly addressed by the storyteller as "you", "my friend" (6), "Mr. Investigator" (18), "Mr. Student Detective" (20), among others, and is revealed as carrying a copy of "Meursault's book"

13 Original: "Aujourd'hui M'ma est encore vivante" (11).
14 Original: "Un Arabe bref, techniquement fugace" (13).

(131) in his schoolbag (4). Significantly, Harun's pretend act of "writing back" is revealed to be directed less at Camus's *L'Étranger* per se than at a pre-text whose plot loosely mimics that of Camus's classic.

Halfway through the book, the narrative uncovers that, in contrast to what happens in *L'Étranger*, Meursault is released after his murderous deed in 1942 and his condemnation to death; he then goes on to achieve fame by describing his homicide in a book entitled *The Other* (Daoud 2015, 127). As if preparing to "write back to the centre" in typical postcolonial fashion, upon his first encounter with his anonymous and silent listener, Harun tells him that he learnt the language of Meursault, his brother's murderer, so he could "speak in the place of a dead man [...], finish his sentences for him" (1) and more generally, so he could "tell the story Musa was never able to tell" (4). But Harun appears to almost self-consciously rehash and recycle hackneyed postcolonial tropes so he can later on derail them. Initially stating that his aim is to appropriate "the murderer's words and expressions" as "[his] *unclaimed goods*" (2; original emphasis),[15] the narrator clearly frames his storytelling as a postcolonial act of restitution and re-purposing, associating the language of his brother's murderer with "stones from the old houses the colonists left behind" that he can now use to "build [his] own house, [his] own language" (2). At a later point in his one-sided confession, though, Harun complicates his earlier statement, presenting the French language as a buffer zone with his illiterate mother, who, following Musa's death, invariably constructs her deceased son as "an invincible, long-awaited hero, a kind of savior" (Daoud 2015, 16), so Harun "feel[s] guilty for being alive" (35). Associating the French language with the desire to know more about his brother's death while bypassing Mama's "monstrous torrents of [...] made-up tales" (37), Harun eventually confesses that he learnt French because he wanted to be able to read two newspaper clippings that his illiterate mother "kept religiously folded in her bosom" (120)[16] and that purportedly retraced the details of Musa's

15 Original: "[son] *bien vacant*" (12; original emphasis).

16 Original: "[les deux coupures de journaux] que M'ma gardait religieusement pliées dans sa poitrine" (130).

death. Harun then perfects his mastery of French with Meriem, an Algerian teacher from Constantine who becomes his lover for a few months in 1963, and who is the first to bring to his attention that, unbeknownst to Mama, the story of his brother's murder had in fact been consigned all along to a famous book written by Meursault and published two decades earlier, in 1942. In other words, loaded as they are with colonial ramifications, and granted that they are "tilt[ed] sideways" (132) by Meriem or "read from right to left" (7), "Meursault's book" (131) and the French language end up representing, for Musa, a means of acquiring historical knowledge beyond the grasp of Mama, who, after her first-born's death, has abandoned herself to "the macabre pleasure of a never-ending period of mourning" (37), so much so that his mother is perceived by the storyteller to impose a "strict duty of reincarnation [of his dead brother]" (41) onto him, even to "resent [him] for a death [he] basically refuse[s] to undergo" (36).

Relying on Abdel-Jaouad's remark that, in postcolonial Maghrebi writings in French, the figure of the mother is either glorified and/or tied up to the subjugated and colonized nation, Mary Poteau-Tralie and Suzanne Miller (2020) aptly remark that Daoud's novel subverts this dynamic, in that the mother here "becomes a metaphorical figure representing the inexorable pull of Algeria's past on any effort to go beyond it, to forge something new from the ashes of tragic history" (3). But there is more to it than that. As many critics have noted, in Algeria, the fact that official history is written by the party in power since Independence, namely the FLN, accounts for many distortions and blank pages in contemporary history. These blank pages range from the silencing of the role of the pro-independence and competing party MNA (*Mouvement national algérien*/Algerian National Movement) during the anticolonial struggle, to the problematic memory of the military coup and so-called *"redressement révolutionnaire"* (revolutionary redress) that saw Colonel Boumédienne overthrow the historic leader of the FLN, Ahmad Ben Bella, and install himself as president from 1965 to 1978 (Harbi 1980), to the hushing up of the use of torture and physical mutilation during the decade-long civil war of the 1990s between the authoritarian regime and a variety of Islamist, secular and Berber political groups (Prochaska 2006, 266–67). In many ways, Mama's impossible mourning, her unsurpassed power over Harun, and her infinite variations on "one deceptively wonderful tale" (Daoud 2015, 15)[17] that idealize her dead son but annihilate her live one thus mirror the lethal and myth-like character of state-sanctioned memory in contemporary Algeria, a country where the glorious narrative of heroic resistance to the French has been appropriated and instrumentalized by the FLN to valorize its post-independence position, naturalize single-party rule (1962–89), enforce military power, and "unify" issues of national identity.

This is not to say that Harun is "nostalgic for French Algeria", as he vehemently makes clear (31). Rather, following Sami Alkyam (2019), I would like to contend that Harun is critical of both colonial power and of postcolonial Algeria, while hopelessly longing for the advent of a plural Algeria. Possibly incarnated by Meriem, a "free, brash, disobedient" and bookish Algerian woman whom Harun meets following Independence, but whose type "has disappeared in this country today" (Daoud 2015, 135),[18] the notion of a plural Algeria increasingly recedes into the distance now that Islamism appears to constitute the only alternative to the corrupt authoritarian regime, causing Harun to feel that he is stuck "between Allah and ennui" (131). Interestingly for my purposes, the leading Algerian historian Mohammed Harbi (1992) explains that there has been an unfortunate carryover between the colonial period, where the FLN strategically imagined the Algerian nation "in an extremely simplistic fashion" to unify against the French, and the postcolonial period, where national identity still congeals around Arab identity, "thus excluding the diversity of origins and cultures that are at the base of Algerian identity" (28–29; my translation). So, it is no accident that Harun's drunken rantings problematize his self-identification with the very notion of Arab-ness: "*Arab*", as Harun muses. "I never felt Arab, you know. Arab-ness is like

17 Original: "un seul conte faussement merveilleux" (25).

18 Original: "[Meriem] appartient à un genre de femmes qui, aujourd'hui, a disparu dans ce pays: libre, conquérante, insoumise" (145).

Negro-ness, which only exists in the white man's eyes" (Daoud 2015, 60; original emphasis).[19] Raging at the state of the postcolonial nation in a "dive" which is officially called Djebel Zendel (25), that is, a mountain that served as a safe haven for *fellaghas* (FLN guerrillas) during the anticolonial struggle, but which is now ominously dubbed "The Titanic" (25) by its regulars, Harun unsettles state-sanctioned notions of national identity as he emphasizes the plurality of influences shaping his surroundings: "The song is Oranian, the beer's Arab, the whiskey's European, the bartenders are Kabyles, the streets are French, the old porticos are Spanish" (22).[20]

But Harun's commentary on the many unfortunate carry-overs between the colonial and postcolonial also carries further gendered undertones. Mocking the implicit binary opposition at play in "Meursault's book" (131) between the French Algerian Marie—a character who was "brought up in a greenhouse of impossible innocence" (62)—and the sister of "the Arab", a prostitute whom the narrator reads as "a distant symbol of our land, plowed by customers and passersby" (62), the storyteller remarks that had his interlocutor bumped into him a few decades ago in the same café in Oran, he, too, "would have served [him] up" another version of this binary "with the prostitute slash Algerian land and the settler who abuses her with repeated rapes and violence" (62). However, Harun notes that he has "gained some distance now" (62–63).

To return to my earlier point that Daoud's novel gives a refreshing twist to the maternal metaphor by eschewing the trope of the mother as saint and/or victim who is tied up to "the subjugated and colonized nation" in Maghrebi postcolonial writing, it is worth mentioning that, in an attempt to unsettle the ways in which the figure of the (asexual) mother and that of the (over-sexed) prostitute are utilized to represent never-possible ideals of national purity in colonial

19 Original: "*Arabe*, je ne me suis jamais senti arabe, tu sais. C'est comme la négritude qui n'existe que par le regard du Blanc" (70).

20 Original: "cette chanson est oranaise, la bière arabe, le whisky européen, les barmans sont kabyles, les rues françaises, les vieux portiques espagnols" (32).

and postcolonial discourses alike, Harun significantly merges the figure of the originator *and* that of the prostitute in an "obscene vision" (13) of Oran. Indeed, for Harun, the city "faces the sea with its legs apart, its thighs spread, from the bay to the high ground",[21] a high ground where he often goes to visit a "luxurious and fragrant" garden in which, "down there", he detects "the scent of a woman's sex, a giant, worn-out one" (13). Foregrounding a "vast labyrinth of Spanish and Turkish galleries", as well as vegetal entanglements with "roots of centuries-old trees" (12–13) that are likened to "giant, naked, suspended flowers" (13), the hyper-feminized and luxuriant garden faces the sea, so it could be "*inseminated*" (13; original emphasis) by General Létang in 1848. Needless to say, Harun's "obscene vision" operates as a "sexed up" myth of origins in which the genealogy of the Algerian city is reshuffled as being as unrestrainedly lush and fertile as it is impure. Significantly, Harun invokes the similar figure of the "luxuriant prostitute" to gesture towards the circulational detours, historical entanglements and contextual cross-pollinations predating his own "worldly" act of storytelling:

> Picture an old whore dazed by an excess of men; she and this story of mine share some features. It's like a text written on parchment and scattered all around the world; it's brittle, patched up, no longer recognizable, infinitely rehashed—and yet look at you, sitting beside me and hoping for something new, something never heard before. This story does not suit your quest for purity, I swear to you. (51)[22]

In this passage, far from validating binary-reversing postcolonial readings of *L'Étranger*, Daoud toys with the notion that "Meursault's book" (and by extension Camus's classic) is now so ensnared in its

---

21 Original: "[cette ville] a les jambes ouvertes vers la mer, les cuisses écartées, depuis la baie jusqu'à ses hauteurs" (22).

22 Original: "Elle a pourtant quelque chose d'une vieille putain réduite à l'hébétude par l'excès des hommes, cette histoire. Elle ressemble à un parchemin, dispersé de par le monde, essoré, rafistolé, désormais méconnaissable, dont le texte aura été ressassé jusqu'à l'infini—et tu es pourtant là, assis à mes côtés, espérant du neuf, de l'inédit. Cette histoire ne sied pas à ta quête de pureté, je te jure" (61).

various interpretations, re-interpretations, erasures and retellings that it carries with it the "worldly" and impure potential to signify "something new, something never heard before". However, as I have suggested above, "worldliness" and "circumstantiality" are profoundly entangled in Daoud's novel, in that Harun's drunken ravings about "Meursault's book" offer, in fact, a broad narrative canvas, a "text written on parchment" onto which the storyteller can both express his rage towards the "murder-killer" (Meursault/Camus's colonial imaginary) *and* confess his past enmeshment with Mama who, in post-independence FLN-like fashion, has instrumentalized her grief, turning the pre-independence loss of her son into a "marvellous act", a "masterpiece" (34) which keeps Harun (or is it contemporary Algeria?) under her thumb.

The toxic power of state-sanctioned memory stands at the heart of Daoud's representation of the mother-son relationship, and such power is nowhere more lethal than when Harun confesses that he, too, shot a man in July 1962, a few hours after Independence, while significantly "feel[ing] [Mama's] eyes on [his] back like a hand pushing [him], holding [him] upright, guiding [his] arm, slightly tilting [his] head at the moment when [he] took aim" (Daoud 2015, 75). In other words, enmeshed as he is with Mama (or power-drunk as he is on the regime's myth-like version of history?), Harun kills a man while on autopilot, in a way that is reminiscent of Meursault, who kills Harun's brother while "propelled by some blind force, as if he's a robot" (72). Kaplan (2016b) has noted that the form of *Meursault, contre-enquête* is highly influenced by the "I/you" dialectics wielded by Camus in another of his classics, *La Chute*, so it is only fitting that Harun's victim, namely the Frenchman Joseph Larquais, materializes in Harun's courtyard through "the muffled sound of a fall" (Daoud 2015, 80)[23] after having the bad luck of seeking refuge in his house after Independence. By importing one of the most famous sentences of *La Chute* into his (pseudo-)remake of *L'Étranger*, Daoud suggests that the murder of the Frenchman acts on Harun's psyche in a similar way as the

23 Original: "un bruit sourd de chute" (90).

titular "fall" of the woman into the river Seine in Jean-Baptiste Clamence's mind, which retroactively emphasizes Clamence's passivity and consequently shatters his self-image.

In *Meursault, contre-enquête*, Harun feels that his own belated act of revenge is "struck down to the [. . .] level of insignificance" (Daoud 2015, 111),[24] as FLN officials arrest him and then release him while reproaching him, not for having killed a man, but for having killed a man at the wrong time—that is, a few hours after the end of the war. Harun then experiences a sense of the Absurd that brings him back to Meursault's novel, *The Other*. At that point, whole passages from *L'Étranger* are quoted verbatim in Daoud's novel, as if Meursault's rantings against the hypocrisy of society and the lure of religion in Camus's novel had directly travelled from Camus's Meursault to Harun. It is one of the greater paradoxes of Daoud's book that Harun finally discovers that he is "practically [Meursault's double]" (131). At the start of the novel, Harun is incensed that nobody knows his brother's name, even as "everyone declare[s] their empathy with [Mersault's] solitude" (4). At the end of the novel, though, Harun feels that, throughout his life, he has "interpreted all [the] roles [of Meursault's book] in turn"—including, now, that of "the stranger" to an Algeria caught between Islamists and the military rule of the FLN.

Undoubtedly, through Harun's final identification with Meursault, Daoud literalizes the world literature hypothesis that texts continually travel towards meaning, and what is more, that they might even end up complicating (or "writing back" to) the very paradigms that had previously burnt layers of interpretation into them. By regrounding Camus's *L'Etranger* in today's Algeria, Daoud re-historicizes some of the intricacies of the postcolonial period in Algeria and shows that the binaries of classic postcolonial theory are unable to bear witness to the complexities—and the entanglements—of the contemporary moment. Harun's confession of having taken up the place of Meursault prompts us, in turn, to envisage the entangled

24 Original: "[ma vengeance] venait d'être frappée de [. . .] nullité" (121).

"wordliness" and "circumstantality" of Camus's novel. Like Harun, we are thus encouraged to return to Camus's classics, and "read them in a certain way, tilting [them] sideways as though to make invisible details fall out" (132).

Bibliography

Alkyam, Sami. 2019. "Lost in Reading: The Predicament of Postcolonial Writing in Kamel Daoud's *The Meursault Investigation*." *Journal of Postcolonial Writing* 55 (4): 459–71.

Brée, Germaine. 1959. *Camus*. New Brunswick, NJ: Rutgers University Press.

Breen, Gina Marie. 2019. "Neither Algerian, nor French: Albert Camus's Pied-Noir Identity." *Mediterranean Studies* 27 (2): 210–33.

Camus, Albert. 1942. *L'Étranger*. Collection Folio. Paris: Gallimard.

Camus, Albert. 1956. *La Chute*. Paris: Gallimard.

Camus, Albert. 1994. *Le Premier Homme*. Collection Folio. Paris: Gallimard.

Camus, Albert. 1957. *The Fall*. Translated by Justin O'Brien. New York: Knopf.

Camus, Albert. 1958. *Actuelles III: Chroniques Algériennes* [Algerian Chronicles]. Paris: Gallimard.

Camus, Albert. 1995. *The First Man*. Translated by David Hapgood. New York: Knopf.

Camus, Albert. 2013a. *Algerian Chronicles*. Translated by Arthur Goldhammer. Princeton, NJ: Princeton University Press.

Camus, Albert. 2013b. *The Outsider*. Translated by Sandra Smith. London: Penguin.

Carroll, David. 2007. *Albert Camus the Algerian: Colonialism, Terrorism, Justice*. New York: Columbia University Press.

Chrisafis, Angelique. 2018. "France Admits Systematic Torture During Algeria War for First Time." *The Guardian*, 13 September. https://www.theguardian.com/world/2018/sep/13/france-state-responsible-for-1957-death-of-dissident-maurice-audin-in-algeria-says-macron.

Combe, Dominique. 2013. "Camus Postcolonial?" *Revue Sciences/Lettres*, 25 March. http://rsl.revues.org/638.

Cooper, Frederick. 2003. "Postcolonial Peoples: A Commentary." In *Europe's Invisible Migrants*, edited by Andrea L. Smith, 169–84. Amsterdam: Amsterdam University Press.

Daoud, Kamel. 2014. *Meursault, contre-enquête*. Arles: Actes Sud.

Daoud, Kamel. 2015. *The Meursault Investigation*. Translated by John Cullen. London: Oneworld.

Damrosch, David. 2003. "World Literatures, National Contexts." *Modern Philology* 100 (4): 512–31.

Derrida, Jacques. 1995. "There Is No *One* Narcissism: Autobiophotographies." In *Points, Interviews, 1974–1994*, by Jacques Derrida, 196–215. Stanford, CA: Stanford University Press.

Derrida, Jacques. 1998. *Monolingualism of the Other; or, The Prosthesis of Origin*. Translated by Patrick Mensah. Stanford, CA: Stanford University Press.

Dobie, Madeleine. 2016. "We Are in a 'Camus Moment': But What Can the Great French-Algerian Author Teach Us About the World Today?" *Huffpost*, 24 May. https://www.huffpost.com/entry/essay-we-are-in-a-camus-m_b_10124026.

Gurrey, Béatrice. 2005. "Mémoire coloniale: Jacques Chirac temporise" [Colonial Memory: Jacques Chirac Temporises]. *Le Monde*, 10 December. https://www.lemonde.fr/societe/article/2005/12/10/histoire-memoire-politique-la-france-troublee_719817_3224.html.

Harbi, Mohammed. 1992. *L'Algérie et son destin: Croyants ou citoyens?* [Algeria and Its Destiny: Believers or Citizens?] Paris: Arcantère.

Helgesson, Stefan. 2014. "Postcolonialism and World Literature." *Interventions* 16 (4): 483–500.

Helgesson, Stefan, and Pieter Vermeulen. 2016. "Introduction: World Literature in the Making." In *Institutions of World Literature: Writing, Translation, Markets*, edited by Stefan Helgesson and Pieter Vermeulen, 1–20. Abingdon: Routledge.

Hubbell, Amy L. 2015. *Remembering French Algeria: Pieds-Noirs, Identity, and Exile*. Lincoln, NE: University of Nebraska Press.

Huggan, Graham. 2015. "Notes on the Postcolonial Arctic." In *The Future of Postcolonial Studies*, edited by Chantal Zabus, 130–43. Abingdon: Routledge.

Jeune Afrique. 2015. "Massacres de Sétif: 'L'autre 8 mai 1945', la France qui regarde son histoire en face" [The Sétif Massacres: 'The Other May 8, 1945': France is Looking Its History in the Face]. *Jeune Afrique*, 6 May. https://www.jeuneafrique.com/231284/politique/massacres-de-s-tif-l-autre-8-mai-1945-la-france-qui-regarde-son-histoire-en-face/.

Kaplan, Alice. 2013. "New Perspectives on Camus's Algerian Chronicles." In *Algerian Chronicles*, by Albert Camus, 1–18. Translated by Arthur Goldhammer. Princeton, NJ: Princeton University Press.

Kaplan, Alice. 2016a. *Looking for The Stranger: Albert Camus and the Life of a Literary Classic.* Chicago, IL: University of Chicago Press.

Kaplan, Alice. 2016b. "Making *L'Etranger* Contemporary: Kamel Daoud's *Meursault, contre-enquête.*" In *Being Contemporary: French Literature, Culture and Politics Today*, edited by Lia Brozgal and Sara Kippur, 334–46. Liverpool: Liverpool University Press.

King, Adele. 1992. "Introduction: After Fifty Years, Still a Stranger." In: *Camus's L'Etranger: Fifty Years On*, edited by Adele King, 1–15. London: Palgrave Macmillan. https://doi.org/10.1007/978-1-349-22003-8_1.

Moretti, Franco. 2000. "Conjectures on World Literature." *New Left Review* 1: 54–68. https://newleftreview.org/issues/ii1/articles/franco-moretti-conjectures-on-world-literature.

Mukherjee. Ankhi. 2014. *What Is a Classic? Postcolonial Rewriting and Invention of the Canon*. Stanford, CA: Stanford University Press.

Nuttall, Sarah. 2009. *Entanglement: Literary and Cultural Reflections on Post-Apartheid*. Johannesburg: Wits University Press.

Poteau-Tralie, Mary, and Suzanne Miller. 2020. "Maternal Metaphor in Kamel Daoud's Textual Grafting upon Camus's *L'Étranger*." *Postcolonial Text* 15 (1): 1–21.

Prochaska, David. 2006. "The Return of the Repressed: War, Trauma, Memory in Algeria and Beyond." In *Algeria and France 1800–2000: Identity, Memory, Nostalgia*, edited by Patricia Lorcin, 257-76. Syracuse, NY: Syracuse University Press.

Radhakrishnan, Rajagopalan. 2017. "*The Meursault Investigation*: A Contrapuntal Reading." *The Cambridge Journal of Postcolonial Literary Enquiry* 4 (3): 440–56

Said, Edward. 1983. *The World, the Text, and the Critic*. Cambridge, MA: Harvard University Press.

Said, Edward. 1994. *Culture and Imperialism*. London: Vintage.

Sartre, Jean-Paul. 1947. "Explication de *L'Étranger*." In *Situations I*, by Jean-Paul Sartre, 99–121. Paris: Gallimard.

Shatz, Adam. 2015. "Stranger Still." *New York Times Magazine*, 1 April. https://www.nytimes.com/2015/04/05/magazine/stranger-still.html.

Shepard, Todd. 2006. *The Invention of Decolonization: The Algerian War and the Remaking of France*. Ithaca, NY: Cornell University Press.

Simon, Catherine. 2012. "Affaire Camus: Onfray quitte la 'pétaudière.'" [The Camus Affair: Onfray Leaves the "Madhouse"]. *Le Monde*, 17 September. https://www.lemonde.fr/livres/article/2012/09/17/affaire-camus-onfray-quitte-la-petaudiere_1761377_3260.html.

Stora, Benjamin, and Jean-Baptiste Péretié. 2013. *Camus brûlant* [Burning Camus]. Paris: Editions Stock.

Transareal Cities and Literatures Without a Fixed Abode in Assia Djebar, Emine Sevgi Özdamar and Cécile Wajsbrot

Ottmar Ette

Urbanity and Literature

Cities and literature have always been connected in a mutual relationship. The first tablets of the *Epic of Gilgamesh* confront us with an intellectual aim which today we call literature: to grasp the totality of everything that has been created and that has become, and the will to develop awareness of the world by relying on that vision. The first tablets of the epic tell us about the hero's travels, which take the city of Uruk as their point of departure, and how he traverses the depths of space and time:

> He who saw the Deep, the country's foundation
> [who] knew [. . .], was wise in all matters!
> [Gilgamesh, who] saw the Deep, the country's foundation,
> [who] knew [. . .], was wise in all matters!
> [He] [. . .] everywhere [. . .]
> and [*learnt*] of everything the sum of wisdom.
> He saw what was secret, discovered what was hidden,
> he brought back a tale of the Deluge. (George 2000, 1)

These ancient tablets made of clay, which date back to the end of the second millennium BC and even hint at earlier versions from the third millennium BC (George 2000, xix), develop literature as an ever-mobile world-consciousness which, nevertheless, always traverses and evokes the city. The city proudly appears on the textual stage as a spatial entity, an impressive geographical expanse, at the beginning and the end of the epic:

> [A square mile is] city, [a square mile] date-grove, a square mile is clay-plit, half a square mile the temple of Ishtar:

> [three square miles] and a half is Uruk's expanse.
> (George 2000, 2)

But the great city of Uruk mostly establishes itself through the movements of Gilgamesh, who keeps passing through the city and therefore connects it to the most remote corners of the world.

The *Epic of Gilgamesh*—with its very own history of sources[1]—is the point of departure of a long-lasting literary tradition. Within this tradition, epics and prose often connect the representation of totality to the representation of the city, thereby transforming it into a microcosm-macrocosm relationship. This is to say that the city, like literature—which has always had to deal with the task of representing infinity within a finite, closed frame—becomes part of the microcosm, the place of man-made and worldly creations and their specific forms.

In the late 18th century, under the influence of paradigms such as the end of natural history (Lepenies 1978) and the historicity of all discourses (Foucault 1966), the city was often the object of what one might call an archaeological gaze. Victor Hugo's *Notre-Dame de Paris*, Honoré de Balzac's *Le Père Goriot* and Gustave Flaubert's *L'Éducation sentimentale* are prime examples. This gaze did not confine itself to horizontal movements *within* the city but also privileged vertical, archaeological movements through the strata and stories of a city's history. During the last three decades of the 20th century, however, these strata and stories were in turn replaced by developments which focused on vectors and directionality within history. These transformations, in my view, are clearly and obviously linked to the second and third phase of accelerated globalization.[2] Ever since then, the city has no longer manifested itself as a geographically defined sprawl, *in situ* as it were, but, rather, as arising from within a foundational phenomenon of interrelations. This perspective not only connects cities from different countries, from different cultural areas, to form mobile structures. It also highlights the insular characteristics

1 See in this context the genealogical reflections in Maul (2005, 9–18).
2 See, for more information on these categories, Ette (2004b, 169–84).

of a city—which the *Epic of Gilgamesh* had already made very clear by contrasting city and countryside—as a far-reaching transareal archipelago situation.

The following chapter will work with selected texts by Assia Djebar, Emine Sevgi Özdamar and Cécile Wajsbrot. All these authors have spent their lives going back and forth between Paris and New York, Istanbul and Berlin, as well as Paris and Berlin. This chapter will attempt to elucidate to what extent these literary creations, which we could call literature without a fixed abode (Ette 2016), present advanced vectorial models of the urban. At this point, it is safe to say that these authors create cities that have lost the firmness of their situation, their stability *in situ*, and have transformed into highly "individualized", self-reliant metropolises just because these cities always include and represent *other* cities.

We might very well ask whether it is still possible to understand a city without realizing that it is made up of other cities, a specific combination of various cities—and this does not just refer to the realm of migration. Can we understand a city without being aware of its movements, without knowing that we may not restrict our perspective to archaeological strata, but that we must understand a city's dynamic directionality? Does not literature have the capacity to show us how important it is for us to submit our view of the city to a fundamental epistemological shift, which takes us from a history of space to a history of movement?

The Goethean concept of *Weltliteratur* endured throughout the entire 19th century and the first half of the 20th century and can be understood as a practice of literary activity as well as a theoretical conceptualization of the construction of a global literary system. The practice and concept of world literature began to crumble in the second half of the 20th century, and were brought into question and became historical no later than the beginning of the 21st century. This world literature was replaced by the transareal and polylogical literatures of the world. With their increasing differentiation in francophone, anglophone, hispanophone and lusophone literatures with their own logics, these literatures of the world have changed into a highly mobile and quickly changing multi-logical system, which depends on various entanglements between and across the Global North and the Global South. The metropolises "have become focal points of multicultural, intercultural and transcultural movements, by which the various kinds of cultural juxtaposition can be understood" (Ette 2006, 36), highlighting precisely such entanglements. Dislocation and heterotopia, a constant movement of jumping from one location to another, have created literatures without a fixed abode. This specific type of literature is a concept that will not fit the categories of national literature and migrant's literature, or even world literature. The literatures without a fixed abode have become a traversing, as it were, component of our contemporary literary practice and increasingly of our theoretical engagements with literatures at a global scale.

If we describe the literatures without a fixed abode as a constant process of dislocation, we can grasp the continuation and reinterpretation ("Fortschreibung") of German-language literature as *F:ortschreibung*,[3] which is to say that loci of literature are continued, reinterpreted, multiplied and displaced.

Literature, which from its beginnings was fundamentally and intimately linked to the city, offers us new views of the city by representing real life as its aesthetic essence. As the French semiotician Roland Barthes (2002) put it in a lecture course at the Collège de France, *Comment vivre ensemble*, making his point very clear: that literature is always ahead of the times: "toujours en avance sur tout" (167). Literature is a cultural practice which specializes in being unspecialized concerning discursive and disciplinary dispositions of knowledge. Therefore, literature has much to offer to those scientific disciplines that deal with the phenomenon of the urban. We will use the prospective capacities of literature about the urban to create a new understanding of the city, leading us away from immobile states and estates.

3 This is an orthographic and poetic technique I borrow from the poetry of José F. A. Oliver. For more information on the specifics of this technique, see Ette (2004a, 247).

Assia Djebar, or the City of Streets

Fatima-Zohra Irmalayène was born in 1936 in Cherchell, not far from Algiers. As a writer, she became famous under her *nom de plume*, Assia Djebar.[4] And it is no coincidence that her novel *Les Nuits de Strasbourg*[5] takes place in the heart of that specific geo-cultural space that we must consider the European field of movement *par excellence*. The novel's diegesis, which does not remain restricted to European territory, instead of centring on a landscape, describes the cityscape of the Alsatian city of Strasbourg. In the course of this love story, the city also vividly comes alive as a "soundscape", a "touchscape" and "smellscape".

This city, which in many respects represents a "ville transfrontalière",[6] is the focal point of a story which establishes its temporal frame by referring to the European Middle Ages and the beginnings of French colonialism in Northern Africa. It focuses on the "long" 20th century while creating a spatial structure that uses Strasbourg as a point of departure and goes on to develop a transareal dimension by evoking France, Germany, the Netherlands, but also the North-African "counterpart" to the European coast, especially Algeria. All paths passing through this vast space intersect in Alsace, that is: in Strasbourg, which in Assia Djebar's (1997) book is the place where all roads and paths meet, as the etymology of the word implies (400). This city takes its mythical beginnings from the concept of routes, a *ville des routes*, and seems to have been born from movement. The novel unfolds this phenomenon in a conceptual structure of movement. Therefore, this urban novel, in whose title the German name of the town still peeks out from under the French, does not take any special interest in roots, in the roots and foundations of a clearly defined (and delimited) identity, a concept which claims one isolated source. Rather, the novel highlights the importance of routes, pathways and

4 For more information on the work of this Algerian-born author, see Jürgs (2015).
5 See my extensive analysis in Ette (2010b).
6 See in this context the very interesting essay by Wolfgang Asholt (2005).

movements which create the subject, the city, the network of streets with no beginnings or endings.

The structure of the novel is a symmetrical one. It begins with a prologue, ends with an (implicit) epilogue and presents the main narrative as a sequence of nine nights. And it comes as no surprise that the fifth chapter—which marks the centre of the text—is entitled "Le Fleuve, les ponts" and urges us to interpret the cityscape as a *landscape of theory*. As a logical consequence, the prologue of the novel, "La Ville", places the city at the centre of the reader's attention. But at the same time, *centre-ville* turns out to be a *centre vide*, as the first-person narrator crosses town for a last time, shortly before daybreak: a city-centre which was abandoned by its inhabitants in September 1939, while the German Wehrmacht prepared its assault and Strasbourg, east of the famous Maginot-line, seemed an inevitable military sacrifice. Again, the concept of movement reappears, even though these are movements of a different sort, namely persecution, migration and delocalization. The novel's incipit speaks of these movements: "Everyone, at once, outside, on the pavement and along the streets, is an army, a mob, a stampede" (Djebar 1997, 11).[7]

The people flee, but the streets and the statues remain. Apart from the French troops in the barracks and the officials who have been left behind to take care of the abandoned city, only the statues remain. They stare down upon the deserted city from bridges, churches and pedestals, enveloping it in the network of their gaze. Even though the statues seem "indifferent" (Djebar 1997, 14) to the human population, like the buildings, churches or bridges, their gaze comes alive very quickly: Their eyes take note of the changes. They sense the silence, even revolt against the "strange mutism" (17) of a soundscape that has deadened abruptly. They cannot foresee that they will be "dismantled, crushed, put into storage, deported" (17),[8] once the city has been sealed off, "immerged in this void" (18). It was

7 Original: "Tous, d'un coup, au-dehors, sur le pavé ou par les routes, c'est une armée, une horde, un exode".

8 Original: "déboulonnées, concassés, transportées à la remise, deportees".

not until June 15, 1940, that the Nazi troops crossed the Rhine at Colmar, reaching Strasbourg four days later. The novel repeatedly mentions the Prussian occupation of Strasbourg in 1870, when the French fought for the city. The prologue ends with the French capitulation on June 22, 1940 (35).

But the Algerian author's reflective recollection of European history does not end here. The abandoned city of Strasbourg—which is hardly ever mentioned in German or French history-books—confronts the reader with a puzzling lesson. Fifty years after these events, the novel's Algerian protagonist aims to solve this riddle: a question which has not lost any of its relevance in the 21st century as it asks how we might live together peacefully, respectful of our differences, and share the experience of our lives despite our long history of wars and bloody conflicts.

This is a fundamental question for the future. It has taken hold of our cities, which function as dynamic, amplifying spaces and which we can no longer grasp just by searching for their roots. In an essay published in February 2009, entitled *Le dérèglement du monde* and translated as *Disordered World*, Amin Maalouf (2011), who was born in Lebanon and lives in France, grasped this problematic extremely well: the challenge of living together peacefully with others. This is how he put it:

> Will a way be found for the world's populations—which evolution has forced into permanent contact with each other despite all their differences of religion, colour, language, history and traditions—to coexist in peace and harmony? The question is a real one in every country and every city, as well as on a global level. And at present, the reply remains uncertain. (233)

How can our cities respond to that challenge, and what would an adequate reaction look like? If we want to say something about this, we should try to find out how Djebar's novel confronts the reader with multi-, inter- and transcultural entanglements. The first chapter, which introduces the protagonist, shows us Thelja, a young woman who lives in Paris and who will soon turn into a foreigner in Strasbourg, "l'étrangère" (Djebar 1997, 41). The novel presents her pattern of movement as a voluntary, double delocalization: from Algeria to Paris, and from Paris to Strasbourg. After traveling on the night train, Thelja arrives at the Alsatian capital before daybreak and immediately begins to roam the streets of still-deserted Strasbourg (50) with its cobblestones, statues, churches and public squares. But she takes care not to enter the centre of medieval Strasbourg and stays away from the cathedral. The stroll through town makes it clear that all the novel's processes of understanding and reflection are spatial processes. Thelja's approach to the city mirrors the way Djebar approached it on the structural level of the novel: *Centre-ville* makes its appearance as *centre vide* and transforms into a space for patterns of movement. The young woman has come to Paris funded by a stipend in art history. Now, the mobile cartography of Strasbourg becomes the setting for nine amorous nights which she spends with an Alsatian called François who is 20 years older. Their relationship remains confined to the nine nights.

Obviously, Djebar's translingual writing in a language other than her mother tongue places a special emphasis on the choice of language. While Thelja masters two languages which her lover does not speak or understand, colloquial Arabic and Berber, François speaks a language and a dialect that she does not understand, namely German and Alsatian. They communicate in French, which becomes the language of their loving relationship but nevertheless does not erase the other languages and dialectal expressions. It is important to note that this symmetrical structure hides an asymmetry: while French is François's mother tongue, it is a foreign language to Thelja (though also homely and familiar).

Les Nuits de Strasbourg is about an urban experiment of cohabitation. Within the confines of a given stretch of space and time, the book tries to establish, with literary means, conditions under which it becomes possible to share the experience of life in difference. In this sense, it does not view difference as an external "disturbance", but as an erotic contact-zone and area of friction. Carefully established antagonisms, especially sexual, cultural and linguistic, create a feeling of tension which does not limit itself to the erotic and which is transposed to the cityscape as the couple moves from one hotel to the other.

The bed is at the centre of Djebar's experimental literary assembly. In *Les Nuits de Strasbourg*, it is not a specific, individualized bed, but a sequence of different beds in different hotel rooms and—when other couples appear in the novel—apartments. As an abstract concept of space and functionality, the bed turns into a privileged place in which love and life take their course: it is the focal point of all forces, motions and patterns of movement traversing Djebar's fascinating novel. Barthes (2002) has already emphasized the bed's enormous relevance in literature and cultural history (155). The bed is the place where the poetry and movement of a couple's life are at home. There can be no doubt that *le lit*—along with the bedside lamp which begins to play an important part in the second night and provides the lighting (and complete darkness) for the various "bed-scenes"—is the true home to the delights, deceptions and duties of those who inhabit the pages (and beds) of this novel. Differences between the sexes, generations and the basic world views of religions, cultures and languages, always at the root of bloody confrontations, remain alive in the novel and—in a *mise en abyme* of the urban—are set in motion: the history of conflict between orient and occident is not portrayed in a static way, in an attempt to find its roots, but *vectorized* spontaneously.

The novel was written with the historical context of seemingly endless massacres in Algeria in mind. Djebar's writing and her life-knowledge are her way of resisting these developments. This is why most of the macro-historical events evoked in the novel represent the failure of leading a peaceful life with others. On a global level, the nations involved in the First and Second World Wars spread the unease to their colonial possessions; on the level of interconnected areas, French colonialism gave rise to the political relationship between France and Algeria; on an international level, there was a string of wars, for example between France and Germany; on a national level, bloody power-struggles in politically independent Algeria or the rule of the Red Khmer; on a regional level, confrontations between the inhabitants of the two banks of the Rhine; on a local level, tensions and violence between migrants from suburban housing projects and the bourgeois middle-class. We could go on and mention more conflict zones from the novel, such as the tension between different religious groups, members of different cultures and the battle of the sexes. Djebar's novel about the city of Strasbourg is anything but an idyllic representation of peaceful cohabitation.

The nine chapters of the main body of *Les Nuits de Strasbourg* unite these conflicts on two levels which are kept separate graphically by the typography: italics for the nights, regular print for daytime. The days are dominated by the French and European metropolis Strasbourg, its fluvial setting between the banks of the river Ill and the mighty Rhine. Countless canals, with their locks, bridges and small piers, cut through the old part of town. The medieval city centre contrasts with a number of very different suburban neighbourhoods. Needless to say, this landscape of a city also mirrors the wars and colonial history of the country, deportations and persecution, the migrations of workers and the quest for political asylum. People belonging to the most diverse communities and groups come together here, provoking conflict, but also sharing their knowledge—which is often delocalized or translocalized knowledge—with the city. Strasbourg is a European metropolis, and, for that reason, it can no longer be understood or explained adequately by focusing only on Europe or France, let alone Alsace: within a vectorial understanding of urbanity the streets of the city of Strasbourg form a worldwide network of routes characterized by interacting cultural and literary imageries of the Global North and the Global South

As opposed to Paris, however, Strasbourg is a regional, not a national capital. As a border-city, a national perspective sees it in a peripheral part of the country. At the same time, Strasbourg is the seat of the European Parliament and has taken up a central position in the process of political and economic unification. Therefore, the novel correctly designates Strasbourg as the "navel of Europe" (Djebar 1997, 350)—not just a body-metaphor of centrality, but also a type of relation beyond the individual body that refers to the European and global dimension. After all, this has also left its footprint on the architecture of what was once a sleepy Alemannic town.

But Djebar's novel does not depict Strasbourg in harmonious shades. Marginalized communities, such as the migrants from Hautepierre, who—like young Djamila—live under the constant threat of xenophobia, are one of its themes. Another example is the rape and murder of the local girl Jacqueline, who is rehearsing a performance of *Antigone* with migrants and feels attracted to young foreign men. And, nevertheless, the cityscape of the Alsatian and European city of Strasbourg (including the "Europe Bridge" leading to the town of Kehl in Germany's Baden region, with no need for passports, but a huge French flag on the German side—a reminder of the Second World War) symbolizes the hope for new forms of cohabitation, representing multilingualism and respect for the other's difference. The city and the cityscape of Strasbourg, with its magical array of canals, locks, streets and bridges, make it clear that—as Amin Maalouf (1998) has it in his essay on "murderous identities"—one can no longer privilege one single *appartenance* or identity. Instead, the city stands for a widely unfolded web of affiliations. An urban landscape of theory arises: the novel repeatedly mentions the canal's locks, which connect, but do not melt or eradicate difference.

Every figure in the novel is endowed with its very personal life-knowledge. Therefore, due to their highly diverse cultural, religious, national, linguistic, sexual or social affiliations, the dramatis personae create a true microcosm of multifarious forms and norms of life-knowledge. Her life in the interstice of the oriental and occidental worlds gives Thelja a nomadic[9] approach to knowledge, which also expresses itself in the rules François learns about during their first rendezvous:

> We find ourselves, he and I, at the same café-restaurant, but I, I depend on changing the hotel every night. As I have the whole day for roaming the ancient streets randomly, I choose this or that quarter

9 For more information on the concept of the nomadic in the work of Assia Djebar, see Calle-Gruber (2005).

> at a whim… I have suggested to him this game, from the first evening on… I don't tell him my choice of the night until the moment of dinner! … Why? Maybe it's a way of making him feel, every night, that he must become a nomad! Without attachments, like me, but in his own city, the one of his past, the one where he works! Maybe that way he will sense, every morning, how ready I am, at every moment, to leave: I have not come for a "liaison", how they say here, I… (Djebar 1997, 108–09)[10]

This quotation shows that nomadic movement is one of the book's fundamental elements. After all, Thelja's strategy of using the transit-spaces of hotel rooms is an experiment that attempts to turn her lover into a nomad, despite the fact that he—who was born and raised in Strasbourg—has inherited a fixed place of residence within the confines of "his" city. It is yet another cunning strategy aiming to free our couple from the weight of inherited historical baggage, making room for the pleasurable experience of free movement—a constellation which the concept of literature without a fixed abode helps uncover.

Djebar's *Les Nuits de Strasbourg* was written in a space somewhere between Strasbourg, Paris and Louisiana, in a state of exile from Algeria and in the interstices between different worlds. This condition has long-since transformed the Algerian author's literary production into a form of writing without a fixed abode. The author's oscillating movement between different locations of literary production went hand in hand with a well-considered choice of language, which had its point of departure in her multilingual homeland where Berber and colloquial and written Arabic had to make room for French, the colonial language. It comes as no surprise that Thelja (like

10 Original: "On se retrouve, lui et moi, au même café-restaurant, mais moi, je tiens alors à changer chaque nuit d'hôtel. Comme j'ai toute la journée pour arpenter les rues anciennes au hasard, je choisis tel ou tel quartier selon mon humeur… Je lui ai proposé ce jeu, dès le premier soir… Je ne lui dis mon choix de la nuit qu'au moment du dîner!… Pourquoi? Peut-être une façon de lui faire sentir, chaque soir, qu'il doit devenir nomade! Sans attaches, comme moi, mais dans sa propre ville, celle de son passé, celle où il travaille! Peut-être qu'ainsi il ressentira, chaque matin, combien je suis prête, à chaque instant, à partir: je ne suis pas venue pour une 'liaison', comme on dit ici, je…"

the author herself) uses mainly French but reveals her multilingualism by relying on Arabic or Berber expressions and metaphors as well.

Thelja's expeditions through Strasbourg do not only take place at night. During the daytime, she feels at home in a multilingual urban soundscape. Here, in the Alsace region, she is confronted with two languages she does not know, as opposed to François, who is fluent in German and Alsatian. At the same time, French—the language of the colonizers—turns out to be the language of her liberation (which is also a sexual liberation). To her, this language is not associated with ties and dependencies, because she uses François to free herself from the male linguistic domination of *Français* which she tries to interpret as a female concept (Djebar 1997, 225). Strasbourg/Straßburg, the city of streets, becomes a city of languages. They intersect and overlap without establishing a fixed territory. Shouldn't we view the double designation of the city as a hint at (linguistic and cultural) vectorial patterns?

The act of writing in a language which is not one's mother tongue creates a specific form of writing without a fixed abode. It introduces a nomadic element into the language the author has chosen, which was once the language of sedentary people. This process follows the same pattern as the experience François undergoes when he becomes a nomad in his hometown for nine nights. The things which once "naturally" belonged to or resided in this space change when the nomad is present: what was once sedentary and stable becomes dynamic. In the novel, François is struck by the fundamental realization that he must change his perspective on his hometown and its history, that new paths and movements have appeared, and that he must observe and understand these phenomena if he is to understand his hometown correctly. Structures of other cities have long since overlapped with structures of the city of Strasbourg. *Les Nuits de Strasbourg* demonstrates how the new transareal circulation of knowledge is creating a networked European history of movement traversed by the Global South.

It no longer makes sense to try and grasp Europe as a firmly defined territory. Whoever aims to understand this continent will have to be aware of the fact that—*in* motion (Bade 2000) and *as* movement (Ette 2001)—Europe, and especially its larger cities, arise and are born from the movements which cut across and traverse it. If we want to switch perspectives from a European history of space to a history of movement, the literatures of the world in general and the literatures without a fixed abode will play a central part in the process of establishing the new perspective. These literatures without a fixed abode record and create vectorized life-knowledge and insights on how to share our lives with others. These two types of knowledge are linked to literary representations of patterns of movement which allow us to understand Europe *simultaneously from the inside and the outside*.

The ninth and last episode of the "Strasbourg nights" projects the "Franco-Arabian entanglement" ("enchevêtrement franco-arabe", Djebar 1997, 100), which Thelja and François practice by enlacing their tongues and bodies onto a transareal relation between Algeria and Alsace: "Alsagérie", in a tender neologism the book presents and plays with (353).[11] The country's multilingualism is a double one, ignored by the maps, but anchored in the life-knowledge of the protagonists. It unfolds a space of movement which enables the novel to develop a structure displaying a plurality of logics and new forms of knowledge on how to share our lives with others (which we must renegotiate constantly). The loving designation Alsagérie/Alzagérie unites the two languages, tongues and bodies: "a happy couple, a couple making love" (373). Algeria is no longer imaginable without Alsace, and Alsace no longer without Algeria: both regions embody and arise within one another, meeting in the city of streets, the city of languages. A country encompasses many other countries, a city many other cities: the long history of urbanity and literature leaves no doubt that the history of the city should no longer be conceptualized in

11 Concerning the border-crossing and transnational perspective, see Asholt (2005), Barbé (2001), and Vialet (2002).

terms of space, but in terms of movements. The literary text has become a living, mobile cartography of the city.

Emine Sevgi Özdamar, or the Double City

In November 2004, when she was asked whether her escape to Germany from military dictatorship in Turkey was also an escape to the German language, Emine Sevgi Özdamar (2004) said:

> Yes. One always hears that people lose their mother tongue when they are forced to live in a foreign country. But I believe that people sometimes lose their language in their homeland. When times are bad, language lives through a bad experience. I felt as if Turkish words had fallen ill during the military dictatorship. I had the feeling that I had gotten tired, very tired in my own language. (23)[12]

This passage comes from an interview which the Turkish-born author gave on the occasion of winning the Kleist prize, but her trilogy of novels[13] also reflect Özdamar's painful experiences with her mother tongue. It also becomes clear that her writing, which has won her a number of prizes, does not allow her to separate her mother tongue from the fatherland. Özdamar's literary language works like a system of interconnected tubes, in a *translingual* and, at the same time, *transcultural* sense: Özdamar suffered a shock from the military dictatorship, fell seriously ill and suffered a breakdown on all levels of life and communication, which nevertheless inspired her impressive literary *traversal* of different languages and cultures.

Özdamar was born in 1946 in Malatya. The title of her 1992 debut novel—*Das Leben ist eine Karawanserei hat zwei Türen aus einer kam ich rein aus der anderen ging ich raus* (*Life Is a Caravansarai,*

12 Original: "Ja. Man erzählt immer, daß man in der Fremde die Muttersprache verliert. Ich denke, man kann auch die Sprache im eigenen Land verlieren. In schlimmen Zeiten macht die Sprache eine schreckliche Erfahrung. Ich hatte das Gefühl, dass die türkischen Wörter während der Militärputschzeit krank wurden. Ich hatte das Gefühl, dass ich in meiner Sprache sehr, sehr müde geworden war".

13 The first-person narrator from Özdamar's novel *Seltsame Sterne starren zur Erde* uses almost the exact same words to reflect upon language. See Özdamar (2003, 23).

Has Two Doors, I Came in One I Went Out the Other)[14]—features two doors which leave no doubt that, for Özdamar, space—including the epochs of her life—is always an area of transit, a place of transition with more than one exit and more than one system of reference and communication. This is also how we will have to conceptualize the architecture of her (literary) cities.

Before we set out on our analysis of Özdamar's cities, we should remark that the entire text is characterized by constant geographical displacement and migration, but also by constant diatopical and diastratical linguistic variation between different cities in Turkey. The text begins by evoking the train full of soldiers, which carries the first-person narrator and her pregnant mother deeply into the Anatolian heartland, and the "train of whores" (Özdamar 1999, 379) which marks the beginning of the eighteen-year-old girl's voyage to West-Berlin. Intralingual processes of translation[15] puncture the family's movements across Turkey. The text emphasizes the peculiarities of the Turkish dialects the family encounters during its translocal and transregional migrations. These migrations through Turkey anticipate the transnational movements of the narrator by highlighting intralingual translations which point to posterior translingual developments.

The movements of a pendulum are typical of the patterns of movement we find in the novels of Özdamar. In 1998, she published the second part of her trilogy of novels, which bears the title *Die Brücke vom Goldenen Horn* (*The Bridge of the Golden Horn*). This is one of the things the book says about the city on the Bosporus that connects two continents:

> In 1967, there still was no bridge between Asia and Europe. The ocean kept the two shores apart, and whenever the water was between me and my parents, I felt free. [. . .] The Asian and the

14 For more information on the following remarks, see also Ette (2007).
15 For more information on intralingual translation, see Jakobson (1971, 260).

> European parts of Istanbul belonged to two different countries. (Özdamar 1998, 222)[16]

The constant movement of oscillation between these two "countries" quickly turns into an everyday and commonplace procedure allowing the first-person narrator to keep writing her professional, intellectual and sexual coming-of-age novel[17] far away from the parental home and its mechanisms of control. At first, the difference between Asia and Europe appears to be a fundamental one; but the protagonist and thousands of commuters on the ferries overcome this separation on a daily basis. Like the movement of a weaver's hand, the ferries constantly connect the two parts of the city, which are so important in the life of this 20-year-old woman. They create a texture, a text resulting from an interminable process of trans-portation and translation. This process of translation does not settle down in a clearly delineated "in-between". Instead, the interstitial space becomes a space of movement, filled with a constant spatial and temporal come and go.

It is quite amazing how precisely and meaningfully Özdamar transferred this model of Istanbul to the Berlin neighbourhood of Mitte in the 1970s. In *Seltsame Sterne starren zur Erde* (*Strange Stars Stare at the Earth*), the divided city, still broken up into different sectors, separates into two realms. Like Asia and Europe, the eastern and western blocks stand in seemingly eternal hostility, two cities and "countries" separated by their political systems and militarized borders. The Berlin wall has taken up the place of the Bosporus strait; the Berlin S-Bahn replaces the ferry boats. In the S-Bahn train, the young Turkish woman with a tourist visa and no permanent place of residence takes another 20-minute ride from one side of the wall (painted with countless graffiti pictures) to the other. She is an actress and was

16 Original: "Zwischen Asien und Europa gab es damals, 1967, noch keine Brücke. Das Meer trennte die beiden Seiten, und wenn ich das Wasser zwischen meinen Eltern und mir hatte, fühlte ich mich frei. [...] Die asiatische und die europäische Seite in Istanbul waren zwei verschiedene Länder".

17 Irmgard Ackermann and Nazli Hodaie (2011) consider *Die Brücke vom Goldenen Horn* a "novel of personal development" ("Entwicklungsroman").

temporarily imprisoned by the Turkish regime, which then made it impossible for her to perform in her homeland. Until she receives a three-month visa from the government of the East German capital, she shares an apartment in West Berlin, where she experiences a sense of community and support similar to her parental home. Even though it becomes clear that this apartment in the neighbourhood of Wedding and its inhabitants, which she portrays lovingly and humorously (and with a pinch of salt), mean a lot to her, the protagonist nevertheless finds personal fulfilment in East Berlin. It is here that she can enter into "her" Brechtian world of theatre and where, after obtaining her visa, she stays with another young woman, a setting she also renders in great detail.

Again, the city seems to be definitely split into two different "countries" and "blocks". But as opposed to Istanbul, contact between the two parts of the city does not remain limited to telephone calls and the occasional gaze—between the eastern and western, Asian and European sides. Instead, the two sides become interwoven by daily trips on the S-Bahn trains. After divorcing the husband, she married in Istanbul, the protagonist travels back and forth between a number of apartments and lovers—who pop up, only to disappear again. The title of the book refers to a poem by Else Lasker-Schüler. As this poem's leitmotiv has it, "*Mit brennenden Armen die Liebe suchend*" (Özdamar 2003, 9),[18] the protagonist remains without a fixed abode. In more than one respect, Berlin is the city of her desires—and yet, Istanbul remains.

In the novel, the urban space of Berlin provides the setting for literally contact-free *multicultural* coexistence and for a wide variety of *intercultural* relationships: mutual contacts between linguistically, culturally and socio-politically diverse groups. Translations remain present in the life of the protagonist. They occur in private and professional, oral and written contexts. The protagonist works for the

18 Else Lasker-Schüler's line expresses the longing for love and the protagonist's search for her own identity. Robert P. Newton translates this line as follows: "seek out love with arms of burning" (Lasker-Schüler 1982, 105).

Siemens company, translating for Germans and Turks, and she supplies imprisoned Turkish actors with notes from a pupil of Brecht, Benno Besson. But while she acts as a "messenger" between two groups, between two separate linguistic (but also social, cultural and political) communities, she gradually discovers her own language. Crossings and mergers occur constantly in this peculiar language.

If one takes a closer look at the spatial structures and patterns of movement in Özdamar's texts, it becomes clear that the lexical level is a structure in which words cover deeper structures of other words, while on the level of space certain locations cover deeper structures of other places. Istanbul is always present in Berlin—and this is not a hint at what we might call "Little Istanbul". Rather, the movements in this particular city cover up movements which took place at another point in time in another city. These movements follow their own choreography, their own logic. It is important to realize that in Özdamar's writing hermeneutic processes and developments are not just spatialized, but simultaneously *vectorized.* All of the movements taking place in the present are an accumulation and record of prior movements while they also anticipate movements which will take place in the future.

In this sense, the poetic prophecy of the protagonist's husband—whom she left behind in his cottage in the woods on the Asian side of Istanbul—partly fulfils itself. As his former wife seemed to turn her back on Istanbul, he said the following: "Neither will you discover new land, nor new seas. The city will follow you. You will roam the same. Streets, grow old in the same neighbourhoods" (Özdamar 2003, 56).[19]

It comes as no surprise that even this same cottage, which one could discern from the European shore (28), also has a counterpart in Berlin: shortly after the cottage in Istanbul (where she spent many happy months with her husband) appeared in one of her dreams, an

19 Original: "Du wirst keine neuen Länder entdecken, keine anderen Meere. / Die Stadt wird Dir folgen. Du wirst durch dieselben Straßen / Streifen, in denselben Vierteln alt werden". As the author points out, this is an excerpt from a poem by Konstantinos Kavafis.

East German colleague from her camera crew invites our protagonist to his "lonely cottage in the forest" (113). Desperately trying to stay calm, she has to tell herself that "this is not the same forest" (113). From a cinematic point of view, these are countless fade-ins and fade-outs which give Istanbul a presence in Berlin, making it appear on all levels and present to all senses. A broken water pipe on Unter den Linden makes the protagonist recall a lime-tree that stood next to the cottage in Istanbul. In one of her associative strings of thoughts, our first-person narrator connects this recollection to literature—a Turkish poet whom she befriended—and love (95–96). On the one hand, the protagonist has a hard time imagining the two parts of Berlin as one. On the other, she quickly begins to consider the border between West and East Berlin "one great ocean" (18), as in Istanbul—and this ocean asks for acts of trans-lation. The "morning hours" and the "smell" of the East Berlin streets make the protagonist recall the Turkish metropolis (81): "the smell of coal and automobile exhaust, like in Istanbul" (81), a transareal "smellscape". And when she sees a movie from the USA featuring Rod Taylor, she suddenly remembers it as one of her "childhood experiences in Istanbul" (123). Images, sounds and smells from the city on the shores of the Bosporus keep surging in. Every object, every sensual impression is capable of creating the sensation of fading overlaps between Istanbul and Berlin. A "Bridge Unter den Linden", so to speak, just by looking at *Die Brücke vom Goldenen Horn* and *Seltsame Sterne starren zur Erde*. One city is always present within the other: combining love and literature, it followed the migrant's footsteps and has no vertical or archaeological connection to the older strata of Berlin history but links it horizontally to other locations and latitudes.

The cities and their divided structures are written into the other, and the travels of the protagonist keep interlacing them. The structure of the living quarters might serve as an example. The temporary living quarters for Turkish women in Berlin, which is changed phonetically to "Frauenwonaym"[20] during the protagonist's first stay in Berlin, anticipates the living conditions she confronts during her second stay in the city on the Spree. These temporary residences with their clear subdivisions, sexual and gendered borderlines, appear as a parodic and paradoxical mirror-image in the shared apartment in the Wedding neighbourhood, where new roommates begin their stay—as in the residence for women—by doing the dishes and quickly learn that fraternization will not be tolerated. All along the novel, collective living arrangements create worlds of their own, a kind of urban space of transit, which can transform into a *phalanstère* for a limited period of time. Only when a friend attempts to leave the official residence for women does the narrator realize that Berlin "had not really existed for us so far" (Özdamar 1998, 63): "We had had our Wonaym, and the Wonaym had nothing to do with Berlin. Berlin was what was outside of the Wonaym".[21] A city of secret groupings and impenetrable places?

Words beneath words, places beneath places, movements beneath movements, living quarters beneath living quarters, events beneath events, cities beneath cities: *Das Leben ist eine Karawanserei, Die Brücke vom Goldenen Horn* and *Seltsame Sterne starren zur Erde* are chronological narratives of a life and the historical contexts surrounding it, such as the contradictory processes of modernization begun by Atatürk in Turkey, the life-experience of the generation of 1968, the Cold War and—on the horizon—the conflicts aroused by left-wing terrorism in Germany and the fall of the Berlin Wall. But the novels also show that, apart from these syntagmatic elements, the paradigmatic structures of constant fading and overlapping are decisive for the hermeneutic processes taking place in them. The techniques of fading in and out and of inscribing one phenomenon into the other make it clear that the European side of Istanbul, on both sides of the Bosporus Bridge, cannot be conceptualized without taking

20 We find this spelling in the title of the first chapter of the first section of Özdamar (1998, 11).

21 Original: "Wir hatten unser Wonaym, und dieses Wonaym war nicht Berlin. Berlin begann erst, wenn man aus dem Wonaym herausging".

the Asian side into account as well. The same is true of West and East Berlin, Berlin and Istanbul, Germany and Turkey.

The books do not limit their scope to intercultural dialogue but are expressions of transcultural interlacing and traversal, a choreography of movements across a number of cultures. This is not to say that these movements guarantee euphoria and enjoyment. Very often, they are represented as being very tense and disturbing. We find fractal, multiple and disjunctive patterns, which nevertheless adopt "insular" forms and structures. In the literatures of the world and, specially, in the literatures without a fixed abode, these patterns fulfil a fundamental role. And this also amounts to saying that the vectorial mobility of all references and relationships does not take place in a continuous, but in a discontinuous, fragmented post-Euclidean space (Ette 2005). The structures and constructions of the cities we have observed so far are located in this particular type of space. Özdamar was careful not to centre her trilogy of novels on national spaces but on two urban areas on the seam between eastern and western history, between two continents and two spheres of political power—facts which have changed the topography and infrastructure of these cities. Shouldn't we say that these urban spaces are islands, even entire archipelagos, which, because they are part of a network of relations, show us what the vectorized hermeneutics of urban spaces looks like?

Cécile Wajsbrot, or Life in the Archipelago of Cities

The analysis of *Les Nuits de Strasbourg* showed how the evacuation of the Alsatian capital in 1939 left an abandoned cityscape behind. In its centre, around an island created by the small river Ill and its network of bridges, the statues were connected by a web of gazes: "The statues, they have eyes. They observe. They wonder: the air has changed, imperceptibly; the light that, in previous days, sparkled and danced only to weaken, little by little, and hide, is now transformed: an abstraction, it seems" (Djebar 1997, 16).[22]

The statues have long since established their own realm of signs within the human world of signs. Only when the—fleeting—human beings have fled does this realm unveil its richness and obstinate uniqueness. Djebar's cityscape suggests that the web of gazes which has materialized between the works of art no longer requires the presence of humans.

Cécile Wajsbrot lives in Paris and Berlin, commuting between the two capitals. In August 2008, she published the novel *L'Ile aux musées*. No less fascinating than Djebar's book, this narrative does not only show us the statues from the outside but also unveils what we might call their inside. And Wajsbrot's statues dwell in a place without human residents: Berlin's Museumsinsel, or museum island.

The narrative's spatial and temporal frame is dominated by the quite different, even contrasting (and therefore also complementary) cityscapes of Paris and Berlin, at the heart of which one finds (as in Strasbourg) an urban island, the Ile de la Cité and Berlin's Museumsinsel. The statues cast a web of gazes over these cities, unbeknownst to the people who hurry by, or live below. They are part of our daily lives, but as we pass under their gaze, do we ever look the statues in the face?

This is exactly where the novel begins. Should not literature heighten our awareness of things that have become invisible due to their omnipresence? The novel gets right to the point in the first chapter:

> We keep watch, even if no one pays attention to us—and maybe it is easier to do so if no one looks. Our destiny is strange. Before our birth, we were the object of negotiations, of decisions, of changes of mind, of compromises, you fight yourselves for having the right

22 Original: "Les statues, elles, ont des yeux. Elles regardent. Elles s'étonnent: l'air a changé, imperceptiblement; la lumière qui, chaque jour d'autrefois, scintillait et dansait pour, peu à peu, s'affaiblir et se terrer, la voici métamorphosée: une abstraction, semble-t-il".

> to bring us into existence, but once we are there, our presence obtrudes and yours is effaced, the roles are inverted—you are the pretexts and the space belongs to us.
> The space belongs to us and we keep the watch. We are made of stone, of bronze, we are made of granite or marble, we are on the bridges, on top of buildings and in front of museums, we are in the gardens, as signs of warning, we are in the recesses—but immobile, with our gazes fixed. (Wajsbrot 2008, 10)[23]

This passage not only emphasizes the omnipresence of the statues, but also their semiotic properties as signs, an aspect the novel highlights more than once. Their makers are unaware of their dominance of physical space, and they do not take note of the fact that the statues belong to a spatial and temporal domain which goes beyond the frame of individual human experience: "We are there for centuries" (11). As in many of Cécile Wajsbrot's novels—and one can easily point to a number of intratextual references in *L'Ile aux musées*—the presence of the other—be it animals or the arts, as the white owl of *Mémorial* or Romantic art in *Caspar-Friedrich-Strasse*—unveils an other-logic (of art and nature) which supersedes humanity and the coordinates of human life. Beyond the gaze of human beings, the statues' webs of gazes create relationships which traverse space and time.

The statues know about the castles and palaces of humankind. They know of buildings that served to represent power and glory, and of their destruction. They tell the story of the collections stashed away in the Louvre or the Altes Museum (Wajsbrot 2008, 12);

---

23 Original: "Nous montons la garde, même si personne ne nous prête attention—et peut-être est-il plus facile de veiller quand personne ne regarde. Notre destin est étrange. Avant notre venue au monde, nous sommes l'objet de tractations, de décisions, de revirements, de compromissions, vous vous battez pour avoir le droit de nous donner existence mais une fois que nous sommes là, notre présence s'impose et la vôtre s'efface, les rôles s'inversent—vous êtes les prétextes et l'espace nous appartient. L'Espace nous appartient et nous montons la garde. Nous sommes en pierre, en bronze, nous sommes en granit ou en marbre, nous sommes sur les ponts, en haut des édifices ou devant les musées, nous sommes dans les jardins, en signes avant-coureurs, nous sommes dans les niches—mais immobiles, le regard fixe". For an in-depth analysis of the novel, see Ette (2009).

they know history and its many stories, but the statues themselves have not entered the realm of the historical and cannot become historical facts. They may not be reduced to the presence of their objective existence, nor to the objective existence of their presence: "You are in the present. We are in the presence" (11).[24]

Given this form of presence, which amounts to more than merely being present, the locus of human reality seems precarious and unstable. Against the backdrop of a history of wars and catastrophes, the statues seem to suggest a planetary future from which mankind has disappeared, as they speak of a past in which mankind had still not appeared: "Before, there was an island, and even before, wetlands, the earth surrounded by waters" (Wajsbrot 2008, 11).[25] This genesis starts with water and soil. And we discern a future in which the ships and boats of mankind no longer navigate these waters, the airplanes of mankind no longer cross the sky of this planet (229). Only the statues will remain, "the last witnesses of your aspirations" (229). They will become the true inhabitants of the city, true subjects in the man-made urban realm of signs. This is probably why all human figures in the novel resemble rough and hurried sketches, nameless people on their quest for a little love and community. Their world is temporary and unstable: In the eyes of the statues, their fleeting contours are nothing but traces, only the shadows of a presence which remains confined to the present tense.

Wajsbrot's novel *L'Ile aux musées* offers elements from a history of the Berlin Museumsinsel, which it then puts into a transhistorical perspective. In the discourse of historiography, the history of the Museumsinsel—notwithstanding eastern and western ideological perspectives—sounds like this:

> The island is situated in the Berlin city-centre, with the river Spree on its eastern, and one of its arms—Kupfergraben—on the western shore. In the early 15th century, it was a spot favoured by its location between the two merchant cities of Berlin and Cölln. When in

24 Original: "Vous êtes dans le présent. Nous sommes dans la presence".
25 Original: "Avant, il y avait une île, avant encore, des marais, la terre cernée par les eaux".

> 1417 the Counts of Nuremberg, who were Hohenzollerns, became the rulers over Brandenburg, they transformed the island into a new base for their dynasty. (Schade 1987, 7)

An island between swamps and sand in the interstice between two Brandenburg centres of commerce. *L'Ile aux musées* mentions this history in a condensed fast-forward motion, rendering it in a couple of lines: step by step, the island became the king's orchard, a botanical garden, and finally—upon royal decree in 1797—it was connected to the city by bridges and transformed into the museum island (Wajsbrot 1997, 12).

But if we define an island as a space surrounded by water and therefore subject to a fundamental infrastructural discontinuity—namely the need to switch one's mode of transportation when arriving at or leaving the island—then we could also pose the question whether or not the Berlin Museumsinsel really is an island in the strict sense of the term. From this perspective, the answer is simple: even before the so-called Altes Museum ("Old Museum") was built on the urban island between 1825 and 1830, the island had already ceased to be an island. It was no longer a peripheral place but had taken root in the city-centre, with bridges connecting it to the mainland. Therefore, one of the anonymous protagonists rightly remarks: "I darted for this museum island because I felt like being on an island, but it is an urban island with nothing insular about it, connected by bridges where cars circulated" (Wajsbrot 2008, 38).[26] An urban island, accessible via a network of bridges and (in the cases of the Bode Museum and the Pergamon Museum) small bridge-like elements (Schade 1987, 22, 23): a paradoxical non-island. But the voices of the statues insist that this is an insular *île urbaine* which maintains a relationship to other islands all over the world:

> You are on an island, you seem to be forgetting about it—we know that there are far-away islands separated from all ground, islands without bridges in the middle of the sea and you need boats and

26 Original: "[J]e me suis précipitée dans cette île aux musées parce que j'avais envie d'être sur une île mais c'est une île urbaine qui n'a rien d'insulaire, reliée par les ponts où circulent des voitures".

> hours on boat to reach them, we know that some never arrive there, that there are shipwrecks. We know that on some of them live gigantic statues of which no one knows the origin. (Wajsbrot 2008, 83)[27]

The island is a multi-dimensional phenomenon because it is an element in a globally networked *island-world*, which is also the *world of islands* and therefore a world apart. This perspective not only arises on a global but on a local level as well, given the fact that, historically, one would also have to consider the cityscape of Berlin an island, or an assembly of islands, and that—if this is acceptable—the question as to where the "true" centre of the city is located comes up:

> Our island was wrested from the wetlands, like the entire city, the cesspits were dried, the ground was levelled, then the bridges were built to connect the different parts of the city, what now seems like their centre used to be at the exterior and what seems excentred now was the city itself. On our island you have built other islands because the museums are a sort of cloister in which you locked the history of time. (84)[28]

Wilhelm von Humboldt, Karl Friedrich Schinkel and Aloys Hirt, but also the sculptors Gottfried Schadow and Christian Daniel Rauch, were the fathers of this island (Schade 1987, 12–13). For over a century, its buildings were enlarged and reconstructed, which means that the reduced geographical space of the island houses a chain of museum-islands, a string of cultural islands bridging the space between Berlin and the cultures of the world.

---

27 Original: "Vous êtes sur une île, vous semblez l'oublier—nous savons qu'il y a des îles lointaines coupées de toute terre, des îles sans pont au milieu de la mer et qu'il faut des bateaux et des heures de bateau pour les atteindre, nous savons que certains n'y arrivent jamais, qu'il y a des naufrages. Nous savons que sur certaines habitent d'immenses statues dont nul ne connaît l'origine".

28 Original: "Notre île fut gagnée sur les marais, comme toute la ville, les fosses d'écoulement furent asséchées, le terrain aplani, puis des ponts furent construits pour relier les différentes parties de la ville, ce qui en paraît aujourd'hui le centre était alors à l'extérieur et ce qui semble aujourd'hui l'excentré était la ville même. Sur notre île vous avez construit d'autres îles car les musées sont des sortes de cloîtres dans lesquels vous enfermez l'histoire du temps".

The inter- and transcultural relationships of the statues, which originated in various epochs and spaces, societies and cultures, form the basis upon which Wajsbrot's novel erects a bridge. By doing so, the novel attempts to foresee and anticipate the future of museums in the neighbourhood of Berlin Mitte and in other places, for example, the construction of the Humboldt Forum that was launched in 2012, four years after the novel's publication. It was built in the vicinity of the Museumsinsel (which has been awarded the status of world cultural heritage by UNESCO) and opened on December 16, 2020. Situated on what was once the location of the royal palace, the "Humboldt Forum" attempts to question cultural hierarchies and creates an even more dynamic openness for the cultures of the world. *L'Ile aux musées* uses literary means to offer answers to the question how people might share their lives and cultural world views in the future. The book presents a specific utopia. The novel begins an open polylogue between the cultures, which draws its energy from a place that we may no longer consider the centre of the city, but that is nevertheless a special field of interplay between cultural island-worlds. Even though the architecture still reminds us of times in which great archaeological projects were fuelled by an imperial mindset, aiming to document and represent grandeur and expansionist politics in the capital of the recently founded German Reich, this epoch is over once and for all.

"The Caller", *Celui qui appelle*, appears at the beginning of Cécile Wajsbrot's novel. The statue's silent cries seem to have met many ears, many new interlocutors. The novel creates a space in which the figures from the inlays on the Pergamon altar communicate with the statues, reflecting on World War II and establishing a transhistorical world of statues which "The Caller" inhabits as well. Did "The Caller", erected in February 1989, have something to do with the fall of the bleak Berlin Wall a couple of months later? The novel's short opening chapter seems to suggest something like this: "Six months after the installation of the eternally immobile man with the eternally open mouth, the Berlin Wall fell" (Wajsbrot 2008, 9).[29]

Wajsbrot's *L'Ile aux musées* is an insular bridge of cultures, born from a number of different islands and connected to a worldwide array of islands. Starting from this concept, it establishes museum-islands differing in specific temporal structures. This makes *L'Ile aux musées* a perfect literary and cultural fractal which resembles and repeats itself, thereby placing an island under more islands, a story under more stories, a city under more cities, hiding and revealing them at the same time. Thus it comes as no surprise that, in a reference to "these mathematicians who say that the coast of Finistère is infinite" (Wajsbrot 2008, 106), located at the centre of the book, we encounter the name of the father of fractal geometry, Benoît Mandelbrot (1991). *L'Ile aux musées* is an impressively dense aesthetic and ethical work displaying an open, polylogical structure: a (hi)story within a fractal island of islands.

The novel seems to suggest that not one story, or one place is ever forgotten on this island. Whatever has been destroyed, whatever is absent is still present just because it is absent. Wajsbrot's literary production represents an aesthetic of absence.[30] It represents the past—as the omission of the name David in the title of her novel *Caspar-Friedrich-Strasse* suggests—in a way that makes us aware of the blank space, of deferred meaning, of destruction. It introduces us and the world to the invisible islands under the islands, the hidden cities under the cities. The wars of Alexander the Great connect to the Cold War; the fall of Troy (which is one of the novel's earliest themes) and the wars in Iraq and Afghanistan are elements of this structure, which the novel represents—as literature does—as specific vectorial figures of movement. This is a presence which exceeds all limits of the human present.

29 Original: "Six mois après l'installation de l'homme éternellement immobile à la bouche éternellement ouverte, le mur de Berlin tombait".

30 See in this context Ette (2010a); see also the eighth chapter of Ette (2016).

Wajsbrot's novel not only show us an archaeological perspective, which uncovers different strata of history in a vertical movement, but it also creates a dynamic cartography of movement. A horizontal perspective tracks deportations and migrations which always cause an overlapping of physical spaces and even link the representation of one place to another place. The history of space must be replaced by a history of movement if we want to understand these increasingly frequent phenomena of de- and reterritorialization.

One would not necessarily have to think of the other and still well-connected urban island of Paris, the Ile de la Cité, if one wanted to say about the Berlin Museumsinsel: *Une île peut en cacher une autre* (An island can hide another). A city is more than its local history, and its depth. It is also a vectorial phenomenon, a mobile and dynamic network in a plane of transareal scale. This city under the city displays polylogical properties which, concerning its museums and artworks, create the open structure of a worldwide archipelago. This archipelago carries the imprint of all living cartographies and choreographies, with its acts of destruction and absences. Is a museum not a space of movement in which the activity of collecting which occurred in different places passes over into the activity of collecting in *one* place? Could we ever understand the space of a museum if we only concentrated on its static, architectonic space, without taking the transversal movements generating this space into account?

It is a logical step to consider the statues and their memory of stone, whose presence does not just remain confined to the present tense but is open to all the existing pasts and futures, islands as well: "We are islands, too—if you want to reach us, you have to step on our shores" (Wajsbrot 2008, 85).[31] Every single statue follows its own logic, has its own history and figures of movement. And these figures of movement are less rooted in territoriality or origins, than in a pattern of vectors that makes them explicable as a history of movement. The mountain of the fortress of Pergamon and the museum island of

31 Original: "Nous sommes des îles aussi—pour accéder à nous, il faut nous aborder".

Berlin are intrinsically connected in a transareal way. One could not imagine the "Alte Museum" without the older Louvre.

As a big-city novel, *L'Ile aux musées* makes it very clear that a city like Berlin cannot be represented or understood if the perspective remains limited to the city's archaeology, to its growth in one specific place. It is more important to reveal its vectorized patterns, its historically accumulated patterns of movement which project themselves into the present and future. This helps us see the city as a complex, constantly shifting picture of movement. A city has no roots but is born from its routes.

This perspective is not just about relations and their concomitant movements. It deals with continuous overlaps and blends in the true sense of the words: in and under the city, a different city appears, turns into an experience and a way of life, while each of these two cities must always refer to the other if they are not to remain equivocal and elusive. A city creates an image of itself by constituting itself as a fractal, setting many cities in motion within itself.

Wajsbrot's autobiographical experience as a commuter between Paris and Berlin is decisive: the book approaches Franco-German relationships and creates an especially tight web of connections between the urban spaces of the French and the German capital. But *L'Ile aux musées* also configures its title-giving location by blending and overlapping it with the island at the centre of Paris, the Ile de la Cité, and the Louvre. However, the structure of the two islands is quite different. The island in Paris is densely populated and does not fall apart into a string of museums. But the book integrates it into an urban landscape of museums and connects it to the mainland through the gaze of its statues. This perspective connects the islands as mirror-images of insular structures and as complementary elements in a Franco-German contrast. This can teach us—and is this not the true task of literature?—to follow different logical structures *simultaneously* in our thinking, which would allow us to develop a world-consciousness in a plurality of logical systems.

This type of complementary contrast not only serves as a spatial and cognitive model for the cities of Berlin and Paris, constantly changing and mirroring itself. It also applies to the statues, which enter into an intense dialogue between the cities of Berlin and Paris, and to the two anonymous couples of lovers who appear as flickering configurations of a lover's discourse while they discover and lose themselves between the two cities. The two cities and the urban islands of Paris and Berlin overlap and generate mobile cartographies. In the interstices between these cartographies, fragments of a discourse of love quietly appear. These fragments unfold fleetingly (ephemerally, as if they were fleeing something) before the backdrop of art, *under* the gaze, in more than one sense of the term, of the marble, granite or bronze statues. At the end of the novel, in its *excipit*, the lemma of "Panta Rhei" throws its shadow on these human and all-too-human relationships of anonymous lovers:

> She has returned to the central alley and is part of the flow of pedestrians who walk up to the gate as if they were following the course of a river. One of the gates is closed, the other is still half-opened. A guard is waiting for the garden to be empty to actually close it. From a distance, we hardly distinguish her from the others, from afar, there are only silhouettes. She is gone, everyone is gone. The gate closes. And we are here. We stay. (Wajsbrot 2008, 229–30)[32]

What unfolds *en filigrane* as a web of emotions in the course of the novel, while the reader learns about random encounters and plans for a visit to the museums and exhibitions, comes back together on itself at the end of the novel, when the park becomes the playful and precise narrative enactment of these emotions. They come together as a stream, representing the notion that everything we create, feel and experience is in flux, transitory like a trickle of water at the pedestal of age-old art.

---

32 "Elle a regagné l'allée centrale et fait partie du flux des promeneurs qui remontent vers la grille comme en suivant le cours d'un fleuve. L'une des grilles est fermée, l'autre, encore entrouverte. Un gardien attend que le jardin soit vide pour le fermer vraiment. De loin, nous la distinguons à peine des autres, de loin, il n'y a que des silhouettes. Elle est partie, tout le monde est parti. La grille se referme. Et nous sommes là. Nous restons".

But what remains when the absent reveals itself as such by its absence? The web of gazes and emotions is transformed into the web of experiences that art creates. It is sublated, transformed into and remembered in the art of literature, which can never withdraw completely from the peripeties of human (hi)stories, but also never remains confined to them. Like the Berlin Museumsinsel, with the "Humboldt Forum" on the former palace grounds, *L'Ile aux musées* is an enduring and fascinating expression of this knowledge which can tell us how to live and share our lives with others: it is anchored in space and time, but as the artistic creation of potential experiences, it transcends them brilliantly.

The mobile cartographies of urban spaces and urban dreams create a semiotic realm which can draw on a long tradition of urbanity and literature. The urban space of movement gives rise to an awareness or consciousness for the world which condenses all epochs and spaces, as they appear in the microcosm of the city and the macrocosm of literature, into *one* place, like a Borgesian Aleph, or like Gilgamesh, who keeps returning to the city of Uruk. In a sense, literature is always ahead of the times (Barthes 2002, 167), and in this sense literature can guide our present perception of the city into the future, while the act of reading and its movements insert and release the future in our perception of the present:

> [*See*] the tablet-box of cedar,
> [*release*] its clasp of bronze!
> [*Lift*] the lid of its secret,
> [*pick*] *up* the tablet of lapis lazuli and read out [. . .]. (George 2000, 2)

Bibliography

Ackermann, Irmgard, and Nazli Hodaie. 2011. "Emine Sevgi Özdamar." In *Kritisches Lexikon zur deutschsprachigen Gegenwartsliteratur* [Critical Encyclopaedia of Contemporary German Literature], edited by Heinz Ludwig Arnold and Hermann Korte. München: Edition text + kritik database.

Asholt, Wolfgang. 2005. "Les villes transfrontalières d'Assia Djebar" [Assia Djebar's Cross-Border Cities]. In *Assia Djebar, Nomade entre les murs... Pour une poétique transfrontalière* [Assia Djebar, Nomad Between Walls... For a Cross-Border Poetics], edited by Mireille Calle-Gruber, 147–60. Paris: Maisonneuve & Larose.

Bade, Klaus. 2000. *Europa in Bewegung: Migration vom späten 18. Jahrhundert bis zur Gegenwart* [Europe on the Move: Migration from the Late 18th Century to the Present]. München: C.H. Beck.

Barbé, Philippe. 2001. "Transnational and Translinguistic Relocation of the Subject in 'Les Nuits de Strasbourg' by Assia Djebar." *Esprit Créateur* 41 (4): 125–35.

Barthes, Roland. 2002. *Comment vivre ensemble: Simulations romanesques de quelques espaces quotidiens. Notes de cours et de séminaires au Collège de France, 1976–1977* [How to Live Together: Novel Simulations of Some Everyday Spaces. Notes from Lectures and Seminars at Collège de France, 1976–77], edited and annotated by Claude Coste. Paris: Seuil—IMEC.

Calle-Gruber, Mireille, ed. 2005. *Assia Djebar, Nomade entre les murs... Pour une poétique transfrontalière* [Assia Djebar, Nomad Between Walls... For a Cross-Border Poetics]. Paris: Maisonneuve & Larose.

Djebar, Assia. 1997. *Les Nuits de Strasbourg: Roman*. [Strasbourg Nights: A Novel]. Arles: Actes Sud.

Ette, Ottmar. 2001. "Europa als Bewegung: Zur literarischen Konstruktion eines Faszinosum." [Europe as a Movement: On the Literary Construction of a Fascination]. In *Europa: Einheit und Vielfalt. Eine interdisziplinäre Betrachtung* [Europe: Unity and Diversity. An Interdisciplinary Approach], edited by Dieter Holtmann and Peter Riemer, 15–44. Münster: LIT Verlag.

Ette, Ottmar. 2004a. *ÜberLebenswissen: Die Aufgabe der Philologie* [Knowledge for Living: The Task of Philology]. Berlin: Kadmos.

Ette, Ottmar. 2004b. "Wege des Wissens: Fünf Thesen zum Weltbewußtsein und den Literaturen der Welt" [Ways of Knowing: Five Theses on World Consciousness and the Literatures of the

World]. In *Lateinamerika: Orte und Ordnungen des Wissens. Festschrift für Birgit Scharlau* [Latin America. Places and Orders of Knowledge. Festschrift for Birgit Scharlau], edited by Sabine Hofmann and Monika Wehrheim, 169–84. Tübingen: Narr.

Ette, Ottmar. 2005. "Von Inseln, Grenzen und Vektoren" [Of Islands, Borders and Vectors]. In *Grenzen der Macht, Macht der Grenzen* [Borders of Power, Power of Borders], edited by Marianne Braig, Ottmar Ette, Dieter Ingenschay and Günther Maihold, 135–80. Frankfurt am Main: Vervuert.

Ette, Ottmar. 2016. *Writing-Between-Worlds: TransArea Studies and the Literatures-Without-a-Fixed-Abode*. Translated by Vera M. Kutzinski (Original: *ZwischenWeltenSchreiben. Literaturen ohne festen Wohnsitz*, 2005). Berlin and Boston, MA: De Gruyter.

Ette, Ottmar. 2006. "Literatures Without a Fixed Abode: Figures of Vectorial Imagination Beyond the Dichotomies of National and World Literature." In *ArabAmericas: Literary Entanglements of the American Hemisphere and the Arab World*, edited by Ottmar Ette and Friederike Pannewick, 19–68. Frankfurt: Vervuert.

Ette, Ottmar. 2007. "Über die Brücke Unter den Linden: Emine Sevgi Özdamar, Yoko Tawada und die translinguale Fortschreibung deutschsprachiger Literatur" [Across the Bridge Unter den Linden. Emine Sevgi Özdamar, Yoko Tawada and the Translingual Writing of German Literature]. In *Exophonie: Anders-Sprachigkeit (in) der Literatur* [Exophony: Other-Lingualism in Literature], edited by Susan Arndt, Dirk Naguschewski and Robert Stockhammer, 165–94. Berlin: Kadmos.

Ette, Ottmar. 2009. "'L'Ile aux musées' oder die verborgenen Choreographien der Anwesenheit" ['The Museum Island' or the Hidden Choreographies of Presence] In *Observatoire de l'extrême contemporain: Studien zur französischsprachigen Gegenwartsliteratur* [Observatory of the Extreme Contemporary: Studies in Francophone Contemporary Literature], edited by Roswitha Böhm, Stephanie Bung and Andrea Grewe, 257–70. Tübingen: Narr.

Ette, Ottmar. 2010a. "'Caspar-David-Friedrich-Straße': Cécile Wajsbrot oder die Ästhetik der Abwesenheit" ['Caspar-David-Friedrich-Street': Cécile Wajsbrot or the Aesthetics of Absence] In *Du silence à la voix: Studien zum Werk von Cécile Wajsbrot* [From Silence to Voice: Studies on the Work of Cécile Wajsbrot], edited by Roswitha Böhm and Margarete Zimmermann, 223–40. Göttingen: V&R Unipress.

Ette, Ottmar. 2010b. "Experimente des ZusammenLebensWissens in den Literaturen ohne festen Wohnsitz: Assia Djebar und die Straßburger Nächte" [Experiments of Conviviality in Literatures Without a Fixed Abode: Assia Djebar and the Strasbourg Nights] *Littérature(s) sans domicile fixe/Literatur(en) ohne festen Wohnsitz* [Literature(s) Without a Fixed Abode], edited by Wolfgang Asholt, 13–51. Tübingen: Narr.

Foucault, Michel. 2002. *Les Mots et les choses* [The Order of Things]. Paris: Gallimard.

George, Andrew, transl. 2000. *The Epic of Gilgamesh: The Babylonian Epic Poem and Other Texts in Akkadian and Sumerian.* London: Penguin.

Jakobson, Roman. 1971. "On Linguistic Aspects of Translation." In *Selected Writings II: Word and Language*, edited by Stephen Rudy, 260–65. The Hague: Mouton.

Jürgs, Britta. 2015. "Assia Djebar." In *Kritisches Lexikon zur fremdsprachigen Gegenwartsliteratur* [Critical Encyclopaedia of Contemporary Foreign Language Literature], edited by Heinz Ludwig Arnold and Hermann Korte. München: Edition text+kritik database.

Lasker-Schüler, Else. 1982. *Your Diamond Dreams Cut Open My Arteries: Poems by Else Lasker-Schüler.* Translated by Robert P. Newton. Chapel Hill, NC: University of North Carolina Press.

Lepenies, Wolf. 1978. *Das Ende der Naturgeschichte: Wandel kultureller Selbstverständlichkeiten in den Wissenschaften des 18. und 19. Jahrhunderts* [The End of Natural History: Changes in Cultural Self-Evidence in the Sciences of the 18th and 19th Centuries]. Frankfurt: Suhrkamp.

Maalouf, Amin. 1998. *Les Identités meurtrières*. Paris: Bernard Grasset.

Maalouf, Amin. 2011. *Disordered World: Setting a New Course for the Twenty-First Century*. Translated by George Miller. London: Bloomsbury.

Mandelbrot, Benoît B. 1991. *Die fraktale Geometrie der Natur* [The Fractal Geometry of Nature]. Translated by Reinhilt Zähle and Ulrich Zähle. Basel: Birkhäuser.

Maul, Stefan M. 2005. "Einleitung" [Introduction]. In *Das Gilgamesch-Epos* [The Epic of Gilgamesh], edited by Stefan M. Maul, 9–18. München: C.H. Beck.

Özdamar, Emine Sevgi. 1998. *Die Brücke vom Goldenen Horn* [The Bridge of the Golden Horn]. Köln: Kiepenheuer & Witsch.

Özdamar, Emine Sevgi. 1999. *Das Leben ist eine Karawanserei hat zwei Türen aus einer kam ich rein aus der anderen ging ich raus* [Life is a Cavanserei: Has Two Doors I Came in One I Went Out the Other]. Köln: Kiepenheuer & Witsch.

Özdamar, Emine Sevgi. 2003. *Seltsame Sterne starren zur Erde. Wedding—Pankow 1976/77* [Strange Stars Stare at the Earth. Wedding—Pankow 1976/77]. Köln: Kiepenheuer & Witsch.

Özdamar, Emine Sevgi. 2004. "Wir wohnen in einer weiten Hölle.' Interview with Nils Minkmar" ['We Live in a Vast Hell'. Interview with Nils Minkmar]. In *Frankfurter Allgemeine Sonntagszeitung*, 21 November: 23.

Schade, Günter. 1987. "Die historische Entwicklung der Berliner Museumsinsel" [The Historical Development of Berlin's Museum Island] In *Die Museumsinsel zu Berlin* [The Museum Island of Berlin], edited by Peter Betthausen, 6–47. Berlin: Henschelverlag.

Vialet, Michèle E. 2002. "Between Sound and Fury: Assia Djebar's Po etics of 'l'entre-deux-langues'." *Symposium* 56 (3): 149–62.

Wajsbrot, Cécile. 2002. *Caspar-Friedrich-Strasse*. Paris: Zulma.

Wajsbrot, Cécile. 2005. *Mémorial*. Paris: Zulma.

Wajsbrot, Cécile. 2008. *L'Ile aux musées* [The Island of Museums]. Paris: Editions Denoël.

Heterodox Maps of World Literature and South-to-South Dialogue in Caribbean Writing

Jan Rupp

In the introduction to his study *Frontiers of the Caribbean*, Philip Nanton (2017) emphasizes "the need for reimagining the Caribbean in a world context" (1). Further, he asks the question: "how can a small, increasingly ignored, dependent region contribute to the dominant debate of the late twentieth and twenty-first centuries—i.e. the impact and meaning of globalisation?" (1). While Nanton reflects on sociological and political concerns, his opening observation might equally serve to address literary ones. Has the Caribbean also dropped from attention in the context of world literature specifically, relegated to a small region between the Americas? In conversation with the late V.S. Naipaul at the Jaipur Literature Festival (JLF) in 2015, at an event titled "The Writer and the World" (borrowing from Naipaul's 2002 essay collection), Indian-born, British-based author Farrukh Dhondy (2015) suggested as much: "I can recall their names, but they seem to have disappeared" (JLF, 14:00 to 14:05), he observed of Naipaul's fellow writers who contributed to the "post-war rise of the West-Indian novel" (Ledent 2011, 1382) in the 1950s and 1960s. "The only writer that has really survived from that time is, respectfully, yourself, and it [Naipaul's work] has made an international impact, rather than the provincial impact of stuff from the Caribbean" (JLF 2015, 15:40 to 15:52), Dhondy expanded to the Nobel laureate's nodding consent.

To be sure, this take on the life and times of Caribbean world literature was afforded by the occasion of paying homage to the ageing writer's œuvre, as much as seeking to conduct a literary critical argument. Yet the terms invoked and the broad temporal horizon opened up by Naipaul's long career—his international impact vs. the provincialism of "stuff from the Caribbean"—resonate provocatively with current debates over world literature and the attempt to envision or revise this concept from a Global South perspective. No doubt, questions of universal value and international impact continue to be at the heart of World Literature Studies, but they have been complicated by growing scepticism as to how and where such a reputation is earned and granted. In recent projects of "re-mapping world literature" (Müller et al. 2018) in and from the Global South, well-trodden loops of circulation and the idea that aspiring writers need to pass through European or western centres in the "world republic of letters", as suggested by Pascale Casanova (2004), are no longer taken as given. Here, the Jaipur Literature Festival as a novel hub of world-literary entanglements adds an interesting location and tension. Ever since its inception in 2006, the Jaipur Literature Festival has "attracted both critical praise and derision" (Chakravorty 2014, 2). While thriving on spectacle, superstars and Indian cultural stereotypes, the festival has also been commended for its "effort to integrate Dalit, subaltern, and vernacular issues" (3), redressing the lingering dominance of English and Anglophone writing in the Indian and world-literary scene. Moreover, a number of satellite festivals around the globe have meanwhile been established, forging new connections "internationally with 'India-themed' cultural events in Europe, North America, Africa, and Asia" (Ståhlberg 2019, 57). Much has been made of the paradox that despite being a postcolonial writer, Naipaul represents a rather old world order, as his own well-documented views and the controversies he sparked in critical circles attest. Thus, recalling the late Naipaul's appearance at a festival that foregrounds lateral South-South connections as much as existing North-South and western circuits of world literature offers a timely point of departure to explore trajectories and travels of Caribbean writing in a Global South context.

In this chapter, I will trace both temporal and geographical dimensions by revisiting Sam Selvon's novel *An Island Is a World* (1955) before returning to the Jaipur Literature Festival to discuss the work of Kei Miller and Marlon James as refracted through their reading and commentary at the Festival's 2016 instalment. Selvon's second novel, *An Island Is a World*, is one of his more domestic works.

A fictional portrait of Trinidad in the decolonization era, it explores metropolitan links, like the better-known *The Lonely Londoners* (1956), but it simultaneously tracks additional pathways and centres, notably surrounding the island's Indian community. Selvon's novel lends itself to recent contributions in World Literature Studies which have sought to extend the circulation model by broaching world literature as a matter of literary production and artistic world-making. Resonating with Global South perspectives, Selvon's world-making in *An Island Is a World* can be seen to anticipate alternative imaginaries on a world scale, apart from the rather static and uneven relationship between North and South either in the circulation model or in materialist approaches to world literature.

As resident writers in the UK and US respectively, Kei Miller and Marlon James are placed firmly in a paradigm of "transcultural world literature" (Schulze-Engler 2007), representing a "new genre of writing which has never been national, often written by diasporic authors, which is promoted by international publishers for a world market-place" (Young 2011, 215). Both have won prestigious literary awards, with Kei Miller (2014a) receiving, among others, the Forward Prize for Poetry for his collection *The Cartographer Tries to Map a Way to Zion*. Marlon James's (2014) novel *A Brief History of Seven Killings*, a fictional account of the attempted murder of Bob Marley in 1976, was awarded the 2015 Man Booker Prize, arguably the ultimate accolade and sign of world-literary status accorded to postcolonial English-language writers in the west. While both Miller and James draw from their experience of Jamaica, where they were born and brought up, their writing can safely be characterized as "global in scope, concerned with both Western and non-Western subject matter" (Young 2011, 215). Both authors and their works are well-travelled on North-South circuits of world literature, and they epitomize the Global South's hemispheric interconnections with diasporic contexts of "the South contained within North" (Müller et al. 2018, 3). At the same time, I deliberately set out to view their work through a prism of South-to-South dialogue at the Jaipur Literature Festival, which will include discussion of the festival's programme and self-understanding as an alternative forum of world writing from below.

From Selvon to Miller and James, this chapter will foreground itineraries and routes of exchange between the Caribbean and India while certainly not losing sight of other coordinates, including historical entanglements within the Caribbean, caused by displacement and migration between Africa, India and Latin America. Moreover, I will draw on "three axes of analysis" (Müller et al. 2018, 4) distinguished in similar endeavours, two of which pertain to literary production and circulation respectively. Aspects of "writing" or literary world-making as well as institutional matters of "book markets" and the world-literary system (4, 6), including literary festivals and awards, will inform my two case studies of Selvon and subsequently Miller and James. On a more theoretical note and to frame my analysis, I will next turn to the third axis, formed by "epistemologies" and maintained by the "circulation of knowledge, ideas and concepts" (8). This axis focuses on intellectual exchanges within and between South and North rather than primarily literary ones, with decolonial theory and critical border thinking as prominent examples. [1] Not least, this degree of epistemological interchange across hemispheric borders has prominently involved the very concept of world literature itself and the large, productive scale of revision that the latter has undergone from postcolonial or Global South perspectives.

World Literature in and from the Global South: Epistemological Adjustments

It should be emphasized that much of world literature's current circulation as a critical debate and concept carries a postcolonial inflection, despite the fact that postcolonial and Global South scholars are among its fiercest sceptics.[2] Even slightly predating the current

1 See also the references to Walter Mignolo's (2000) work in Nanton (2017).

2 See, *inter alia*, Mufti (2016) and Abu-Lughod (1998).

renaissance of World Literature Studies from the early 2000s onwards, triggered by the important interventions of Franco Moretti (2000) and David Damrosch (2003), among others, Homi Bhabha (1994) speculated about the beginning of a new phase, following on from the pronouncements of origin figures like Goethe and Marx "where, once, the transmission of national literatures was a major theme of world literature" (12). In its place, "perhaps we can now suggest that transnational histories of migrants, the colonized, or political refugees—these border and frontier conditions—may be the terrains of world literature" (12). Bhabha emphasizes the role of new themes and transnational experiences in this early proposition of postcolonialism as world literature, a paradigm whose prospects have been treated with reservation by many other contributors. Institutional constraints and biased canons in World and Comparative Literary Studies, the dominance of English and the power of western-based publishing houses have all been cited as obstacles to an alternative curriculum of world literature. Globalization, which apart from transnational migration has arguably helped most to put world literature on the critical agenda again, is likewise eyed with suspicion as an economic doctrine and a thinly-veiled rerun of western dominance. However, such an understanding represents only part of what has always been a more diverse field: "World Literature, by covering a broad and open semantic spectrum, allows for the application of postcolonial approaches" (Müller et al. 2018, 2). Well before dealing with themes, contents and texts, this semantic openness has been exploited for epistemological concerns, seeking to redress basic terms of debate such as "world" and "globe" to begin with.

Gayatri Spivak's (2003) alternative notion of "planctarity" is a much-quoted case in point. Opting for the planet as a more appropriate referent for comparative and world-spanning critical endeavours, Spivak moves beyond what she sees as a narrow canon of comparative literature, as well as away from western ideas and practices of globalization. Similarly intervening at conceptual levels, Pheng Cheah (2014) pits "world against globe" in the title of a programmatic essay, in which he differentiates two fundamentally opposed understandings of world literature as attached to the two terms. "Globe" for Cheah is shorthand for world literature as global circulation and commodification according to a neo-colonial, capitalist order. It conceives of "the world in terms of spatial circulation, the paradigmatic case of which is global capitalist market exchange" (Cheah 2014, 303). "World", by contrast, stands for "an alternative notion of world literature as an active power of world making that contests the world made by capitalist globalization" (303). Rather than an external, sociological criterion, or a mode of circulation after the fact of literary creation, world literature is thus "reconceived as a site of processes of worlding" (303) and returned to the very ways in which literary works may make and remake the world as a matter of their text-internal configuration. World is a "temporal category" (303) of a creative process for Cheah, different from the idea of world-literary status as ex post facto spatial circulation.

Processes of literary world-making and worlding have been attended to in a range of recent contributions in World Literature Studies. Conducive to the project of envisioning world literature from the Global South, these have involved arguing for a pluralization of both literary worlds and world literatures: "The critical endorsement of the world-making potentialities of literature allows us to enact a systematic and not merely terminological shift from world literature (*Weltliteratur*) to *world literatures*" (Neumann and Rippl 2017, 3). Emphasis on literature's potential for "planetary imagination" (Spivak 2003, 96) and its capacity to provide "windows on the world" (Damrosch 2009, 6) brings a range of new and lesser-studied traditions of writing into the fray, such as from the Anglophone South. Conceptually, world literature can be extended to at least three levels: plural poietic worlds, the far-flung itineraries of writers' lives and the global flows of their works' distribution and reception. In this light, world literatures are no longer construed "as a canon of globally circulating works but as open, inherently pluralised texts that are both shaped by and modelled on processes of circulation, translation and exchange" (Neumann and Rippl 2017, 3).

Caribbean writing and its entanglements with multiple Caribbean spaces world-wide (Boyce Davies 2013) can be seen as a paradigmatic case of Anglophone world literatures, shaped by and simultaneously shaping local as well as global settings of production and circulation (Rupp 2017). From a materialist and ecocritical perspective, the Caribbean has been ascribed pivotal significance as a tradition of writing that registers world-ecological developments. In the introduction to their edited volume *The Caribbean: Aesthetics, World-Ecology, Politics*, Chris Campbell and Michael Niblett (2016) point out the Caribbean's role as a central location and theatre of the capitalist world-system from the time of New World discovery and colonialism onwards. Yoking together world systems theory, ecology and world literature, Campbell and Niblett argue that Caribbean writings, however local in outlook, have world-literary value in that they speak to larger developments of global capitalism and its ecological repercussions almost by default (3). Cheah (2016) accords a similar place to postcolonial and Global South literatures more generally: "Literature of the postcolonial South is an important modality of world literature [. . .] because the sharp inequalities created by capitalist globalization and their devastating consequences [. . .] make the opening of other worlds a matter of the greatest imperativity" (11). As Cheah argues, the "tension between cosmopolitanism and globalization, world and globe, is most acute in postcoloniality because far from holding a world together, capitalist globalization incorporates people outside the European world-system by violently destroying their worlds" (11–12).

While Cheah similarly highlights the impact of the capitalist world-system, he differs from materialist approaches in granting literature a more active role in relation to it. Campbell and Niblett (2016) posit capitalist world-ecology "as the matrix within which all modern literature takes shape" (8). In this slightly deterministic though typically Marxist view, literature is primarily being left to "register" (8) the workings of capitalist globalization. In Cheah's (2016) account of postcolonial South world writing, literature's relative autonomy and potential for contestation is an important extension, seeing that "material conditions are part of the processes of worlding in which the novels are immersed and which they participate in and actively contest" (16). Insisting on literature's worldliness, Cheah rejects any "sharp separation of aesthetic form from referential content" (16). Yet, as much as acknowledging the inscription of material conditions, he emphasizes literature's reciprocal capacity for "worldly intervention" (16), realized in agentic processes of worlding and world-making.

In keeping with his reformulation of world as a temporal category, Cheah (2016) focuses on "alternative temporalities" in his reading of novels from the postcolonial South, foregrounding their "intense preoccupation with narrativity and time" (17). At the same time, he highlights intersecting concerns when observing that "non-Western temporalities" may "generate alternative cartographies that enable a postcolonial people or a collective group to foster relations of solidarity and build a shared world" (17). Indeed, literary world-making involves a larger "array of imaginative manoeuvres, such as the creation of new, non-Eurocentric geographies and the tentative entanglement of heterogeneous places into networks of reciprocal exchange" (Neumann and Rippl 2017, 11). Further aspects of literary worlding may consist in articulating planetary imaginaries and "other, minor forms of cosmopolitanism [...] that can alert readers to new modes of transcultural conviviality" (11). Not least, "literary world-making also resides in a number of poetic practices and transcultural aesthetics that bring together different literary traditions" (11). As a case in point, Birgit Neumann (2018) analyses the use of Caribbean Creole in Sam Selvon's 1956 novel *The Lonely Londoners* as a vehicle for the novel's "vernacular cosmopolitanism" (239). In particular, she points out the stylized nature of Selvon's dialect voice, as a blend of different Caribbean vernaculars and thus as a means of literary worlding and diasporic community-building par excellence.

In my reading of Selvon's earlier *An Island Is a World*, which I shall turn to next, dialect voice also plays a central part in rendering polyglot communities and painting a fictional portrait of Trinidad in the decolonization era. However, my main interest will be in Selvon's meditation on various entanglements between island and world—what Ottmar Ette (2016) has felicitously termed "Caribbean Island-Worlds" (84)[3]—as prominently signposted by the novel's title. As in *The Lonely Londoners*, metropolitan links to the US and the UK loom large, making it possible to read both texts as early accounts of post-Empire migration and globalization. Unlike in the later novel, however, Selvon's world-making in *An Island Is a World* foregrounds island and other Global South locations, rendering alternative geographies of local and South-South relations.

World-Making between Routes and Roots in Sam Selvon's *An Island Is a World* (1955)

Emphasis on routes and roots has served as a fruitful characterization of mobility and dwelling as dialectical factors shaping Caribbean writing (DeLoughrey 2007). Indeed, routes of mass exodus and migration—Middle Passage, indenture, post-imperial exile and contemporary global travel—inform Caribbean imaginaries just like island roots or ancestral homelands. The interplay of routes and roots also resonates in discussions of Caribbean world literatures as vernacular cosmopolitanism in novels like *The Lonely Londoners*. Where Selvon's later work is a clear product of metropolitan tutelage and diasporic themes, *An Island Is a World* presents a complementary picture by refracting global transcultural flows from a more homebound perspective. While many of its characters travel extensively and spend time in metropolitan locations in the west, the book's central concerns lie with island communities and its "palpable Trinidad setting—an absolutely crucial element of *An Island is a World*" (Barratt 1996, 25). Both routes and roots are at the heart of this novel's world-making, too. Yet its concern with island spaces, with the local or landed cosmopolitanism of Trinidad's heterogeneous population and with South-to-South memories of ancestral homelands eventually

3 See Ottmar Ette's concept of "island-worlds" and archipelagos in his chapter of this volume (110-11).

offers an alternative geography. This new map is not only non-Eurocentric, but moreover deemphasizes western and North-South connections in its fictional network of exchange.

As highlighted by its title, Selvon's novel takes up two prominent tropes of Caribbean writings as a "language of landscape" (Phillips Casteel 2011). Both island and world are part of a veritable "lexicon of the Caribbean spatial imaginary" (Phillips Casteel 2011), by which authors have repeatedly turned to local topography to derive literary idioms and styles. Historically speaking, where models and modes of expression from the English canon no longer represented local realities, or if anything prolonged stereotypical images of a tropical garden Eden, Caribbean writers started revisiting the land for scarred memories of forced labour and plantation agriculture. The sea, plantation, hinterland, beach, archipelago and hurricane have since provided innovative elements of form and genre. Like these other topoi, both island and world serve as "multivalent image[s]" (483), offering rich and multi-faceted tropes of world-making. Thus, "the island can be read either as insular, bounded and confining or as opening out to the sea and beyond" (484). In Antonio Benítez-Rojo's (1996) model of the "repeating island" and the Caribbean as a "meta-archipelago" (4), the island opens out as far as to the world at large and is mapped onto a global scale, as a central element of "dynamic states or regularities that repeat themselves globally" (2). From this perspective, the island is a world and vice versa, to speak with the title of Selvon's novel, which can also be read as local manifesto of the island as a world unto itself or a self-contained miniature world. Many if not most of these meanings are drawn by Selvon's *An Island Is a World*, including potential tensions between island and world.

Converging as well as conflicting images of world and island are invoked right at the beginning, as the prologue introduces the novel's central character and focalizer's morning routine: "Every morning when Foster awoke, it was the same thing. The world spun in his brain" (Selvon 1955, 8).[4] Foster's restless mind is caused by a

4 All quotations are taken from the 1955 edition of Selvon's novel.

familiar angst at the Caribbean's marginal position and small island status. It is aggravated by a situation in which the region's place in the world at large is challenged by social and technological developments of globalization in the decolonization era. Foster's confusion is tellingly staged and illustrated through several spatial operations, by which his perception first zooms out to a global scale or world map and then as far as the universe to get to grips with Trinidad's location and significance:

> He imagined the island of Trinidad, eleven and a half degrees north of the equator. He saw it on a globe, with the Americas sprawled like giant shadows above and below, and the endless Atlantic lapping the coastlines of the continents and the green islands of the Caribbean. (8)

The smallness of Trinidad is pictured as "a mere dot on the globe" (8). As the passage further scales the heights of the universe, Foster's disorientation is interspersed with a paradoxical desire to control and influence the way of the world: "He was lying down in the dot and thoughts radiated from him like R.K.O. introduce their films with a radio station broadcasting into space" (8). All of a sudden, spatial constellations are reversed and Foster is transformed into a giant arising from his dot on the world map: "Foster was big and the globe was small, spinning off there in space. Sometimes he gave the globe a blow with his fist and he shattered it. And sometimes he put out a finger and he stopped it spinning" (8). Foster's dizzying roller coaster of emotions from his "sense of insignificance and alienation" (Barratt 1996, 27) to megalomania bespeaks his wish to conquer and "go out in the world" (Selvon 1955, 4), overcompensating for nagging doubts about Trinidad's de facto marginality: "The world, in reality, consisted of the continents—the world was London, New York, Paris, and the big cities [. . .]. Who was interested in a few thousand people living on an island?" (257).

Like his brother Rufus, who emigrates to the US, Foster does eventually go out in the world, completing a familiar journey along South-North routes of postcolonial migration to live in London: "the sense of entrapment and rootlessness, the smallness of the colonial world, alienation, escape, and disillusionment—these are the major obsessions of almost all of the characters in *An Island Is a World*" (Barratt 1996, 27). Deviating from the post-war novel of migration, however, Foster later on returns to Trinidad, with the novel turning into a spiritual *Bildungsroman* in the process. While the homeland remains a nostalgic yet ultimately elusive and unfeasible destination in the novel of migration, which is forever torn between old and new homes, the hero's return in *An Island Is a World* clearly involves a reappraisal of community and island origins when reading Selvon's novel as a *Bildungsroman*. Foster's reverse journey is crucial to the book's world-making, and in its wake the protagonist's initial meditation on island and world undergoes a significant change. Foster's sentimental education is foreshadowed by his encounter with Father Hope, who is a well-travelled man himself but has deliberately settled down as an island priest. Clearly not by coincidence, it is from the figuratively named priest and his eloquent discourse that the novel derives its title: "'People are the same all over the world,' Father Hope said. 'It does not matter where you are, you encounter sadness, happiness, love, hate. An island is a world, and everywhere that people live, they create their own worlds" (Selvon 1955, 93). This insight will come to resonate as Foster embarks on and completes his quest, with a final twist that resolves his restlessness and small islander inferiority complex. At the end of the novel, after Father Hope has died and left all his possessions to Foster, the prodigal son emerges as the priest's material as well as spiritual heir, making peace with his big world aspirations:

> Looking through the windscreen, he tried to shake off the despondency he felt. He could see the world spinning ahead of them. It was as if they were going towards it, but it kept its distance. Somehow it didn't seem to matter anymore. (288)

While withholding any neat sense of closure, the novel's ending no doubt places special emphasis on Caribbean islands as Global South locations, reformulating assumptions of place and world stature which privilege western and South-North routes of escape. Adding to this non-Eurocentric outlook, the latter part of the book includes telling descriptions of Trinidad's polyglot population as a minor cosmopolitanism within, balancing external cosmopolitan links with the western world and throwing into relief "the region's [. . .] privileged perspective on another major challenge and reward of occupying a glocal world—that of living together in difference" (Donnell 2012, 54). As part of his spiritual journey, Foster comes to realize and appreciate the invariably complex and yet tolerant and convivial community he grew up in: "He had been brought up as a Trinidadian—a member of a cosmopolitan community who recognized no creed or race, a creature born of all the peoples in the world, in a small island that no one knew nothing about" (Selvon 1955, 257). This fictional portrait of Trinidad is further elaborated when members of the island's Indian population contemplate joining the "Back to India" (197) movement after India's independence: "A flame of nostalgia began to spread. Men who had forgotten who they were dusted their memories and began to talk about going back home" (196). The novel in no way naively celebrates the prospect of reclaiming national origins by returning to the ancestral homeland.[5] In fact, the Back to India movement runs a risk of dividing the community and Foster feels a "strange emotion in his heart. He was one of them, and yet he couldn't feel the way they did, nor share the kinship they knew" (256). Yet despite these ambivalent undertones alerting the reader to the precarious fabric and painful history of Trinidad's cosmopolitanism, the retrieval of South-to-South connections is significant, as an attempt to "represent and imaginatively coordinate communities and nations within, as well as across, geographical space" (Donnell 2012, 54). It clearly establishes a sense of possibility and connectivity in an alternative geography of hemispheric exchange that is markedly different from North-South routes of travel. Just like Foster's return to Trinidad, which remedies or at least serves to reassess its marginality

5 After the abolition of slavery, some 500,000 Indians migrated to the Caribbean to compensate for the loss of slave labour. A good third of this number returned to India after the end of indentured servitude in 1920 and India's independence in 1947.

as "a small island that no one knew nothing about" (Selvon 1955, 257), ancestral links with the vast space and rich cultural legacy of India contribute to compensating for Caribbean backwardness.

For all the agency of literary worlding, it can hardly be denied that world literature is also part of "an apparatus of production with a worldwide reach", a world-literary "system [...] marked by inequality" at that, which "requires an analysis of the geopolitical order and the implied material dimensions, as the power-relations at play" (Müller et al. 2018, 2–3). In this connection it is intriguing to note that literary visions of non-western and non-Eurocentric networks of exchange in the Global South, such as in novels like *An Island Is a World*, are increasingly being matched by an emerging institutional structure, where, apart from the book market and publishing policies, literary festivals such as the Jaipur Literature Festival serve as an important catalyst.

Caribbean Voices at the Jaipur Literature Festival

Founded by Namita Gokhale and William Dalrymple in 2006, the Jaipur Literature Festival has seen rapidly growing numbers of visitors and internationally acclaimed speakers by the year. On its website, it is presented as "the greatest literary show on earth" (JLF n.d.), preserving a grassroots policy of "core values [that] remain unchanged; to serve as a democratic, non-aligned platform offering free and fair access" (JLF n.d.). Not a lot of scholarly writing on the festival exists as yet, but extensive journalistic coverage and, not least, a rich visual archive of televised readings and debates facilitated by social media platforms have significantly raised the festival's profile and its influence as a beacon of the Global South literary world.

Writing about the Jaipur Literature Festival in 2011, Jocelyn Watson (2012) echoes its self-understanding as an alternative forum of world literature from below, both with respect to minor voices from the Indian subcontinent and beyond: "The Festival, while encouraging best-selling writers in English, has created a space for local languages and the examination of works with a strong social content in indigenous languages and through translations" (50). In particular, Watson is interested in possibilities for Indian women writers from marginalized positions of gender and class to draw attention to their causes. Demonstrating the festival's democratic potential through wide-ranging interviews with writers and her own participant observation, Watson points out its merits as "the world's largest free literary festival" and concludes: "That it can encourage, stimulate and promote diverse cultural expressions, vernacular languages and translations and new forms of communication across the globe is surely to be applauded" (55).

The Festival's 2016 instalment featured a strong Caribbean connection, with Booker Prize winner Marlon James and two other 2015 Booker contenders, the shortlisted writer Sunjeev Sahota and longlisted novelist Anuradha Roy, together discussing their work and reading from their books. In a second appearance, James debated traditions of Caribbean prose and poetry with fellow Jamaican poet Kei Miller, who has eloquently written about matters of Caribbean and world writing in essays and scholarly articles, too. Both events centred on lingering inequalities and western strongholds in the contemporary publishing world, yet they were testament to emerging world-literary connections across the Global South at the same time. Thus, in conversation with Indian poet and writer Tishani Doshi, James and Miller address familiar difficulties of having to channel their work through publishing houses in the US and Europe, including sometimes limiting expectations as to particularly publishable subject-matters and styles to be taken up by authors from the postcolonial world. In the talk, entitled "From Jamaica to Zion", both recall having to leave home to make a career and establish themselves as writers to begin with. An issue of long standing, the lack of a major home-grown publishing industry has featured in many reviews of James's *A Brief History of Seven Killings*, as a motive for "why Marlon James had to get out of Jamaica to win the Booker Prize" (Wright 2015). For "Jamaica's book industry is generally seen as a hobby, and even the most talented writers struggle to make enough sales" (Wright 2015). While James lives as an expatriate writer in Minnesota,

Miller has similarly followed the northbound journeys of his books and taken up residence in Glasgow and London respectively. Part of the reason is simply practical, to do with not being able to sustain a literary infrastructure and critical mass of readers across an archipelago of islands: "It's just not possible to have Penguin Caribbean in the way you have Penguin India, we just don't have those kinds of numbers" (JLF 2016, 9:32 to 9:40), as Miller points out when speaking in Jaipur.

Surprisingly enough, Doshi's work is an example to the contrary, placing emphasis on not just a Caribbean, but in fact a Caribbean-Indian book market. Her 2015 collection *The Adulterous Citizen: Poems, Stories, Essays* came out with the House of Nehesi Publishers in St. Martin. Doshi's Caribbean publication and her appearance at the St. Martin Book Fair in 2015, at which her collection was launched, constitute some intriguing South-South connections, which are further thrown into relief by Doshi, Miller and James's exchange on a podium at the 2016 Jaipur Literature Festival. The St. Martin publishing house may not be a match for a major publisher like Penguin, but Doshi, Miller and James are clearly representative of the increasing travel of writers and their work along lateral South-to-South pathways. Doshi's collaboration with a Caribbean publishing house and her conversation with Miller and James in Jaipur at least qualify the idea that writers from the Global South invariably have to follow their books to publishing opportunities in the metropolitan North.

Apart from benefiting from a metropolitan literary culture, critics have attributed the world-literary success of James's *A Brief History of Seven Killings* to the novel's virtuoso performance of Jamaican patois alongside Standard English. Assembling a multitude of voices from more than 70 characters to tell the story of an attempted assassination of Bob Marley in the 1970s, James's use of dialect voice is not unlike Selvon's vernacular cosmopolitanism. Following in the footsteps of Claude McKay and Louise Bennett in a Jamaican tradition more specifically, James creates a truly transcultural idiom "that does not sacrifice identity in seeking to globalise narratives for the sake of book sales" (Wright 2015). At the same time, the vernacular has meanwhile become a central and particularly sellable aesthetic of successful transcultural world writing in English. Moreover, James's prize-winning novel "challenges conventional notions of 'postcolonial' writing, and introduces all kinds of boundary crossing" (Nanton 2017, 123) in terms of genre and world-literary affiliation. This includes transgressing boundaries between literary and genre fiction, as well as taking in influences from US popular culture rather than working through Caribbean-English legacies. James himself has described his work as "post-post-colonial", referencing "a new generation of, well, newish generation of writers, where we're not driven by our dialogue with the former mother country" (quoted in Mayer 2015). James's depiction of Kingston's 1970s underworld and the formula of literary crime fiction are reminiscent of Aravind Adiga's *The White Tiger* (2008), another Booker Prize-winning novel. The question of whether the appeal of rough authenticity in the two novels constitutes a new world-literary currency for writings from the Global South was an added South-South parallel featuring in Doshi, James and Miller's conversation.

As for Miller's work, connections across the Global South as highlighted from the vantage point of the Jaipur Literature Festival concern, among others, Zion, the eponymous African dreamland of Jamaican Rastafarianism that features in his poetry collection *The Cartographer Tries to Map a Way to Zion* (2014). If the "link between Caribbean literature and African literature sometimes gets underplayed" (JLF 2016, 49:13 to 49:18), as James observes, Miller's literary meditation on Zion goes some way towards restoring this link and filling in blanks. This concern with map-making, borders and transcultural linkages is present in Miller's life and work throughout, and like James he utilizes an aesthetic thriving on local and global influences. As he has observed in a critical essay, "those of us lumped into this strange category of 'world writers', might find it useful, even exciting to occasionally turn our attention to very local practices" (Miller 2014b, 340). Similarly, speaking in Jaipur, he "insist[s] that you can write a large literature from a small place" (JLF 2016, 45:30

to 45:35), adding that "I definitely see myself as a Caribbean writer" (JLF 2016, 44:56 to 44:58). Taken together, the various criss-crossing lines of connectivity retraced by Doshi, Miller and James in their work from the vantage point of the Jaipur Literature Festival are highly telling. Eventually, they stand to yield a heterodox map, recognizable in parts, but more varied, expansive and multidirectional than conventional global circuits, and so are highly conducive to envisioning and re-mapping world literature from the Global South.

Conclusion: New Writing in a Global South World

In the light of this extended and sprawling map, it is ironical that the late V.S. Naipaul should have taken such a dim view of Caribbean world writing at the Jaipur Literature Festival, of all places. Arguably, the Nobel laureate's appearance marked a moment of generational change in more than one sense, because with new understandings of world, world literature and entanglements across the Global South the conditions of being a writer in the world have been shifting, too. The new generation of writers including Miller, James and many other Caribbean and Global South writers are beginning to explore a different landscape from former "world republics of letters", with an emphasis on understudied linkages between supposedly marginal, non-Eurocentric and frontier locations in the Caribbean and India. South-South perspectives in the work of these and other writers of this generation, such as Caribbean poets Ishion Hutchinson and Vladimir Lucien, clearly merit further discussion. As Nanton (2017) concludes his analysis of "compare-and-contrast that extends beyond the insular and restricted geography of regional writing" in the Caribbean: "Frontier analysis starts from the common ground that the region shares with the rest of the world" (124). Viewing Miller's and James's work through the lens of the Jaipur Literature Festival provides some compelling and highly symbolic illustrations of that common ground. True, the world literary system continues to be marked by lingering divisions and inequalities, but it is also an evolving framework from below as "literary festivals become part of the global landscape" (Watson 2012, 56) in novel and unexpected ways, among other institutional structures. The fact that the Jaipur Literature Festival is seeking to make an impact also as a touring and travelling festival, with satellite events being organized in other global literary centres like New York, further underscores this development.

As I hope to have shown, epistemological revision and literary world-making are at the heart of re-mapping Caribbean world writing in and from the Global South. Increasingly, material developments are coming to complement the alternative kind of world-literary, postcolonial South visions that I have traced back to the founding 1950s moment of novels like Sam Selvon's *An Island is a World*. At a time of nascent or accelerating western-style globalization in the post-World War II, post-Empire world, Selvon's novel gives prominence to alternative locations and itineraries in the South, gesturing towards a shared hemispheric consciousness meanwhile circulating under the sign of Global South. The fact that the novel contributes to a mapping of this Global South world *avant la lettre* is a measure of its world-making power and world-literary vision. It can thus be grouped among "opuses [that] have a global reach beyond Eurocentrism, not in the literary market, but in their global sensitivity and consciousness, through the settings where they take place and the worldviews they present" (López-Calvo 2018, 18). Indeed, Selvon's novel bears out recent attempts of reformulating and re-mapping world literature from the Global South. By focusing on the world-making power of writing and literary creation as much as on institutional frameworks of global circulation and reception, rereading this lesser-known 1950s text instructively serves to "investigate the links and trajectories that interconnect and energize world regions like the Global South, which have been marginalized by most of the recent studies on the topic of World Literature" (Müller et al. 2018, 3). This will be even more plausible regarding the time of publication in the 1950s, where no patent Global South links existed then in terms of the literary market, contrary to North-South circuits of metropolitan tutelage that Selvon himself travelled on as a diasporic writer in

England. Far from singing a swansong, Caribbean writers are turning new pages in a Global South world literature a good half-century on.

Bibliography

Abu-Lughod, Janet. 1998. “Going Beyond Global Babble.” In *Culture, Globalization, and the World-System: Contemporary Conditions for the Representation of Identity*, edited by Anthony D. King, 131–37. Minneapolis, MN: University of Minnesota Press.

Barratt, Harold. 1996. “An Island Is Not a World: A Reading of Sam Selvon's ‘An Island Is a World’.” *ARIEL: A Review of International English Literature* 27 (2): 25–34.

Benítez-Rojo, Antonio. 1992. *The Repeating Island: The Caribbean and the Postmodern Perspective*. 2nd edition. Translated by James Maraniss (Original: *La isla que se repite: El Caribe y la perspectiva posmoderna,* 1996). Durham, NC: Duke University Press.

Bhabha, Homi K. 1994. *The Location of Culture*. London: Routledge.

Boyce Davies, Carole. 2013. *Caribbean Spaces: Escapes from the Twilight Zones*. Champaign, IL: University of Illinois Press.

Campbell, Chris, and Michael Niblett. 2016. “Introduction: Critical Environments: World-Ecology, World Literature, and the Caribbean.” In *The Caribbean: Aesthetics, World-Ecology, Politics*, edited by Chris Campbell and Michael Niblett, 1–15. Liverpool: Liverpool University Press.

Casanova, Pascale. 2004. *The World Republic of Letters*. Translated by M.B. DeBevoise (Original: *La République mondiale les Lettres*, 1999). Cambridge, MA: Harvard University Press.

Chakravorty, Mrinalini. 2014. *In Stereotype: South Asia in the Global Literary Imaginary*. New York: Columbia University Press.

Cheah, Pheng. 2014. “World against Globe: Toward a Normative Conception of World Literature.” *New Literary History* 45 (3): 303–29.

Cheah, Pheng. 2016. *What Is a World? On Postcolonial Literature as World Literature*. Durham, NC: Duke University Press.

Damrosch, David. 2003. *What Is World Literature?* Princeton, NJ: Princeton University Press.

Damrosch, David. 2009. "Introduction: All the Time in the World." In *Teaching World Literature*, edited by David Damrosch, 1–11. New York: Modern Language Association.

DeLoughrey, Elizabeth. 2007. *Routes and Roots: Navigating Caribbean and Pacific Island Literatures.* Honolulu: University of Hawai'i Press.

Donnell, Alison. 2012. "The Island and the World: Kinship, Friendship and Living Together in Selected Writings of Sam Selvon." *Journal of West Indian Literature* 20 (2): 54–69.

Ette, Ottmar. 2016. *Writing-Between-Worlds: TransArea Studies and the Literatures-without-a-fixed-Abode.* Translated by Vera M. Kutzinski (Original: *ZwischenWeltenSchreiben. Literaturen ohne festen Wohnsitz*, 2005). Berlin and Boston, MA: De Gruyter.

Jaipur Literature Festival (JLF). n.d. "About." Accessed 3 November, 2021. https://jaipurliteraturefestival.org/about.

Jaipur Literature Festival (JLF). 2015. "#JLF 2015: The Writer and the World." 28 January. YouTube Video, 1:00:23. https://www.youtube.com/watch?v=IW9D5pxCSwg.

Jaipur Literature Festival (JLF). 2016. "#JLF 2016: From Jamaica to Zion." 28 January. YouTube Video, 59:34. https://www.youtube.com/watch?v=cgr_sLIHnpc.

James, Marlon. 2014. *A Brief History of Seven Killings.* New York: Riverhead Books.

Ledent, Bénédicte. 2011. "West Indian Fiction." In *The Encyclopedia of Twentieth-Century Fiction, Vol. 3: World Fiction*, edited by John Clement Ball, 1382–85. Chichester, NH: Wiley-Blackwell.

López-Calvo, Ignacio. 2018. "Worlding and Decolonizing the Literary World-System: Asian-Latin American Literature as Alternative Type of *Weltliteratur*." In *Re-mapping World Literature: Writing, Book Markets and Epistemologies between Latin America and the Global South*, edited by Gesine Müller, Jorge J. Locane, and Benjamin Loy, 15–31. Berlin and Bosten, MA: De Gruyter.

Mayer, Petra. 2015. "Marlon James Wins Man Booker Prize." NPR, 13 October. http://www.npr.org/sections/thetwo-way/2015/10/13/448397179/marlon-james-wins-man-booker-prize.

Mignolo, Walter D. 2000. *Local Histories/Global Designs: Coloniality, Subaltern Knowledges and Border Thinking*. Princeton, NJ: Princeton University Press.

Miller, Kei. 2014a. *The Cartographer Tries to Map a Way to Zion*. Manchester: Carcanet Press.

Miller, Kei. 2014b. "If I Could Write This on Zinc, I Would Write It on Zinc." *Journal of Commonwealth Literature* 49 (3): 333–41.

Moretti, Franco. 2000. "Conjectures on World Literature." *New Left Review* 1: 55-67.

Müller, Gesine, Jorge J. Locane, and Benjamin Loy. 2018. "Introduction." In *Re-mapping World Literature: Writing, Book Markets and Epistemologies between Latin America and the Global South*, edited by Gesine Müller, Jorge J. Locane, and Benjamin Loy, 1–12. Berlin and Bosten, MA: De Gruyter.

Mufti, Aamir A. 2016. *Forget English! Orientalisms and World Literatures*. Cambridge, MA: Harvard University Press.

Naipaul, V.S. 2002. *The Writer and the World*. New York: Alfred A. Knopf.

Nanton, Philip. 2017. *Frontiers of the Caribbean*. Manchester: Manchester University Press. DOI: 10.26530/OAPEN_622381.

Neumann, Birgit. 2018. "Vernacular Cosmopolitanism in Anglophone World Literatures: Comparative Histories of Literary Worlding." *Arcadia* 53 (2): 239–57.

Neumann, Birgit, and Gabriele Rippl. 2017. "Anglophone World Literatures: Introduction." *Anglia* 135 (1): 1–20.

Phillips Casteel, Sarah. 2011. "The Language of Landscape: A Lexicon of the Caribbean Spatial Imaginary." In *The Routledge Companion to Caribbean Literatures in English*, edited by Michael A. Bucknor and Alison Donnell, 480–89. London: Routledge.

Rupp, Jan. 2017. "Caribbean Spaces and Anglophone World Literatures." *Anglia* 135 (1): 140–58.

Selvon, Sam. 1955. *An Island Is a World*. London: Allan Wingate.

Schulze-Engler, Frank. 2007. "Theoretical Perspectives: From Post-colonialism to Transcultural World Literature." In *English Literatures Across the Globe*, edited by Lars Eckstein, 20–32. Paderborn: Fink.

Spivak, Gayatri Chakravorty. 2003. *Death of a Discipline*. New York: Columbia University Press.

Ståhlberg, Per. 2019. "The Jaipur Literature Festival and Its Critics: World Literature as Social Practice." *Anthropology and Humanism* 44 (1): 54–69.

Watson, Jocelyn. 2012. "The Struggle to be Heard." *Wasafiri* 27 (3): 50–56.

Wright, André. 2015. "Why Marlon James Had to Get Out of Jamaica to Win the Booker Prize." *The Guardian*, 15 October. https://www.theguardian.com/commentisfree/2015/oct/15/marlon-james-jamaica-booker-homophobic.

Young, Robert J.C. 2011. "World Literature and Postcolonialism." In *The Routledge Companion to World Literature*, edited by Theo D'haen, David Damrosch, and Djelal Kadir, 213–22. New York: Routledge.

Movements, Diasporas, Entanglements: Traces of the Brazil-Angola Slave Trade in Contemporary Voices

Eduardo Jorge de Oliveira and Ana Sobral

> Although these two communities had practically lost contact with each other since the beginning of the century, in cultural terms their members became Africans of Brazil and Brazilians of Africa.
> (Verger 2002, 24; our translation)

Pain as a Historical Refrain: The Cheapest Meat in the Market

In the album *Do cóccix até o pescoço* (From the Coccyx to the Neck), the Afro-Brazilian pop-funk singer Elza Soares (2002) included the provocatively titled song "a carne" (the meat)[1] which directly addresses one of Brazil's most pernicious and enduring troubles, namely structural racism. The oft-repeated chorus, with which the song also opens, announces: "The cheapest meat in the market is Black meat".[2] Soares's high-pitched, grainy voice carries an uncomfortable weight that is underscored by the lines' heptasyllabic structure. The repetition could be interpreted at first hearing as recalling all the chants from the colonial era until now, a kind of musical continuity reflecting the violence perpetrated against Afro-Black communities in Brazil,

1 Essentially, the Portuguese term "carne" means both "meat" and "flesh". While the latter would seem more appropriate to refer to people, we chose the previous to highlight the ways in which enslaved Africans were dehumanized. Therefore, throughout this essay we will consciously use the term "meat" as a way of criticizing the racialization of enslaved Africans in Brazil. The term "flesh" will be reserved for occasions where it seems more applicable to our argument.

2 Original: "A carne mais barata do mercado é a carne negra". All poetry and rap translations are ours.

which remains similarly unbroken. However, the reduction of Blackness to meat and thus to a market commodity is made all the more disturbing in the opening scene of the music video, which shows close shots of half-naked Black women and men being slapped by a white woman in elegant clothing. The Black characters remain passive, although clearly expressing pain and even anger, thus highlighting the power imbalance between them and the white woman. Soares delivers the message boldly, directly facing the camera. Her voice does not so much sing as shout, stretching the vowels in "carne" (meat) and "negra" (black), in a manner reminiscent of an actual street market situation—as if the speaker herself were a vendor, pushing her wares. The street market situation is mixed with the "rhythmic cry of the slave" (Du Bois quoted in Abreu 2018, 130),[3] which, according to Martha Abreu, frames the relationship between the Atlantic World and the American continent. Elza Soares transports the meat not only as a symbol, but also as a symptom. In this sense, the song relates to Homi Bhabha's (1986) introduction to *Black Skin, White Masks* by Frantz Fanon, in which Bhabha criticizes traditional leftist intellectuals' tendency to read "questions of race and sexuality" as mere "symptoms of petty-bourgeois deviation" from classical leftist topics such as "'class', 'state' and 'party'", when in fact such questions revealed much larger symptoms of colonial oppression (vii). Through the rhythm of poetry, rap and performances like that of Elza Soares, all these questions are reorganized in a song. The history of the Black people and their music point to the symptoms, singing where it hurts.

The situation depicted in "a carne" evokes memories of one of the defining historical periods of Brazilian society. Indeed, many scholars argue that Brazil's entire social and economic make-up bears the traces of colonialism and the capitalist exploitation of land, resources and most importantly of labour, which found its foremost

3 W.E.B. Du Bois declared in *The Souls of Black Folk* in 1903: "And so by fateful chance the Negro folk-song—the rhythmic cry of the slave—stands to-day not simply as the sole American music, but as the most beautiful expression of human experience born this side of the seas" (quoted in Abreu 2018, 130).

expression in the massive spatial structures of the sugar plantation, the gold, iron and metal mines, and coffee plantations (Schwarz 1977; Lienhard 2002, 131–53; Gomes and Schwarcz 2018; Wisnik 2018). By placing the Black characters in a contemporary urban environment (most actions take place on a sports ground), wearing modern clothing, the music video effectively collapses the distance between present and past. In sum, "a carne" indicates that little, if anything, has changed since the abolition of slavery in Brazil in 1888.

Equating Blackness with a market commodity furthermore suggests its inclusion in a complex market chain. If Blackness is indeed "meat", who is buying and selling it? For what purposes? On the other hand, if it is "the cheapest", what use value is attributed to it? These uncomfortable symptom-related questions point in turn to both the transnational dimensions of slavery and the profound consequences of reducing enslaved people to the status of mere things that can easily be discarded and replaced by new ones. The terrifying thing about "a carne" is its historical accuracy: the expression itself could easily have been used by Portuguese slave traders who carried millions of enslaved Black men, women and children across the Atlantic to work in Brazil, the most important and profitable Portuguese colony in the New World. Most of these captured and enslaved people left Africa from the port of Luanda, in Angola, a major node in the triangular trade. This degrading commercial system is at the very origin of Afro-Brazilian experience, identity, memory and culture. It also points to the specific significance of the South Atlantic as a space of production of commodified bodies.

In September 2018, the authors of this chapter came together to organize an event that closely reflected our ongoing scholarly concerns, as well as our origins. As a white Brazilian and a white Luso-Angolan, we are profoundly aware of the deep colonial structures and entanglements that have sustained our countries of origin and that have contributed to the constitution of our own subjectivities as individuals and scholars. Our academic positions at the University of Zurich, in the departments of Romance and English Studies respectively, allowed us to connect our interests and expertise in a unique way. And so we invited two artists from Brazil and Angola, whose spoken-word poetry and rap performances largely revolve around issues of Blackness, in turn reflecting their own direct experiences and their origins. Under the title *"Boca Também Toca Tambor"*[4]*—Movements, Diasporas, Entanglements*,[5] we hosted an evening with the Brazilian poet Ricardo Aleixo and the Angolan rapper Diamondog at the legendary Cabaret Voltaire in Zurich, a space known for its irreverent artistic events since the rise of the Dada movement in the early 20th century. We wanted to bring back some of that irreverence through the performances of Aleixo and Diamondog,[6] both of whom strongly foreground issues of history, memory, power and race in their works. In short, we wanted to view particular entanglements of the Global South through the special prism of the spoken word and the rhythm of the (embodied) voice. This foregrounds our interest in what Diana Taylor (2003) has termed the "repertoire"—essentially verbal as well as non-verbal practices such as spoken word, prayers, song and dance, which are "transmitted 'live' in the here and now to a live audience" (24). As Taylor argues in *The Archive and the Repertoire*, the repertoire has in fact been vital as a mode of resistance and resilience for many colonized peoples.

In this chapter we reconstruct partially that evening at Cabaret Voltaire through a close reading of the poems, raps and performances of Aleixo and Diamondog. We are particularly interested in how the actual enforced movement of Black people from Angola to Brazil, which has left such deep scars in Afro-Brazilian identity, has been articulated and translated by the artists into a unique vocal and embodied performance that in effect reworks and reframes the trauma of the South Atlantic slave trade. Taking on the perspective

4 "The mouth also plays the drums". We have opted for a literal translation, to convey the message of the event—but in the process the rhythmic play with words of the original Portuguese, which replicates the sound of a drum, is unfortunately lost.

5 A film of the event at Cabaret Voltaire can be found on SWITCHtube (*"Boca Também Toca Tambor"* 2018).

6 Diamondog's rap music only exists in performance. The tracks he performed at Cabaret Voltaire have not been officially recorded or released.

of the Global South, our intention is to foreground the specificities of the Afro-Brazilian experience, one that sheds light on different regimes of exploitation and even racialization. Thus, we wish to probe the topic through a more comparative approach in literary and cultural studies, as a way of countering narratives that tend to obliterate regional specificities.

In many ways, the memory of the transatlantic slave trade has been largely made public and even globalized through African American and, to a smaller degree, Caribbean cultural expressions. While the parallels between the colonial systems of plantation slavery in the USA and Brazil are extremely relevant, in this chapter we argue that there are also important specificities to the Afro-Brazilian experience that require a more nuanced approach. Just looking briefly at the numbers of Black deaths through police intervention in Brazil and the USA in the last years illustrates this: whereas in the USA about 400 people were killed by police officers between 2010 and 2012, in Brazil, police forces killed about 2000 people in 2012 alone. The majority of these victims were Black (Garcia-Navarro 2014). Indeed, in Brazil the statistics show an alarming increase in the deaths of Black people. These deaths are closely linked to social class: poor Black people are more exposed to the violence of the State. There are numerous examples of police brutality, the most recent being the shooting of eight-year-old Agatha Felix in Rio de Janeiro (Phillips 2019). Elza Soares's song is still painfully relevant as we write this chapter.

Such numbers beg the question: what makes Brazilian Black lives apparently so disposable? And more importantly for us, how do artists such as Aleixo and Diamondog react to and indeed act against such circumstances? What role does the voice play in this process, as a means of retrieving a buried past? How does the voice relate to the tortured meat of the slaves and their descendants? We feel that the frame of the Global South offers a possibility for unravelling these entangled histories. As Russel West-Pavlov (2019) puts it, the concept of the Global South "works like a deictic marker, linking discourses, places and speakers in such a way as to generate new subject positions, fields of agency, and possibilities of action" (2). In examining the dialogue that emerged between Aleixo and Diamondog's performances, we wish to explore precisely these aspects of the Global South.

Our contribution is intended also as an intervention in the world literature debates, one which foregrounds the importance of orality. We lean partially on Franco Moretti's (2000) notion of world literature as "one and unequal" (56), highlighting the entanglements between "cultures that belong to the periphery of the literary system" and the European (and Eurocentric) literary canon (58). The focus on entanglements first set off by capitalism's global mercantilist system is of course crucial to our analysis, and therefore we will read Aleixo's and Diamondog's performances as part and parcel of "the literature of the modern capitalist world-system", as the Warwick Research Collective (2015) defined world literature in its manifesto-style study *Combined and Uneven Development* (27). Yet we want to shift away from these scholars' interest chiefly in *written* literary productions, which tends to foreground what Moretti identifies as the "western formal influence", for example in the rise and adoption of the novel in many cultures peripheral to the Eurocentric literary system. Instead, we are interested in forms of expression that such an approach tends to ignore, where the body, the voice and the live performance take centre stage. Indeed, while world literature scholars tend to focus on what David Damrosch (2003) calls the circulation of literary works "beyond their culture of origin" (4), a movement that implies the materiality of texts as printed (and often translated) manuscripts, we claim that the circulation of oral narratives through the embodied voices of performers should be regarded as an integral part of world literature.[7] This is particularly relevant as the current dominance of audio-visual media establishes what Walter Ong (2003) called "secondary orality" as the leading mode of global communication and

7 As Sandra Bermann (2012) points out in direct reference to David Damrosch's above-quoted statement: "Whole archives of world literature are oral rather than printed, and so are seldom considered for transmission in print form" (175).

propagation of narratives and representations. We believe that a focus on embodied orality, whether through Aleixo's performance poetry or Diamondog's rap,[8] leads to a hierarchical inversion of sorts, in which the age-old traditions of oral communication are prioritized over the more Eurocentric written literary forms. This in itself has consequences for the ways the entanglements of the modern capitalist world-system are framed and represented.

A Distinct History: The Black Atlantic from a Global South Perspective

It has often been pointed out that Paul Gilroy's (1993) influential concept of the "Black Atlantic", powerful as it is, was almost exclusively concerned with entanglements between cultures and experiences in the Northern Hemisphere, most notably the Afrodiasporic people of the US and the UK (Chrisman 2012, 23–58). The critique of Gilroy's study reveals a concern expressed by some scholars about the tendency of certain case studies to inspire overgeneralizations. In many ways, this reveals the limitations of our own academic specialization, an issue that the authors of this chapter reflected on when organizing the event with Ricardo Aleixo and Diamondog at Cabaret Voltaire. Coming from Lusophone and Anglophone studies, but at the same time sharing a complex cultural and linguistic link based on our origins, we saw in this event the potential to bring together two areas of study that do not often meet.

Of course, there are obvious and very important parallels between Brazil and the USA, the countries and cultures that we have

8 Rap music itself, especially in the form of lyrics, has more recently caught the attention of literary scholars. See for example Bradley (2009). This study, however, is limited to rap in the USA. When it comes to thinking about rap music as a global phenomenon, linguists have taken the lead, exploring the contributions of rap music and hip hop culture in general to the articulation of economic, social, political and historical entanglements through language use itself. See for example Alim, Ibrahim and Pennycook (2008).

closely researched and taught about in the past years in our respective departments. Both exemplify the "New World" as it was envisioned by the European colonial imaginary in the 16th to 19th centuries. And in spite of differences in specializations—Brazil having a far greater focus on precious metal mining than the USA—both developed into leading plantation economies that largely sustained the colonial metropolises in Portugal and the UK. Most importantly, these plantation economies could only prosper through their heavy reliance on slave labour, which constituted the backbone of the economies of the colonies.[9] Thinking about these spaces together reveals all the more clearly the exploitative apparatus of colonialism and, concomitantly, the impact of the rise of capitalism on a world scale.[10]

Having said that, by focusing on the important parallels between these spaces, we also tend to obfuscate the differences. We feel that the Global South frame allows for a constructive emphasis on those differences. To begin with, the Global South has emerged as an alternative not only to the now largely negatively connoted (and often

9 A brief look at numbers illustrates this point. According to calculations by Justin R. Buciferro (2013), by 1850, Brazil included roughly 1.5 million people of European origin and 3.5 million people of African origin. The USA, in a census conducted in 1850, registered a population of roughly 23 million, of which 3.2 million were slaves and about 400,000 were "free colored" (285–317). See also the *Statistical View of the United States* (DeBow 1854).

10 Colonialism was a necessary step in the early formation of industrial capitalism. In the first volume of *Capital*, Karl Marx (1967) defines colonialism as a stage of "primitive accumulation", stating that: "The discovery of gold and silver in America, the extirpation, enslavement and entombment in mines of the aboriginal population, the beginning of the conquest and looting of the East Indies, the turning of Africa into a warren for the commercial hunting of black-skins, signalised the rosy dawn of the era of capitalist production. These idyllic proceedings are the chief momenta of primitive accumulation. On their heels treads the commercial war of the European nations, with the globe for a theatre" (915). Slavery reveals a contradiction about capitalism itself: it was essential to boost the development of European societies or the north of western civilization. Once capitalism had developed this system, however, the practical way established by the birth of the western international market was to abolish practices of slavery in countries like Brazil.

misunderstood) notion of the Third World, which itself bears the history of the Cold War, but also to the ways in which postcolonial studies have sometimes been conducted. As West-Pavlov (2019) puts it, "Global South studies has the potential to shift postcolonial studies away from its frequent fixation on 'discourse', important as this may be, to include more material aspects of imperialism and inequity" (17). In our discussion of the Afro-Brazilian experience and the voicing of the "Black meat", we wish to probe some of the implications of thinking more thoroughly about inequities.

It is by looking at the Southern Black Atlantic specifically, as it links Angola and Brazil, that we feel those "material aspects" can best come to the fore, a crucial step in our exploration of the commodification of Black Brazilian bodies and its consequences, which are still widely felt today. To begin with, the Brazil-Angola link is itself illustrative of the ways in which a Global South frame influences our reflections on colonialism and globalization. The entanglements between Angola and Brazil are so knotted that, during the heyday of transatlantic mercantilism, they could hardly be thought of separately. This merging of South Atlantic spaces was itself part and parcel of a complex global commodity chain. Patrick Wolfe (2016) quotes a revealing saying from the colonial period: "whoever says sugar says Brazil and whoever says Brazil says Angola" (120).

Indeed, one of our key arguments is that the Southern Black Atlantic has a distinct history: one that places the value of the Black "meat" (here a powerful metaphor for the labouring body itself) over the value of Black "blood" (as a metaphor for ancestry). This perspective has been recently advanced by Wolfe's comparative analysis of racism in different colonial contexts, *Traces of History: Elementary Structures of Race*. Wolfe's insights provide an important frame for our discussion. As he puts it, "subjugated populations are racialised in distinct but complementary ways that together sustain the overall dominance of European colonisers" (117). A brief look at the racialization of Afro-Brazilians illustrates this.

It is important to reiterate here that no other country in the New World imported such a high number of African enslaved people as Brazil did (de Alencastro 2018, 57–60; Rodrigues 2018, 343). The majority of the people captured by or in the name of Portuguese slave merchants—around 3.6 million or 75 percent according to Luis Felipe de Alencastro—were loaded upon Portuguese slave ships in Angola, thus turning the Angolan coast and the portal town of Rio de Janeiro into "the largest slave-producing poles in the Atlantic" (de Alencastro 2018, 58).[11] Consequently, Brazil saw an incredible influx of enslaved Africans: "of each hundred people disembarking in Brazil during that period [between 1500 and 1850], 86 were African slaves and fourteen were colonialists and Portuguese immigrants" (60). Slave labour was first heavily employed in the mines, then in large sugar and later coffee plantations. For Marquese (2018), this variety of exploitative activities granted slavery in Brazil a certain "plasticity". By the end of the 18th century, the leading Portuguese colony in the Americas in fact

> manifested in a relatively uninterrupted continental space all the combined economic activities observed in the other slave economies in the New World: the plantation agriculture of the British and French Caribbean and the meridian Atlantic colonies of North America; the mining, fishing and production of supplies of Spanish America; the urban services of the major Atlantic coastal cities. (207)

Brazil thus emerges as a unique and central global player, one whose slavery-based economy profoundly influenced South Atlantic as well as global relationships. Indeed, this distinctive position in the world economy was, according to Marquese (2018), crucial in making Brazil

---

11 Our translation. The original expression in Portuguese, "polos negreiros", is linguistically quite relevant and difficult to translate accurately. The term "negreiro", used in Portuguese to refer to the slave ships ("navios negreiros"), has as its root the term "negro", i.e. Black. The suffix "eiro", on the other hand, is used to indicate productive actions, such as in "obreiro" ("obra" meaning construction, i.e, construction worker) or "banqueiro" (banker). The most literal translation of "negreiro" into English would thus be "Black-producing", a term that is disarmingly honest: the slave ships were indeed the sites where Blackness was turned into a racial reality, i.e., where African captives were dehumanized and transformed into commodities, as Sowande M. Mustakeem (2016) argues in her important study *Slavery at Sea: Terror, Sex and Sickness in the Middle Passage*.

"the last nation in the Western hemisphere to abolish slavery" (209). This happened as late as 1888, i.e. 50 years after the British Empire and 40 years after the French Empire officially abolished slavery, and 23 years after Juneteenth in the USA.[12] Well after the transatlantic slave trade had been outlawed in Britain and France (in 1814), Brazil continued importing enslaved people from Africa,[13] an activity that only ceased gradually in the early 1850s after a naval blockade by the British (Wolfe 2019, 116). Such commercial interests led to a unique system of racialization.

The Brazilian slave economy relied mostly on the sustained importation of enslaved Africans. One reason for this was the lower cost of the significantly shorter transatlantic journey between Angola and Brazil, combined with a reduced number of middlemen between the ports, since "the Portuguese controlled both ends of the Brazil slave trade" (Wolfe 2019, 121). The affordability of enslaved Africans, the "cheap meat" in Elza Soares's song, was compounded by the "immediate financial returns on putting an African to work on a Brazilian sugar plantation which were much higher than in the case of a Virginian tobacco plantation" (122). This essentially made "investing in a Brazilian slave a shorter-term risk" (134).

It is this exceptional physical violence that needs to be considered in its intersection with the epistemic violence of racial discourses in Brazil. Because of the "much lower" price of enslaved people captured in Africa who were sold with an increment when arriving in Brazil—slave ships were consistently overloaded, and those who survived the crossing of the Atlantic "arrived in extremes of ill health" (Wolfe 2019, 122). Teetering on the brink of death, the enslaved Africans formed a most fragile subjectivity that was further undermined by the constant turnover of slaves in the mines and on

12 'Juneteenth', a portmanteau of June and nineteenth—also known as 'Freedom Day', 'Liberation Day' or 'Jubilee Day'—is a holiday celebrating the emancipation of enslaved people in the USA.

13 For Marquese (2018), the rise in European demand for coffee played a key role in the Brazilian refusal to abolish slavery—indeed, without the cheap labour of enslaved Africans on the Brazilian coffee plantations, coffee in Europe would not have become affordable (209).

the plantations. Wolfe's observations on the debilitating effects of cheap slave "meat" on the Brazilian colonial market are valuable for our understanding of both the past and the present condition of Afro-Brazilians. Because their apparently disposable bodies were so closely linked to labour in the mines and on the plantations, once slavery was abolished on Brazilian territory, Afro-Brazilians were themselves often regarded as little more than a disturbance. Wolfe argues: "Brazilian authorities acted as if, along with slavery, they had also dispensed with the slaves" (134). It is as if the survival of enslaved Africans and their descendants had not really been factored into the constitution of the (postcolonial) Brazilian nation. This brutal history of dehumanization in the name of commercial profit in a global market has had dire consequences still keenly felt today.[14]

In their performance at Cabaret Voltaire, the Afro-Brazilian poet Ricardo Aleixo and the Angolan rapper Diamondog brought many of these historical traces to bear on the present. The encounter was consciously staged as a recovery of the experiences on the Angolan and Brazilian slave ports, one that nevertheless aimed at subverting rather than merely reinstating the violence of selling and buying cheap enslaved "meat". The strong emphasis on history and memory in the work of both artists provided a valuable link between their performances, which gave voice to the Afro-Brazilian community in all its complexities. Importantly, in their interventions and dialogue between performances, both artists also articulated the present experience of Afro-Brazilians, which is steeped in violence. Neuza Santos Souza (1983) summarized this extreme exposure to state violence as the very act of "becoming Black" in her manifesto with the same title. In a nutshell, to become Black is to become a target—conversely, the more of a target one is, the "blacker" one is considered.

14 In the words of the Brazilian literary critic Roberto Schwartz (1992): "The combination of latifundia and unfree labor, given durability by its important role in the international market, and later, by internal politics, stood firm through Colony, Emperors and Regencies, through Abolition, the First Republic, and even now is a matter of debate and bullets" (44).

Performing the Southern Black Atlantic

In spite of the dispiriting topic of South Atlantic slavery and its consequences, which permeated much of the combined performance at Cabaret Voltaire, the evening opened with a highly celebratory note. Ricardo Aleixo's poem "Boca Também Toca Tambor" (The Mouth also Plays the Drums), which gave the event its title, is presented as a manifesto, celebrating the power of using the mouth as an instrument—not only in terms of musicality and rhythm, but also, by implication, in terms of resistance to oppression. In its scope, "Boca Também Toca Tambor" is truly cosmopolitan, hailing such writers and artists as James Joyce, Hugo Ball, Kurt Schwitters and Antonin Artaud, all of whom explored more unconventional ways of using language in their writing. However, for the purposes of our examination, it is particularly relevant that throughout the poem Aleixo includes various references to slavery itself, and more specifically to the restrictions imposed on slaves, such as the interdiction to speak their mother tongue—coupled with the forceful learning of the colonizer's and slave owner's language instead—and the prohibition of instruments, music and religious rituals from different African communities in the plantation. In spite of these boundaries to self-expression, the mouth itself, which can transcend language in its production of pure sound and rhythm, and which can also carry suppressed memories through storytelling, becomes a weapon. On this extraordinary power of resistance through sound, it is worth quoting Martha Abreu's comment on the Afro-Brazilian dance *jongo*, or *caxambu*, which is primarily based on drums. Abreu (2018) notes that many Bantu languages (originating from the territory that is today Angola) in fact contain a number of "expressions and proverbs that relate 'jongo' with 'the mouth's bullet'. The power of the word in verse is a fundamental aspect of jongo" (133; our translation). We could say that Aleixo himself leans on these Afro-Brazilian traditions in his performance of "Boca Também Toca Tambor", on the level of both content and form.

Lines such as "the mouth also keeps secrets" ("boca também guarda segredos") can be read as a celebration of the slaves' resilience: even the enslaved body can hide information from the master, an important practice that allowed slave uprisings to take place. A similar focus on resistance can be found in the line "the mouth spits on the enemy, bites the hand of the aggressor, attacks, pleases, thanks, and also plays drums",[15] which humorously combines several strategies of overcoming oppression—from the more overt acts of violence to the manipulative performance of submission that covers the actual intents—and lands back at the power of drumming as an expression of rebellion. Finally, Aleixo refers more openly to ancestral traditions of slaves and descendants of slaves, such as the storytelling art of Brazilian *akipalôs* and West African *griots*: the first referring to enslaved black women in Brazil who went from plantation to plantation telling tales, the latter to celebrated epic poets who are considered the carriers of oral culture and memory in a number of West African countries to this day. Such figures are depicted in the poem as masters of the word which echoes like a drum,[16] again elevating the power of the voice above the actual content of the storytellers' message. The poem in fact closes in the "New World", as the speaker leads us to the "Caribbean sea", where

> the mouth
> of guillén—his drum—
> covers the sound of the waves with
> an ancestral scream: 'yambambó!'[17]

Aleixo directly references Afro-Cuban poet Nicolas Guillén's (1981) famous 1931 "Canto Negro" (Black Song),[18] which equally evokes the poet's—and many Cubans'—African ancestry by playfully foregrounding "African"-sounding words whose meaning lies in the very sound itself. The signified becomes here the lost origins, the forgotten

15 Original: "boca cospe no inimigo, morde a mão do agressor, agride, agrada, agradece, e também toca tambor".

16 Original: "mestres da palavra que ecoa como tambor".

17 Original: "no mar do caribe a boca / de guillén—o seu tambor—/cobre o som das ondas com/um grito ancestral: 'yambambó!".

18 The Cuban author contributed to the redefinition of black poetics by the sound dimension widely explored in his poetry. The poem mentioned is part of the book *Sóngoro cosongo*, from 1931 (Guillén 1981, 17–18).

language from which the descendants of slaves were brutally uprooted. The imaginary feeding these final lines is that of the Black Atlantic, reverting the crossing from the "New World" back to the African continent. We could thus say that the poem holds special significance for those who truly know what it means to be robbed of their own language, their voices, their identities.

On stage, "Boca Também Toca Tambor" amplifies the subversive power of the voice with the help of echoing and looping effects from a loop station. These translate the transatlantic voyage into sound, while also reinforcing the sense of a returning past, an uncovered history. The playfulness of the poem's lines and sounds is further carried by the joy and lightness expressed by the poet's body on stage. Aleixo smiles frequently, moves rhythmically to the repeated chorus of the poem, performs full control as he decides when to activate the sound effects, how far or close to the microphone to stand, and indeed where on the stage to position himself. Thus, the enslaved "meat" is elevated by the power of the voice and the body, pointing to a vast reservoir of experiences beyond that of oppression and connecting acts of resistance through the voice across a global network.

While the evening was framed by this message of resilience, there were many moments in which the traumatic consequences of colonialism in general and the enslavement of African people in Brazil specifically were brought to the fore. Such is the case of the song "Escravidão" (Slavery) by Diamondog, which notably opens with the enforced journey of enslaved Africans to the New World, only to turn the focus to those who stayed on the African territory and suffered the consequences of colonialism, another form of disempowerment. Diamondog dramatizes here the practice of "linguifam" outlined by Ngũgĩ wa Thiong'o. As Ngũgĩ (2009) famously argued, colonialism "dismembered" the collective identities and memories of colonized and enslaved people by promoting the practices of "linguifam" (linguistic deprivation) in colonized Africa and "linguicide" (linguistic death) in the "New World", thereby effectively disempowering entire communities and cultures (18–19). Like Ngũgĩ, Diamondog associates the linguistic impairment with actual practices of violence against the flesh of the enslaved and colonized people: "they cut with their swords / the flesh of the Africans / they laminated us a bit more and cut out our roots".[19] The violence of these lines is compounded by the very intermingling of physical and mental oppression, as well as literal and figurative meanings.

At the core of "Escravidão" is the elimination of linguistic and by implication cultural identity. Diamondog raps:

> African religions: NO
> Our languages became those of a dog
> They forbade Maymona as a name
> We became Maria and João
> [...]
> Thus was my country in the olden days
> When speaking Portuguese was reason for being proud.[20]

The lyrics reflect the pressure exerted upon the indigenous population to adopt a foreign culture and even feel shame for their own traditions and language. However, the translation of the above lines into English obfuscates a crucial feature, namely the fact that the Portuguese used by Diamondog is interspersed with expressions typical of the northern urban Angolan variant of Portuguese, which has itself been strongly influenced by Bantu languages such as Kimbundo. For "olden days" Diamondog uses "caparandanda", and for "pride" the term "banga", expressions that are foreign to the traditional Portuguese language. The song thus also undermines the very content on the narrative level, as the speaker is able to subvert the suppression of native languages. The attempt at eliminating the African pre-colonial languages does not signify a silencing of the (once) colonized subject. On the contrary: as Aleixo's poems and Diamondog's rap show, language is used precisely to foreground the gap between the

---

19 Original: "Cortaram com seus sabres / as carnes dos Africanos / afiaram-nos mais um pouco e cortaram também as raízes".

20 Original: "Religiões africanas não / Nossas línguas passaram a ser de cão / proibiram Maymona como nome / e passamos a ser Maria e João / [...] assim era o meu país, no tempo do caparandanda / onde falar português, para um preto era motivo de banga".

colonizer and the colonized. Hence also the importance of the estrangement techniques used by Aleixo's loops, echoes and rhythmic games, as well as by Diamondog's specific Angolan Kimbundo-inflected slang. The Portuguese language is here itself fragmented, reshuffled and reinvented.

We could thus read Aleixo's and Diamondog's performances as utmost expressions of the (Southern) Black Atlantic. For Gilroy (1993), this broad term stood for "the stereophonic, bilingual, or bifocal cultural forms originated by, but no longer the exclusive property of, blacks dispersed within the structures of feeling, producing, communicating, and remembering" (3). It is important, however, to highlight once again how much the imaginary explored by these two artists is one that turns our attention to the Angola-Brazil axis and thus foregrounds the Global South as a specific site of violence against the flesh as well as opposition to the reduction of humans to cheap "meat".

This was made particularly visible by Aleixo's performance of the poem "Loa da travessia da Calunga grande" (Song of Praise of the Great Calunga). Set in the Middle Passage, the poem takes on the perspective of a slave chained to the belly of the slave ship, who hears a siren singing outside and believes that she can predict what will happen to him. The "great Calunga" of the title is a direct reference to a Bantu notion, signifying the sea, but also death or hell. Clearly all terms are implied in Aleixo's invocation of Calunga which stands for the immense dangers of the Middle Passage. Indeed, evoking the reduction of the enslaved to cheap "meat", the speaker fears that he may well be devoured by the "beast" that has chained him.[21] The siren's

---

21 Aleixo's speaker echoes the accounts of enslaved Africans such as Olauda Equiano and Mahommah Gardo Baquaqua, both of whom relate the fear they shared with many of the imprisoned Africans on board of slave ships that they were in fact going to be eaten by their white capturers. This instinctive reduction of white commercial interests to cannibalism seems well justified and turns the European fantasies of New World cannibals on their heads. As H.L. Malchow (1996) has powerfully argued, the whole notion of cannibalism as promoted in the European imaginary from the

singing becomes a way of externalizing the profound dread that he feels. Significantly, the speaker identifies the siren according to Angolan/Bantu cosmology, thus reinforcing a sense of rootedness, even though the fury of the sea has already made him forget his own name:

Kianda is her Bantu name and that is how I call for her
I wish that one day her singing would take me to Benguela,
Back to Luanda, I don't care, any place would be good
If Kianda will accompany me
Singing her song to me, even if I don't know
The language that she speaks.[22]

The melancholic longing for home is articulated through Bantu symbols and cultural references, countering the speaker's feeling of being swallowed up by the ship and the sea. Although he has no notion of where he will land or what will happen to him, the translation of his experiences into something he can relate to—the great Calunga sea and the siren Kianda who is believed to dwell along the coast of Angola, especially around the capital Luanda (Cascudo [1965] 2015)—keeps him connected to home, and thus hopeful of an eventual return. Written and performed by a Brazilian, himself a descendant of enslaved Africans, the poem stands as an homage to the original cultural identities carried over to Brazil on the slave ships.

As if in direct response to that poem, Diamondog's rap verse "O bote" (The Vessel) celebrates the cross-cultural pollinations between Angola and Brazil, presenting us a picture of an immensely rich Afro-Brazilian culture that is based on resistance. It is worth quoting in its entirety:

The Vessel
Resistance expressed that marked its presence
In the midst of adversities, life without mercy
We fought and we sought the lost soul

15th century onward is a powerful psychological act of transfer that disavows the actual devouring tendencies of European colonialism itself.

22 Original: "Kianda é seu nome Bantu e é como clamo por ela / Tomara um dia o seu canto me leve para Benguela, / de volta pra Luanda, tanto faz qualquer lugar será bom / se a Kianda quiser me acompanhar / cantando a sua cantiga mesmo que eu não conheça / a lingua que ela pratica".

Cultural influences that marked our days
Words originating from Kimbundo
Fiote, Nhaneca, Nganguela, Yoruba, Umbundo
Capoeira that brought the tripping arts
Ganga Zumba, Zumbi embodied in Master Pastinha
The resistance expressed in the body of those who are militant
Be it in the rap of today speaking of the past and afterwards
With my spiky hair of pride
Sarará [multiracial], black power, a black brother like a Zulu,
Baggy pants and a spray can in the backpack,
Representing on the wall what the DJ does on stage.[23]

The key line for us here is "the resistance expressed in the body of those who are militant", which we again read against the background of the enslaved "meat" made disposable. The body is celebrated on the one hand as a receptacle and carrier of linguistic and cultural influences, reinforcing our discussion above. Here the Angolan influence takes centre stage, as most communities listed in lines 5 and 6 stem from the Angolan territory—the exception being the Yoruba. The song thus provides an extensive map of Angolan spaces, peoples, cultures and languages which resisted the "linguicide" imposed by the transatlantic slave trade and found expression in the resilient bodies of Afro-Brazilians. On the other hand, "O bote" also remembers the body as a concrete vessel of resistance, be it through the practice of *capoeira*—a mock-fight dance brought to Brazil by enslaved people from Angola—or through active revolt against enslavement, represented by the famous *quilombo* of the Palmarés region of Brazil, one of many

23 Original: "Resistência expressa que marcou sua presença / Em meio adversidades da vida sem complacência / Lutou-se e buscou-se da alma perdida / Influências culturais que passaram a marcar o dia/ Palavras oriundas da língua Quimbundo / Fiote, Nhaneca, Nganguela, Yoruba, Umbundo / Capoeira que trouxe bassulas da hora / Ganga Zumba, Zumbi em mestre Pastinha se incorpora / A resistência expressa no corpo de quem milita / Seja no Rap de hoje falando do passado e depois / Com meus cabelos espetados de orgulho / Sarará, black power, um brother preto tipo zulo / Calça caída e mochila com spray / Representa no muro o que no palco faz o Deejay".

runaway slave settlements.[24] Born in the Kingdom of Kongo (now the northern territory of Angola) and forcefully transported to Brazil to work in a plantation, Ganga Zumba was the first leader of this massive settlement, which endured for four decades, and Zumbi was its final leader. Both men have been enshrined in Afro-Brazilian memory and culture as heroes of Black resistance and stand as an important reminder of the enduring struggle of enslaved people against the brutal exploitation of their labour (Farfan-Santos 2016). Diamondog links up this heroic past of the *quilombos* with other expressions of resistance on the cultural level, such as the performances of Mestre Pastinha, one of Brazil's most famous *capoeira* masters, as well as rap music and other hip hop practices such as graffiti spraying. All of these practices are placed in a lineage that leads back to Angola, which turns "the vessel"—at first a seeming reference to slave ships—into an actual carrier of an undying spirit of resistance.

However, that spirit of resistance, of course, is a necessity in the face of contemporary Brazil's treatment of Afro-Brazilians, which reveals disturbing continuities with Brazil's past as a major slave colony. Ricardo Aleixo's poem "rondó da ronda noturna" (Rondo of the Night Watch) captures this reality both semantically and visually.[25]

---

24 "Quilombo" is the generic term used in Brazil to refer to runaway slave settlements. Here we mean the specific quilombo of Palmarés, which was made famous by the bravery of its leader, Zumbi.

25 The visual dimension and the concrete aspect of the words connect Ricardo Aleixo to the visual dimension of poetry in Brazil that was elaborated and disseminated by the group Noigandres (Augusto de Campos, Haroldo de Campos and Décio Pignatari) in the early 1950s. The authors published a journal with the same name. In 1958, in the journal's fourth issue, they published a manifesto entitled "pilot plan for concrete poetry". Throughout the 1960s and 1970s concrete poetry was an inescapable movement for those who deal with the word in its visual, sound and verbal dimension. Ricardo Aleixo incorporated in his poetics the "verbivocovisual" dimension of this group (Campos, Campos, and Pignatari, [1965] 2006).

We have opted therefore to reproduce an image of the poem in Portuguese and provide the translation in a footnote:[26]

Illustration 1: Ricardo Aleixo: *rondó da ronda noturna*
© Ricardo Aleixo

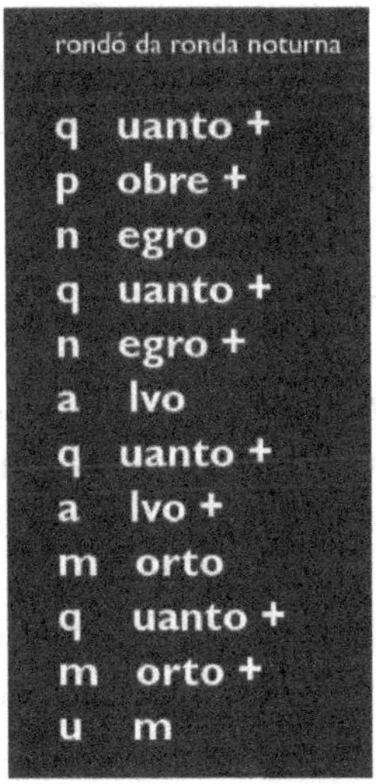
rondó da ronda noturna

q uanto +
p obre +
n egro
q uanto +
n egro +
a lvo
q uanto +
a lvo +
m orto
q uanto +
m orto +
u m

Here we find a mourning dimension, expressed not only in the black background of the poem, but also in the structure of the "broken" words, to which the plus sign (+) is added—in effect exposing the very subtraction of Black lives. Aleixo's poem disturbingly echoes Achille Mbembe's (2019) notion of "necropolitics", which reinterprets Michel Foucault's and Giorgio Agamben's reflections on biopolitics, highlighting the planned act of eliminating lives as constitutive of colonial sovereignty. In Aleixo's interpretation, necropolitics in Brazil becomes "negropolitica", as the risk of death for Black people exists in a semantic space between "necro" (death) and "negro" (black). Against

---

26 Translation: "The poorer / the blacker / the blacker / the more targeted / the more targeted / the deader / the deader / one more". It is impossible to replicate the visual pun produced by the poem's use of the plus sign, called "mais" in Portuguese, which is also the term for the comparative "more" that in English is often expressed through the suffix "-er".

the background of a violent reality, the poet invites the reader and the audience to collectively mourn the countless Black lives exposed to political strategies that keep them, in turn, exposed to death.

In order to overcome the ethical and aesthetic shock of the content, Aleixo does not limit the poem to a semantic dimension. The "broken" or interrupted language also remains open, so that the reader or viewer may access other layers of interpretation, such as the visual dimension and the graphic arrangement of the poem. For example, if we take a historical frame, that game of contrasts can refer directly to a baroque aesthetics appearing in the double reference of the title. The first one is the rondo, a fast and vivacious musical form whose origins date back to the 17th century. The second is an allusion to Rembrandt's painting *The Night Watch*, a term which, in the Brazilian context, denotes a condition of terror for those whose lives are exposed to death according to extermination politics usually not executed in the light of day. Gradually, the plus sign (+) thus acquires the meaning of a rifle's scope following a shooting target. The strongest contrast of the poem is hence the very depiction of the black background as a target. It is precisely as a target that Black life in Brazil may become part of the statistics implied by the poem's additions.

Embodying the Past, Presencing the (Violated) Body

Reflecting on the value of adopting a Global South frame, Dilip M. Menon (2019) defines this wide, heterogeneous space as "a gathering together of memories past into a map for the future" (36). We believe that the combined performances of Ricardo Aleixo and Diamondog at Cabaret Voltaire presented us with just such an opportunity of reflecting on the past and future of Afro-Brazilian bodies and lives. The repertoire, as outlined by Taylor (2003), works here precisely to "[enact] embodied memory" (20). Through the voice, the body, visuals, and the use of music and/or rhythm, Aleixo and Diamondog foreground the importance of nonverbal practices as a way of "[preserving] a sense of communal identity and memory" (20), one that actively resists the colonial archives of written texts reducing the enslaved body to the status of a commodity (as in the case of slave ship logs that merely refer to captured Africans in terms of size, sex and price) or racializing enslaved bodies (as in the Eurocentric scientific treatises of the 19th century on the alleged inferiority of the "African race"). On top of these embodied practices, the artists favour (oral) narratives that actively contradict the historical reduction of Afro-Brazilians to the status of cheap "meat". Indeed, Taylor's (2003) notion of the repertoire could help us reframe the world literature debate outlined above to foreground oral literatures. Taylor's analysis contrasts the written archive with the performed repertoire: here narrative is transmitted—and indeed travels—through the body itself, and it is precisely the endurance of the repertoire and its existence beyond the archive that grants it a strong potential for resisting dominant (written) narratives.

Ever since the 16th century, Black people have been denied social justice in Brazil. On the one hand, racial democracy is still a taboo in Brazil; on the other, a longstanding historical injustice causes descendants of enslaved Africans to live their lives in a permanent state of anxiety. Through the voice, the body, and performance, authors and artists such as Ricardo Aleixo and Diamondog give voice to a memory that has not been lost. There is something in these voices that recalls of one of Portuguese priest and diplomat Antonio Vieira's sermons:

> Whoever saw in the blackness of that night those immense, continuously lit furnaces of the sugar mills [. . .] the noise of the wheels and chains, the people who were the same colour as that night, working briskly and moaning at the same time, without any break or rest: in short, whoever saw the confused and noisy machine and apparatus of that Babylon could not have any doubt, even if he had seen Mount Etna and Vesuvius, that this looked just like hell. (Vieira quoted in Pedrosa and Schwarcz 2014, 352, our translation)

Historically this brutal system still has an impact on the world, and Black people are often still "working briskly". A sermon here is an ambiguous document: a proof of barbarism for African and Afro-Brazilian audiences, a cultural document for "western civilization". As Walter Benjamin (1975) put it, "there is no document of culture which is not at the same time a document of barbarism" (35). Aleixo and Diamondog expose this paradox.

We can think of the evening at Cabaret Voltaire as an exploration of Afro-Brazilian "scenarios", in Taylor's terminology. Taylor (2003) defines "scenarios" as haunting plots that keep resurfacing in the performances of descendants of the colonized, such as "scenarios of discovery" in Latin America (53). This often inspires practices of subversion and even mockery, as the repetition of the scenarios can lead to a re-evaluation of the historic events and their consequences. We argue that Aleixo and Diamondog presented their audience with such a scenario of South Atlantic slavery: this allowed them to reactivate the trauma of dehumanization suffered by enslaved Angolans brought to Brazil, while at the same time celebrating the subversive ways in in which violated Black bodies have resisted total disempowerment. The scenario of South Atlantic slavery thus serves not only to rearticulate the past in the present but also to promote social and political consciousness. This consciousness must be present, even if we are "merely" singing a song like "a carne", by Elza Soares.

Bibliography

Abreu, Martha. 2018. "Canções escravas" [Slave Songs]. In *Dicionário de escravidão e liberdade: 50 textos críticos* [Dictionary of Slavery and Liberty: 50 Critical Texts], edited by Flávio dos Santos Gomes and Lilia Moritz Schwarcz, 130–36. São Paulo: Companhia das Letras.

Aleixo, Ricardo. 2013. *Mundo Palavreado* [Spoken World]. São Paulo: Peirópolis.

Alim, H. Sami, Awad, Ibrahim, and Alastair Pennycook, eds. 2008. *Global Linguistic Flows: Hip Hop Cultures, Youth Identities, and the Politics of Language*. London: Routledge.

Benjamin, Walter. 1975. "Eduard Fuchs: Collector and Historian." Translated by Knut Tarnowki. *New German Critique* 5: 27–58.

Bermann, Sandra. 2012. "World Literature and Comparative Literature." In *The Routledge Companion to World Literature*, edited by

Theo D'haen, David Damrosch, and Djelal Kadir, 169–79. London: Routledge.

Bhabha. Homi. 1986. "Remembering Fanon: Self, Psyche and the Colonial Condition." In *Black Skin, White Masks*, by Frantz Fanon. vii–xxvi. London: Pluto Press.

"Boca Também Toca Tambor" [The Mouth Also Plays the Drums]—*Movements, Diasporas, Entanglements*. 2018. Rhythm and Poetry Rap at Cabaret Voltaire, Zurich, 19 September. https://tube.switch.ch/embed/c743ac2e.

Bradley, Adam. 2009. *Book of Rhymes: The Poetics of Hip Hop*. New York: Basic Civitas.

Buciferro, Justin R. 2013. "A Forced Hand: Natives, Africans, and the Population of Brazil, 1545–1850." *Journal of lberian and Latin American Economic History* 31 (2): 285–317.

Campos, Augusto de, Campos, Haroldo de Campos, and Décio Pignatari. [1965] 2006. *Teoria da Poesia Concreta* [Theory of Concrete Poetry]. São Paulo: Ateliê.

Cascudo, Luis da Câmara. [1965] 2015. "Sereias de Angola" [Mermaids of Angola]. In *Made in Africa*, 10–17. São Paulo: Global Editora.

Chrisman, Laura. 2012. "Whose Black World is This Anyway? Black Atlantic and Transnational Studies after *The Black Atlantic*." In *New Perspectives on the Black Atlantic: Definitions, Readings, Practices, Dialogues*, edited by Bénédicte Ledent and Pilar Cuder-Dominguez, 23–58. Bern: Peter Lang.

Damrosch, David. 2018. *What Is World Literature?* Princeton, NJ: Princeton University Press.

De Alencastro, Luis Felipe. 2018. "África, Números do Tráfico Atlântico" [Africa: Numbers from the Transatlantic Slave Trade]. In *Dicionário de Escravidão e Liberdade: 50 textos críticos*, edited by Lilia Moritz Schwarcz and Flávio dos Santos Gomes, 57–60. São Paolo: Companhia das Letras.

DeBow, J. D. B. 1854. *Statistical View of the United States, Embracing its Territory, Population—White, Free Colored, and Slave-Moral Condition, Industry, Property, and Revenue; the Detailed Statistics of Cities, Towns and Counties; being a Compendium of the Seventh*

Census. Washington, DC: Beverly Tucker, Senate Printer. https://www2.census.gov/prod2/decennial/documents/1850c-01.pdf.

Farfan-Santos, Elizabeth. 2016. *Black Bodies, Black Rights: The Politics of Quilombolismo in Contemporary Brazil*. Austin, TX: University of Texas Press.

Garcia-Navarro, Lulu. 2014. "In Brazil, Race Is A Matter of Life and Violent Death." *NPR*, 9 November. https://www.npr.org/sections/parallels/2014/11/09/362356878/in-brazil-race-is-a-matter-of-life-and-violent-death.

Guillén, Nicolás. 1981. *Sóngoro cosongo y otros poemas* [*Sóngoro cosongo* and Other Poems]. Madrid: Alianza Editorial.

Gomes dos Santos, Flávio, and Lilia Moritz Schwarcz, eds. 2018. *Dicionário da Escravidão e Liberdade* [Dictionary of Slavery and Liberty: 50 Critical Texts]. São Paulo: Companhia das Letras. https://www.companhiadasletras.com.br/trechos/14520.pdf.

Gilroy, Paul. 1993. *The Black Atlantic: Modernity and Double Consciousness*. London: Verso.

Lienhard, Martín. 2002. "África na senzala latino-americana" [Africa in the Latin American Slum]. *Studia Africana* 5: 131–53.

Mbembe, Achille. [2011] 2019. *Necropolitics*. Durham, NC: Duke University Press.

Malchow, Howard. L. 1996. *Gothic Images of Race in Nineteenth-Century Britain*. Stanford, CA: Stanford University Press.

Marquese, Rafael de Biva. 2018. "Economia Escravista Mundial" [World Slave Economy]. In *Dicionário da Escravidão e Liberdade*, edited by Flávio dos Santos Gomes and Lilia Moritz Schwarcz, 203-09. São Paulo: Companhia das Letras.

Marx, Karl. [1867] 1967. *Capital*. Volume 1. Translated by Samuel Moore and Edward Aveling (Original: *Das Kapital*, 1967). New York: Vintage.

Menon, Dilip L. 2019. "Thinking About the Global South." In *The Global South and Literature*, edited by Russel West-Pavlov, 34–44. Cambridge: Cambridge University Press.

Moretti, Franco. 2000. "Conjectures on World Literature." *New Left Review* 1: 54–68.

Mustakeem, Sowande M. 2016. *Slavery at Sea: Terror, Sex and Sickness in the Middle Passage*. Urbana, IL: University of Illinois Press.

Ngũgĩ wa Thiong'o. 2009. *Something Torn and New: An African Renaissance.* New York: Basic Civitas.

Ong, Walter H. 2003. *Orality and Literacy*. London: Routledge.

Pedrosa, Adriano, and Lilia Moritz Schwarcz. 2014. *Histórias Mestiças* [Mestizo Histories]. São Paulo and Combogó: Instituto Tomie Ohtake.

Phillips, Dom. 2019. "Brazilians Blame Rio Governor's Shoot-to-Kill Policy for Death of Girl." *The Guardian*, 22 September. https://www.theguardian.com/world/2019/sep/22/brazilians-blame-rio-governors-shoot-to-kill-policy-for-death-of-agatha-felix-girl-8.

Rodrigues, Jaime. 2018. "Navio Negreiro" [Slave Ship]. In *Dicionário de Escravidão e Liberdade. 50 textos críticos*, edited by Lilia Moritz Schwarcz and Flávio dos Santos Gomes, 343–50. São Paolo: Companhia das Letras.

Santos Souza, Neusa. 1983. *Tornar-se negro—ou: as vicissitudes da identidade do Negro Brasileiro em ascensão social* [Becoming Black—Or: The Vicissitudes of Brazilian Blacks' Identity with Regard to Social Ascent]. Rio de Janeiro: GRAAL.

Schwarz, Roberto. 1977. *Ao vencedor as batatas: forma literária e processo social nos inícios do romance brasileiro* [Potatoes for the Winner: Literary Form and Social Process in the Early Brazilian Novel]. São Paulo: Duas Cidades.

Schwarz, Roberto. 1992. "Misplaced Ideas: Literature and Society in Late Nineteenth-Century Brazil." In *Misplaced Ideas. Essays on Brazilian Culture* by Roberto Schwartz, edited by John Gledson, 19–33. London: Verso.

Soarez, Elsa. 2002. *Do cóccix até o pescoço* [From the Coccyx to the Neck]. Dubas Música.

Taylor, Diana. 2003. *The Archive and the Repertoire: Performing Cultural Memory in the Americas.* Durham, NC: Duke University Press.

Verger, Pierre. 2002. *Fluxo e refluxo. Do tráfico de escravos entre o golfo de Benin e a Bahia de Todos os Santos* [Ebb and Flow. The Slave Trade Between the Gulf of Benin and Bahia de Todos os Santos]. Salvador: Corrupio.

Warwick Research Collective. 2015. *Combined and Uneven Development: Towards a New Theory of World-Literature*. Liverpool: Liverpool University Press.

West-Pavlov, Russel. 2019. "Toward the Global South: Concept or Chimera, Paradigm or Panacea?" In *The Global South and Literature*, edited by Russel West-Pavlov, 1–20. Cambridge: Cambridge University Press.

Wisnik, José Miguel. 2018. *Maquinação do Mundo*: *Drummond e a mineração* [Machining the World: Drummond and Mining]. São Paulo: Companhia das Letras.

Wolfe, Patrick. 2016. *Traces of History: Elementary Structures of Race*. London: Verso.

Re-Envisioning Surrealism from Argentina and Mexico: Julio Cortázar's *Teoría del túnel* and Octavio Paz's *El arco y la lira*

Andrea Gremels

In her monograph *Surrealism as World Literature*, Delia Ungureanu (2018) argues that surrealism should be seen as a global literary phenomenon that may productively be connected with the notion of world literature. For the author, the movements of surrealism correspond to processes of canonization of surrealist works that, in the first half of the 20th century, were gaining a global reach as well as enabling a relational understanding of world literature. Considering the latter, she highlights surrealism's "networks of circulation" (3) across continents, its cultural diversity (10), and the "growing internationalism of Paris" (29) where the movement was born. Surrealism thus appears to be an appealing case study that helps to conceive of world literature as a set of relations and exchanges given its transversal connectivities across different regions of the world. Indeed, a relational and multicentric understanding of surrealism challenges the long-established idea that Paris was surrealism's singular centre. From there it would spread out into the world and "influence" non-European writers, who would then "assimilate" or "adapt" its poetics of the unconscious through their reading of the movement's programmatic declarations, and above all, André Breton's surrealist manifestoes. However, this chapter will go a step further by showing how surrealism's anti-hegemonic and rebellious claims can lead us to re-envision normative and systemic conceptualizations of world literature beyond the confines of centre and periphery. As Melanie Nicholson (2013) has stated, this unidirectional model of influence was rejected by many Latin American writers and artists who dismissed the idea that European colleagues had come to "teach" them about surrealism and instruct them in the techniques of accessing the unconscious (118). Clearly, surrealism's entanglements in the Global South, especially in Latin America, remain a site of tensions and debate—perhaps because until recently there has been little focus on how surrealism has evolved "as world literature" in the Global South apart from the model of unilateral influence.[1]

The present chapter will fill this gap by focusing on Julio Cortázar's and Octavio Paz's re-envisioning of surrealism in their early writings.[2] Their poetological essays, in particular, account for the transnational circulation of modernist ideas beyond Europe and the west, as Susan Stanford Friedman (2012, 501) claims. However, given the controversial attitude of many Latin American writers towards surrealism, it seems surprising that Cortázar (1994a) asserts the avant-garde movement's planetary importance by stating in his 1947 essay "Teoría del túnel" (Tunnel Theory) that "surrealism is cosmovision" (102).[3] In a similar way, Octavio Paz (1973) emphasizes the global relevance of surrealism when he argues in his 1956 essay *El arco y la lira* (*The Bow and the Lyre*) that it postulates an "*idea of the world*" (154; original emphasis).

It is remarkable that both authors re-envision surrealism as an all-embracing world view at a moment when, from a Eurocentric point of view, the surrealist movement was already on the decline. Historically, the surrealist revolution, with its hopes of changing the

1 Ungureanu (2018) includes Argentina—mainly with an emphasis on the writer Jorge Luis Borges—as her only case study from the Global South. Julio Cortázar, however, remains unmentioned by the author although he was much closer to surrealism than his Argentinian contemporary Borges, who never openly sympathized with the movement's ideas.

2 I am referring to Susan Stanford Friedman's (2012) term of "re-vision" here, which she suggests for approaching global modernism. Other terms she uses are "recovery", "circulation" and "collage" (508). She argues against David Damrosch's (2003) perspective on processes of re-vision in world literature, as he assumes that there is always an "isolated original" which is then contested, rewritten, etc. Alternatively, she proposes that re-vision and circulation impact "art *before* and *during* the creative process as well as *after*" (Friedman 2012, 504; original emphasis).

3 Original: "Surrealismo es cosmovisión". All translations from Cortázar's texts are mine.

world by transforming reality through the activation of the unconscious and the power of dreams and irrational drives, seemed to have come to an end: Maurice Nadeau (1989) completed his *History of Surrealism* in 1945; the devastations and exiles of World War II had scattered the movement, which by then had already suffered many discords and divisions between its members. André Breton's *Prolegomena for a Third Manifesto of Surrealism, or Not,* written in 1942, seemed but a weak attempt to revive surrealist ideas, as the "or not" in the title suggests. Provocatively speaking, it looks as if the appraisal of surrealism as "cosmovision" (Cortázar 1994a, 102) or "idea of the world" (Paz 1973, 154) confirms both Latin American writers' belatedness in affiliating with the surrealist movement's revolutionary claims. According to Friedman (2012) "belatedness" functions as a principal label to disregard non-western or postcolonial writers within the debate on global modernism and world literature (513).

In this context, I will argue that it is not principally Cortázar's and Paz's eagerness to catch up—from their supposed position of lateness—with surrealism's claim to irrationalize and poeticize the world that determined their affinity with it. I will argue instead that both writers relate to surrealism not to assimilate or adapt it, but because they consider it unassimilable and inadaptable.[4] For them surrealism is not a school or historical movement but rather a practice in literary nonconformism. In this context, they both stress surrealism's dynamic assumption of the voice of otherness and its different understanding of reality's rules. For this reason, they re-envision surrealism as a *global player* whose "cosmic" responsibility lies in acting against the hegemony of literary norms and a normative world order.[5]

4 With regard to poetry, I agree with Jahan Ramazani (2009) who claims that "[f]or global and transnational studies of poetry [and poetics], we need, in short, dialogic alternatives to monologic models" (12) that go beyond adaptation and assimilation.

5 From the point of view of literary history, both authors' re-envisioning implies a paradox as they go back to surrealism's early claim for a radical rupture with any kind of social or literary norms which, by the 1950s, had already turned into a norm: the historical avant-garde's strategies of rupture betray the norm and set a new norm of betrayal. Cortázar's and Paz's

This chapter moves beyond unidirectional readings in approaching the question of how both authors were influenced by surrealism—specifically that of André Breton—in terms of style and aesthetics, as for example Evelyn Picón Garfield (1975) has done in her study *Es Julio Cortázar un surrealista?* (Is Julio Cortázar a Surrealist?). Instead of engaging with the controversies about their positions within surrealism, I will explore how their surrealist visions in "Teoría del túnel" and *El arco y la lira* contribute to a new understanding of "surrealism as world literature" (Ungureanu 2018) which is explicitly inspired by both writers' reflexions on and exchange within the Global South. Read through Cortázar and Paz, it is surrealism's eccentric philosophy that accounts for its multidirectional and anti-hierarchic dynamics. In this sense, both authors' poetological reflexions on surrealism's place in the world shed new light on systemic or normative models of world literature, especially the one proposed by Pascale Casanova (2004) in *The World Republic of Letters*. In order to gain terrain in the asymmetrical and competitive field of world literature, Casanova argues, writers from the "periphery" have to reach to the "centre", either by adapting its literary norms, or rebelling against them.[6] In this context, she considers Cortázar and Paz as part of the latter category. She describes them as "revolutionaries" (94) or "innovators" (326) who brought new impulses into the "world republic of letters".

However, by claiming a surrealist world vision Cortázar and Paz do not consider themselves as "eccentric" but instead emphasize the general eccentricity of surrealism with its vigorous desire to constantly break conventions, rebel against authority and "advance a sharp critique of Western morals and society" (Ungureanu 2018, 10).

---

essays are not exempt from considering surrealism as a paradigmatic example—and norm—for breaking the rules.

6 Casanova's approach has often been criticized, for example by Susan Stanford Friedman (2012), who argues that even though Casanova sympathizes with minor and "peripheral" literatures, her argument is too "gallocentric" and thus reductionist (502). However, research groups like the Warwick Research Collective (2015) have adopted her model to analyse asymmetries in the world literary field.

Surrealism's anti-centrism and its endeavour to resist hegemony is also what makes it difficult to grasp Cortázar's and Paz's re-envisioning within a postcolonial writing-back paradigm (Ashcroft, Griffiths and Tiffin 1994) that would undermine a European or Global North surrealist "original". For them, surrealism's anti-centrism goes beyond a geographic origin as well as North–South boundaries when it comes to rebelling against hegemony and literary conformity.

Cortázar's and Paz's Search for a "Realidad más Real"

Despite their very different poetics—Paz's essays and poetry are characterized by a high degree of reflexivity (Stanton 2015), whereas Cortázar's mostly fictional writing is situated in the Latin-American tradition of fantastic literature—both authors are concerned with the question of Latin America's modernity, which is reflected in their poetological essays.

Both texts can be considered early attempts of the Latin American writers to explore their own poetics through the genre of the essay. Their reflexion on surrealism is intertwined with an introspective "personal definition" (Stanton 2015, 97) or "personal positioning" (Yurkievich 1994, 16). Yet, in both essays, their poetological self-exploration goes along with a reflexion of their position as modern writers. Rather than expressing an urge to catch up with western modernity, the essays both engage in the exploration and ideation of different modernities—or "multiple modernities" in Shmuel Eisenstadt's (2003) sense—in Latin America that do not exclude irrationalities, atemporalities and disorder. I will argue that the world-embracing significance they attribute to surrealism is closely linked to their reflexions on otherness in the context of their commitment to discover alternative models of modernity from their perspective of the Latin American Global South and its entangled postcolonial history.

When Casanova (2004) refers to Paz's statements on his "backwardness" and "disadvantaged remoteness" that made him realize "that he was inevitably starting behind the other competitors in the field of world literature" (93), she does not take into account the fact that the Mexican poet's considerations of his own—and more generally, Latin American—belatedness in terms of western modernity are acutely polemical. He assumes this controversial position towards Mexico's contradictory modernity from his 1950 essay *El laberinto de la soledad* (*Labyrinth of Solitude*, 1985) to his Nobel Lecture *La búsqueda del presente* (*In Search of the Present*, 1990). Besides, for his evolution as a modern writer, his experiences in India and the USA, as well as his engagement with the Mexican avant-garde of the *Contemporáneos* were as important as his connections to Paris.

The concept of otherness—*la otredad*—is at the heart of Paz's poetics. It is a category that enables him to reflect on postcolonial Mexico's search for a collective transcultural identity between and beyond its indigenous and European heritage. In reference to his poetry, Stanton (2015) emphasizes that Paz's poetics are characterized by the unification of opposites and contradictions (22). In this context, poetry is not only a literary genre by which to express himself, but also a form of reflexivity that allows him to consider the world from different angles and through the perspectives of difference.

Paz's (1990) search for a "real reality" (n.p.) marks his affinity with surrealism. In a similar way, Cortázar (1967) turns to poetry to come to an understanding of reality that he considers a "realidad más real" (a reality more real, 190). It is not surprising that Cortázar sympathized with surrealist ideas, as his work conveys a profound scepticism towards a rationalist world view based on the laws of logic. Cortázar, who lived in Paris from 1951 until his death in 1984, writes in the fantastic tradition of Latin American fiction. Roland Spiller (2009) indicates that Cortázar's use of the fantastic genre corresponds to his transculturality as an Argentinian writer in Paris. Accordingly, fantastic literature's characteristic of "shifting from the familiar into the uncanny and vice versa" follows "a transcultural logic of the other, who, anchored both in Latin America and in Europe, rebels against any kind of order" (213, my translation). Exploring the otherness of reality thus constitutes a means to acknowledge all phenomena that go beyond rationality, logic and control.

For Cortázar and Paz, the poetic world view of surrealism entails a planetary ethics of otherness that moves beyond any historical, cultural and geographical setting. I will demonstrate that their conceptualization of otherness refers to their exploration of multiple modernities and at the same time reflects their transcultural positioning as Latin American writers in the field of world literature.

Much of both writers' poetological exchange took place across Latin America, Europe and also South Asia, because Paz wrote great parts of *El arco y la lira* during his first stay in New Delhi while working at the Mexican embassy in 1952. A considerable amount of his "search" for a different reality is linked to the cultures, philosophies and religious practices he discovered in India. In *El arco y la lira*, he states: "Unlike what happens in Hindu thought, which from the beginning raised the problem of the existence of the external world, Western thought long accepted the world's reality with confidence and did not question what our eyes see" (Paz 1973, 143).[7] Cortázar discovered (South) Asian philosophy much later. Many critics have observed that he turned to Zen-Buddhism as a source of inspiration in his 1963 novel *Rayuela* (*Hopscotch*) and *Prosa del observatorio* (*From the Observatory*) of 1972 (see Wink 2016, 77–94). He undertook his first trip to India in 1957; and almost ten years later, in 1968, came to stay at Paz's house during the latter's second sojourn in New Delhi as Mexican ambassador. Stanton (2006) identifies various moments of intense exchange between Cortázar and Paz that he traces from the early 1940s until the beginning of the 1970s when the writers' friendship became increasingly affected by political discordance (213).

Both writers' reformulation of surrealism as well as their exploration of "alternative modernisms" (Friedman 2012, 511), cannot

7 The quotes of this chapter are taken from *The Bow and the Lyre*, translated by Ruth L.C. Simms (1973). Original: "A diferencia de lo que ocurre con el pensamiento hindú que desde el principio se planteó el problema de la existencia del mundo exterior, el pensamiento occidental por mucho tiempo aceptó confiadamente su realidad y no puso en duda lo que ven nuestros ojos" (Paz 1956, 160).

be separated from their transversal routes between Latin America, Europe, and (South) Asia. Thus, corresponding to Friedman's demand for a globalization of modernist studies, Cortázar's and Paz's South/South and South/North routes illustrate the transversal movements of surrealism in the first half of the 20th century. However, it has to be pointed out that both writers remained outsiders, and never became protagonists, in surrealism's development in Argentina and Mexico from the 1930s until the 1960s.

Cortázar and the Transversal History of Surrealism in Argentina

Considering Cortázar and Paz through the perspective of transversal surrealism requires one to take into account the peculiar national and transnational logics of how surrealism was anticipated, contested and transformed in Latin America. Argentina has the longest history of surrealist activities within Latin America, which began with Aldo Pellegrini's periodical *Que* (What) that ran between 1928 and 1929. The group, formed by young medical students who were outsiders in the literary scene of Buenos Aires, "denounced the materialism, spiritual vacuity, and creative stagnation in their middle-class milieu" (Nicholson 2019, 3) by means of a metapoetic self-reflexivity and aesthetic (self)consciousness that became a characteristic of 20th-century Argentinian literature. While surrealist writing declined in the 1930s and 1940s, there was a remarkable productivity in the visual arts represented by key figures such as Juan Batlle Planas or Roberto Aizenberg. In the years of World War II, Roger Caillois, who was exiled in Argentina, created a francophone supplement of *Sur*—the influential literary journal directed by Victoria Ocampo—called *Lettres Françaises* in issue 3 of which (in 1942) he published French surrealist texts such as *Le dialogue créole* (The Creole Dialogue), written by Breton and the painter André Masson during their visit to Martinique in 1941.[8]

8 Ungureanu (2018) argues that the periodical *Sur* played a major role in spreading surrealist ideas in Argentina. She establishes a connection of exchange between Borges and Breton (80–99).

But the "comeback" of a literary engagement with surrealism in Argentina took place in the late 1940s when Pellegrini founded the periodical *Ciclo* (Cycle) in 1949 and later *Letra y Línea* (Letter and Line, 1953–54), which was published simultaneously with another surrealist magazine, *A partir de cero* (Starting from Zero, 1952–56), edited by Enrique Molina. In the 1960s, "the indefatigable Pellegrini" (Nicholson 2019, 5) still pursued surrealist activities by compiling in 1961 an anthology of 70 francophone surrealist poets from all over the world whom he had translated into Spanish: *Antología de la poesía surrealista* (Anthology of Surrealist Poetry). Pellegrini further organized an exhibition in 1967, *El surrealismo en la Argentina*, which took place at the Instituto di Tella in Buenos Aires and looked back on 40 years of surrealist productivity in the country.

Cortázar is remarkably absent from all these activities. He neither counts among the major protagonists of the Argentinian surrealist "reinvention" of the 1950s (Nicholson 2019, 4), nor did he participate in the activities of the post-war group in Paris gathering around Breton until his death in 1965. The recently published *International Encyclopaedia of Surrealism* (2019) places Cortázar in the rubric "Precursors and Parallels". In his entry, Max Ščur (2019) states,

> although he never openly admitted his affiliation with surrealism, he always stressed his affinities with it and dealt with typical surrealist topics, taking up its methods and artistic challenges throughout his life. Along with his friend Octavio Paz, Cortázar was one of Latin America's most prominent connoisseurs and defenders of surrealism and its general principles. (566)

Dawn Ades et al. (2012) go even further in not only recognizing Cortázar's role as a "connoisseur" and "defender" but also attributing to him "the task of revitalizing the surrealist enterprise and transforming it" (8). It seems that, even though maintaining his distance and even ridiculing certain tendencies of surrealist writing in Argentina for what he saw as the production of meaningless poetry, Cortázar's engagement with both the artistic and the philosophical "challenges" of surrealism (Ščur 2019, 566) turned him into a central voice of surrealist thought in Latin America.

Surrealism without Breton: Julio Cortázar's "Teoría del túnel"

Cortázar's writings are distinguished by their meditation on the phantasmagorical and absurd dimension of everyday life's banality. The literary critic Jaime Alazraki (2007) has classified his writing as "neo-fantastic", arguing that unlike Tzvetan Todorov's (1973) concept of strangeness or abnormality as an irrupting force within the fictional order, in Cortázar's writing fantastic elements are a part of everyday life. In his short stories, in particular, he goes beyond the binary order of fantastic elements by representing them as banal and commonplace regardless of the ambiguity that, according to Todorov, the intervention of the supernatural or the marvellous creates within the fictional plane of reality. His short story "No se le culpe a nadie" (Don't Blame Anyone, [1956] 1994) might serve as a good example of that: the protagonist gets terrifyingly trapped in a woollen pullover while trying to put it on. The realization that there is no way to get out of this impenetrable piece of clothing eventually forces him to commit suicide. This conflict shows that the fantastic element causes severe existential consequences for the protagonist of Cortázar's short story and leads to his death. Cortázar thus intertwines fantastic writing with existentialist questions addressing the meaning and murderous consequences of leading an everyday life. At the same time, his conception of the fantastic is accompanied by a claim that literature should leave the realm of fiction and interfere with everyday life.[9]

This also applies to his re-envisioning of surrealism in "Teoría del túnel". As the subtitle "Notas sobre la ubicación del surrealismo y existencialismo" (Notes on the Location of Surrealism and Existentialism) indicates, he positions himself in the intersection between these two aesthetic and philosophical tendencies. In post-war France, they were polarized, so that there was no way to overcome the gap between the principles of existentialism based on human reality and surrealism's endeavour to alter reality through the imagination. Cortázar's vision of literature postulates a "reconciliation" or "synthesis between the two tendencies", with surrealism belonging to the realm

9 For more information see Gremels and Scheurer (2017, 48–49).

of the "poetic", and existentialism to that of the "scientific" exploration of human existence (Ščur 2019, 567). Hence, he incorporates existentialism into his surrealist world view.

Cortázar's essay is based on a lecture series on French literature that he gave between 1944 and 1945 at the University of Cuyo in Mendoza, where he became a professor in 1943.[10] Written at an early stage, notably before he emigrated to Paris in 1951, "Teoría del túnel" is an attempt to define his own radical understanding of literature and to develop a personal poetics. Saúl Yurkievich (1994) describes the essayistic text as an amalgam between an "analytical review" and a "literary manifesto" (16). Cortázar pursues a philosophical reflexion on and criticism of surrealism within the genre of the essay, avoiding the question of surrealist style that is posed in his short stories and his novel *Rayuela*.

For Cortázar (1994b, 153), surrealism is much more than just a "school" that creates works of art through certain techniques meant to activate the unconscious. Neither does it imply a certain aesthetics of irrationality or the dream. Instead, it reveals an attitude towards life and a "world view" (1994a, 104) able to envision different models of reality. This is important to point out because the critics' divergent opinions on how to link Cortázar's work with surrealism are often related to the question of surrealist style in his fiction. Thus, Garfield (1975) reads his short stories with Breton's theoretical essays, mainly the manifestoes, to analyse how Cortázar practices surrealism on a fictional level, especially with regard to surrealist techniques such as automatic writing or the poetics of the dream. Sara Castro-Klarén (1975), who takes particularly his novel *Rayuela* into account, does not share Garfield's opinion, as she does not detect a style of automatism in Cortázar's writings. However, she observes his affinities with

10 As a Belgian-born Argentinian author who grew up bilingual, Cortázar was by then an important intermediary of French literature and thought in Latin America. He would later also become a mediator of English literature in France, where he not only translated André Gide and Marguerite Yourcenar from French to Spanish but also Edgar Allan Poe and Daniel Defoe from English to French.

the literary (anti-)canon of French surrealism (220)—especially with regard to writers like Arthur Rimbaud, Alfred Jarry and Comte de Lautréamont, all referred to in the 1924 *First Manifesto of Surrealism* (Breton 1969, 16–19, 25–27, 38). According to Ščur (2019), the fact that Cortázar's theoretical approach to surrealism, as reflected in his essays, long remained inaccessible might be one of the reasons why many scholars ascribe his relation to surrealism only to the question of style (566).

In "Teoría del túnel", Lautréamont's poetics are crucial for Cortázar's revision of surrealism. Although the latter thinks that the surrealists' celebration of Lautréamont's oneiric, sexual and visceral writing was exaggerated (he ironically calls it "hypertrophy"),[11] he points out that his scandalous book *Les Chants de Maldoror* (*The Songs of Maldoror*) is "*a poetic presentation of the entire vital range of being human*" (Cortázar 1994a, 96; original emphasis).[12] Lautréamont's text unleashes all the unacceptable, unexplainable, and unfathomable forces inherent in the existential condition of being human. Cortázar claims that, for this reason, *The Songs of Maldoror* must be a model for surrealism, as the text proposes a holistic perspective on the human condition while disrespecting all questions of literary aesthetics, expression and even representation. This turns the book into an "existential manifestation" that fuses all facets of human existence with poetry as a world view. These reflexions mirror his own poetological interrogations of literature's potential to move from words to action, from representation to reality. In this context, poetry is far more than a literary genre: it is a way of life which consists in transgressing the rules of logic.

Thus, surrealism's relevance rests on its potential to go beyond "an aesthetic-literary activity" (1994a, 104), or a "verbal system" and to offer a "*conception of the universe*" (103; original emphasis). Cortázar even ridicules his young contemporaries in Argentina whose

11 "One has become tired of the surrealist's hypertrophies with regard to the Conde [de Lautréamont]" (Cortázar 1994, 96). Original: "Está uno harto de las hipertrofías de los surrealistas a propósito del Conde".

12 Original: "*una presentación poética del entero ámbito vital de un hombre*".

surrealist "tic[s]" lead them "to draw surrealist things that derive from the idea of a distorted reality", as he states in his essay "Muerte de Antonin Artaud" (The Death of Antonin Artaud), first published in 1948 (1994b, 153). For Cortázar, this art ends up reproducing dream-like images already too common and worn out, such as Dalí's famous melting clocks (154). Here, he reacts to the literary scene in Buenos Aires in the mid-1940s when many devoted Argentine artists and writers affiliated themselves with surrealist aesthetics (Yurkievich 1994, 17). But he also remained critical of the surrealist circles in France: the moment surrealists gave way to an artistic vocation, they ended up betraying themselves, he states (Cortázar 1994, 104a). Or, as Castro-Klarén (1975) puts it, "he believes that many [surrealists] took the wrong road and therefore did not get beyond mere syntactical games. Their task—of rescuing reality from rationalist thought—remains unaccomplished" (220).

For Cortázar, surrealism has to go beyond literary expression and artistic style in order to explore reality in its entirety. He sticks to the early and most radically postulated anti-artistic claims of surrealism, and at the same time affirms Breton's search for a new state of mind able to conceive of an "absolute reality" stated in the *First Manifesto of Surrealism*:

> I believe in the future resolution of these two states, dream and reality, which are seemingly so contradictory, into a kind of absolute reality, a *surreality*, if one may so speak. It is in quest of this surreality that I am going. (Breton 1969, 14; original emphasis).[13]

In this fashion, Cortázar (1994a) describes the surrealist as a pioneer "for whom a *certain* reality exists and whose mission consists in finding it" (103; original emphasis).[14] This reality-finding mission is not

13 Original: "Je crois à la résolution future de ces deux états, en apparence si contradictoires, que sont le rêve et la réalité, en une sorte de réalité absolue, de surréalité, si l'on peut ainsi dire" (Breton [1924] 1988, 319).

14 It is this way of continuously (meta-)poetically dealing with reality that leads Laszlo Scholz (1977) to state, "In my opinion, from all influences detectable in Cortázar's poetics, those of surrealism are the strongest. [...]. His conception of an extensive reality coincides basically with the 'surreality' understood as a 'super-reality' that embraces much more

only connected to writing but also resides in "an extraliterary activity" ("una actividad extraliteraria", 1994b, 153), because it is a lived experience, not only an artistic product; an existential condition, not only an artistic vocation. Alongside this reflexion, Cortázar develops his specific poetics in which he "existentializes" literature as an act of transcending language in order to reach out to and affect human experience (Yurkiévich 1994, 24).[15] For this reason, he considers the writer Antonin Artaud, who constantly transmogrified madness into writing and writing into madness, as someone who has accomplished the most difficult state of surrealism. From his point of view, Artaud not only understood but also lived the totality of literature and that of human reality (Cortázar 1994b, 154). In Cortázar's (1994a), understanding the totality of human reality implies the recognition of unfathomable aspects of existence, the absurdity of everyday life as well as an acceptance of the "abysmal zones of humanness" (104).

Like reality, the human condition always unveils the unknown other for Cortázar, "this other that stutters deep inside, that grasps you with its nocturnal nails from below, creeps and debates, legitimately trying to coexist and to be adjoined until the total fusion" (1994b, 155).[16] His poetic world view stresses not only the approval of alternative realities—"everything is and could be a key to access reality," (Cortázar 1994a, 103)[17]—but also emphasizes the necessity to live at the interstices of identity and alterity. Thus, his re-envisioning of surrealism postulates an ethics of otherness, allowing surrealist thought and action take up such a prominent place in his poetics as

---

than the realists thought of" (66, my translation).

15 Yurkiévich (1994) describes Cortázar's poetics as a programme that "takes language to the limit, takes it to the extremes, un-measures it so that the most profound human capacities can be lived out. This language transcends the verbal and transforms it into human totality" (24, my translation).

16 Original: "ese otro que balbucea más adentro, se agarra con uñas nocturnas desde abajo, trepa y se debate, buscando con derecho coexistir y colindar hasta la fusión total".

17 Original: "todo es y puede ser acceso a la realidad".

"conception of the universe" and "cosmovision": it is not just a moment in literary history in which 19th-century positivism is questioned fundamentally (100). Neither does it only reside in the rupture with language that characterizes the avant-garde movements of the 20th century and that he conceives of as a "self-destruction of occidental culture" (67). His theory of the tunnel proposes an almost sacred mission, "a lustral task of restitution" (67)[18] that overhauls all those aspects of (self-)knowledge western modernity has excluded from its rational world view: magic, dreams, madness. For Cortázar, this restitution comprizes a process of inclusion of and fusion with the existential experience of otherness. He thus transforms surrealism into a planetary "magic humanism" (although he remains critical of the term "humanism", as it alludes too much to enlightenment [135]):

> As magic humanism, surrealism rejects all reasonable limits with the certainty that only the dogmas of logic and the small-minded determinist conditions of the gregarious community have refused men to have access to what [surrealism], provisionally, calls super-reality. Its intuition of mankind's reign is childishly Edenic. Childish because surrealists search for a *vision* rather than a *verification* (as the adult's vision). (136; original emphasis)[19]

Ultimately, Cortázar's poetic world view calls for a new order, "a disorder to continue with a re-regulation" (55)[20] which sets up new rules of reality, as it perceives what cannot be grasped, coexists with what cannot be accepted, and constantly explores the constitutive strangeness of human existence that resists "verification".

With his revision Cortázar globalizes surrealism "without Breton" and "without a school" (107). He invites his readers to adopt

---

18 Original: "una lustral tarea de restitución".

19 Original: "Humanismo mágico, el surrealismo niega todo límite 'razonable' en la seguridad de que sólo [. . .] la dogmática lógica y las mezquinas condiciones deterministas de la comunidad gregaria han vedado al hombre el acceso a lo que él, provisoriamente, denomina superrealidad. Su intuición del reino del hombre es puerilmente edénica. Pueril en cuanto el surrealista busca la *visión* antes que la *verificación* (visión del adulto)".

20 Original: "un des-orden a proseguir con un re-ordenamiento".

an eccentric attitude that questions common principles and orders of reality. With his idea of a surrealist cosmovision—that he also calls "magical humanism", a humanism that goes beyond the principles of reason—he claims a literary practice of global non-conformism connected to a world view that never accepts reality for what it is, but rather for what it should be in order to be reinvented. For Cortázar, the cosmic significance of surrealism lies in its transhistorical, atemporal and eccentric call for rebellion against any kind of norm and established order. His vision of surrealism as world literature thus contradicts normative conceptions of world literature like Casanova's, as it becomes clear that there cannot be any central "surrealist norm" that he as a "peripheral" writer either has to assimilate to or rebel against. Neither does there exist a European "original" of surrealism that he could "write back" to as a postcolonial author. Cortázar's "Teoría del túnel" demonstrates instead that it is the essence of surrealism to be anti-centrical and reject normativity from the start. The "cosmovision" implied in surrealism's nonconformity thus opens up new perspectives for conceiving of world literature beyond centres and hierarchies.

Octavio Paz and the Surrealist Entanglements in Mexico

Like Cortázar, Paz did not become interested in surrealism until the late 1940s, when the movement had already traversed Mexico. Antonin Artaud travelled to Northern Mexico's Sierra Madre to participate in the peyote rites of the indigenous tribe of the Tarahumaras in 1936. Breton's visit to Frida Kahlo's and Diego Rivera's famous Blue House in Mexico City's district Coyoacán goes back to 1938. This is where the legendary meeting with Leon Trotsky took place, and together with Trotsky, Breton and Rivera wrote the manifesto *Pour un art révolutionnaire indépendant* (Declaration of an Independent Revolutionary Art) against fascism and totalitarianism at the threshold of World War II. In 1940, the *International Exhibition of Surrealism* was realized in Mexico City, curated by means of a transatlantic collaboration between the Peruvian poet César Moro, the Austrian painter in exile

Wolfgang Paalen, and Breton, who was at that time still living in Rue Fontaine in Paris. In general, the years of war were characterized by intense surrealist activity in Mexico: Alice Rahon and Benjamin Péret from France, the Mexican photographer Manuel Álvarez Bravo, the painter Remedios Varo and the poet and essayist Juan Larrea from Spain, as well as the British-born artist Leonora Carrington, who would permanently settle in Mexico City in 1942, also belonged to the inner circle of the surrealist group.

At the same time, Paz was engaged with his own avant-garde project in Mexico: in 1939 he became editor of the literary magazine *Taller* which was in many ways oriented towards the Latin American modernist group *Contemporáneos* that published a periodical by the same name between 1928 and 1931. Many writers who contributed to *Taller*, such as Luis Cardoza y Aragón, were quite critical of surrealism (Dickson 2019, 96). Paz also "distrusted" surrealist ideas, especially its celebration of the unconscious (Escalante 1997). His position corresponded with the general suspicion with which Mexican intellectuals and artists regarded surrealism. In 1938, Breton was welcomed less than enthusiastically in Mexico City, as articles announcing his arrival in the local press reveal (Gremels 2016, 136). On the contrary, besides the unfavourable situation of a general student strike at the Universidad Nacional Autónoma of Mexico (UNAM), Breton's activities there were practically boycotted by the intellectuals who belonged to the Mexican communist party which, at the time, was still supporting Stalinism. On several occasions, he arrived at the UNAM to deliver speeches on surrealism, to find the doors closed against him. The artists and intellectuals who sided with Breton's anti-Stalinist position—as stated in the *Declaration of an Independent Revolutionary Art*—signed and diffused the public declaration *Al público de América Latina* (To the Latin American Public) which was initiated by César Moro to defend the surrealist movement's leader.[21]

21 The original document is accessible at the André Breton Website (Moro et al. 1938). This declaration is important, as it clearly contradicts Kent Dickson's (2019) claim that "in general, the Mexican arts scene received Breton enthusiastically as a visiting dignitary" (95). However, Dickson

Regarding these entanglements between Mexican and French artists and avant-gardes, the centre/periphery model proposed by Casanova has to be thoroughly questioned. The transversal history of surrealism in Mexico shows that it was not just carried out from Paris into the world, where it influenced "peripheral" writers. It gives an account of diverse positionings and conflictive encounters, and at the same time of multilateral exchange and dialogue. This also holds true for Paz's later friendship with André Breton and Benjamin Péret in Paris, where he pursued his diplomatic career from 1945 to 1951. As surrealism had already traversed Mexico, Paz did not have to leave the Mexican "periphery" to catch up with the avant-garde of the "World Republic of Letters". Moreover, when he came to the French capital after the war, Paris, just like surrealism, was "at its lowest ebb".[22] With many of its members of the pre-war period coming back from exile, the surrealist group had to reorient itself and think about new directions. It also competed with existentialist philosophy which, after the experience of war, provided messages that seemed much more significant than the somewhat outdated idea of an anti-bourgeois revolution carried out through the activation of the unconscious. In this context, Breton was aware that he depended on a surrealist network that would go beyond the borders of France's capital and even those of Europe.[23] Paz, however, never considered

---

also remarks that "there were serious attempts to pave the way intellectually for his visit—anthologies and essays published in literary magazines, with the entire May 1938 issue of *Letras de Mexico* being devoted to surrealism" (95).

22 Jason Wilson (1986) observes, "Paz had arrived in 1945 in a Paris recently occupied, in the grim poverty of the early postwar years, with rationing, recriminations, national humiliations, and the Marshall Plan, a Paris at its lowest ebb, at its least glamorous" (33).

23 This becomes especially clear when reading Breton's *Prolegomena to a Third Manifesto of Surrealism, or Not* (1969), where he locates the vigour of surrealism in the world outside Europe: South America, New Guinea, Egypt and the Caribbean—with Aimé Césaire as the most revolutionary representative (284). He even asserts in the first sentence of this third surrealist manifesto of 1942: "Doubtless, there is too much *north* in me for me ever to be a man to pledge his whole allegiance to anything" (281; original emphasis).

himself an essential protagonist of this international surrealist network. Like Cortázar, he regarded his role within surrealism as rather "tangential" (Paz 1974, 61), in other words, as more of an affinity than an affiliation. Michael Richardson (2019) states:

> Although Paz participated directly in the surrealist movement, and was highly respected within it, he never fully committed to its ideas and in many ways treated it as just one of many influences of which he was subject. Even as he continued to invoke surrealism, often with great passion and insight, increasingly he did so from a distance. (169)

The multiple facets of Paz's entanglements as well as those of his country demonstrate the complexity of encounter and inspiration, approval and disagreement of surrealist exchange between the Global North and the Global South. These entangled relations of surrealism in Mexico, however, did not stop Paz (1973) from acknowledging surrealism's importance as a "vision of the world" (154).

The Other Voice of Surrealism: Octavio Paz's *El arco y la lira*

In terms of style and aesthetics, Paz's work is considered even less surrealist than Cortázar's. Nevertheless, scholars have traced some characteristics of surrealism in his early writings, especially in his poetry, for example, in his 1951 anthology *¿Águila y Sol?* (Eagle and Sun?), which deals with Mexico's extinguished indigenous heritage and its contradictory present (Stanton 2015; Wilson 1986).[24] In *El arco y la lira* Paz explores questions of creativity, inspiration and imagination. In this context, he incorporates surrealism as part of his poetics. Stanton (2015) characterizes the poetological essay as an "interdisciplinary, or even anti-disciplinary" work (356), as Paz creates an intertextual polyphony without any systematic order, evolving his poetics from all kinds of literary, poetic, philosophical and religious references, such as Aztec mythology, Romantic poetry, the Hindu epic

24 For a more detailed account of the controversy of Paz's relationship with surrealism, see Gremels (2018, 129–44).

Bhagavad Gita and the *Upanishads*, existentialist and medieval philosophy, Zen-Buddhism, phenomenology, and surrealism. Cortázar praised this essay enthusiastically because of its polyphonous construction. On July 31, 1956, he wrote a letter to Paz in which he stressed their shared transcultural perspective as Latin American writers:

> Octavio, I think that you have demonstrated something that seems to me the most essential characteristic of the Latin American thinker and essayist—and especially those from Mexico and Argentina. I refer to the possibility that has to be given to us (and of which we do not yet make a lot of use) of understanding and exploring a topic from all angles, without the inevitable reduction to only one way of thinking, to any given culture [. . .]. When it is possible, in a work of this kind, to converge such a vast range of experiences and bring together Europe, Asia and America in one synthesis [. . .], the result is evident: from the beginning to the end, *The Bow and the Lyre* is a beautiful, rich and deep foray [into thinking and writing about poetry]. (Cortázar 2000, 337)[25]

Indeed, when Cortázar stresses the diverse experiences across Europe, Asia and America reflected in Paz's essay, he follows the transversal route that led to its creation. Between 1948 and 1952, Paz pursued his diplomatic career in Paris where his friendship with Breton and also with Cortázar was born. From there, he was sent to New Delhi to work at the Mexican embassy where he spent three months, from January to March, before moving on to Japan. After a year in Asia, he returned to Mexico in 1953, where he received funding to work on his poetological essay *El arco y la lira* (Stanton 2015, 340). He shared

25 Original: "Octavio, yo creo que usted ha mostrado en su libro lo que me parece ser la característica más profunda del pensador, del ensayista latinoamericano—y muy en especial del mexicano y argentino—. Me refiero a la posibilidad que nos ha sido dada (y de la que todavía hacemos poco uso) de conocer y de explorar un tema desde todos sus ángulos, sin la reducción inevitable a un modo de pensar, a una cultura dada [. . .]. Cuando en un trabajo de esta naturaleza se puede hacer converger una gama tan vasta de experiencias, aunar a Europa, el Asia y América en una síntesis [. . .] los resultados no pueden ser que evidentes. Desde el principio al final, *El arco y la lira* es un avance en riqueza, en hondura y en belleza".

his first ideas about this book project with the Mexican essayist Alfonso Reyes to whom he wrote various letters from New Delhi and Tokyo (341–44).

Thus, Paz's attempt to define his poetry and redefine surrealism cannot be separated from his acquaintance with (South) East Asian cultures, literatures and religious practices. This holds especially true for his experience in India which he reflects on from various perspectives in the chapter "The Other Shore" (La otra orilla), initially designed to be the title of his poetological essay. In one passage he evokes his visit to the sacred Hindu town Mutra where he observed a ceremony of hundreds of Krishna devotees singing, dancing and engaging in holy washing. This scene causes awe and consternation in him and inspires him to ponder the validity of his perception of reality: "Strangeness is wonder at a commonplace reality that is suddenly revealed as that which was never seen before" (Paz 1973, 112).[26] His experiences in India mark a fundamental moment of Paz's encounter with cultural difference and enhance his reflexion on otherness which evolves into one of the main components of his poetics.

Paz's ideas on poetry and otherness in *El arco y la lira* might be another reason for Cortázar's appraisal of the essay, as it corresponds to his own poetological engagement with these questions in "Teoría del túnel". Comparing Paz's essay with Cortázar's, I would like to stress a similar reformulation of surrealism that took place between Buenos Aires, Paris, India and México.[27] The authors concur in interrelating surrealism with existentialism, as Stanton (2015) points out, although he assumes that Paz could not have read "Teoría del túnel", which by that time had not yet been published (356–57). But what seems even more remarkable is that they both link surrealism to the idea of otherness and a planetary claim to revise the dominant world view of western modernity.

26 Original: "La extrañeza es asombro ante una realidad cotidiana que de pronto se revela como lo nunca visto" (Paz 1956, 127).

27 In his letter to Paz, Cortázar writes that he will soon travel to India. Contrary to what he announces at the end of October 1956, the trip did not take place until 1957 (Cortázar 2000, 339).

First of all, their revision implies a de-historicization of the avant-garde movement. Paz (1973) is very critical when he speaks of the "revolutionary failure of surrealism" (228) from World War II onwards, which he traces back to its entanglements with communist ideologies. It seems evident to him that the political revolution demanded by communism, and the poetic revolution, postulated by surrealism, are incompatible (228–29). Like Cortázar, he decontextualizes surrealism by recognizing its "power of transformation and [its] capacity to penetrate beneath the historical surface and then reappear again. Surrealism cannot be buried because it is not an idea but a direction of the human spirit" (229).[28]

In a position similar to that of Cortázar, Paz conceives of surrealism as a mode of perceiving the world poetically. Its principal claim is "to transform life into poetry" (225) in order to achieve a "socialization of poetic creation" (226). He even goes as far as to claim that "surrealism does not propose the creation of poems as much as the transformation of men into living poems" (226–27).[29] Thus, surrealism becomes an extra-literary phenomenon, situated in any kind of artistic or literary production but also in life itself. Like Cortázar, Paz rejects any specific form of surrealist style or aesthetics, degenerated to a "recipe" that defines a certain type of artistic creation (227). Furthermore, he criticizes the surrealist method of automatic writing as a means of creating poetry. In his opinion, the poet's creative efforts and his critical spirit can hardly be deactivated and remain passive in order to mobilize solely the unconscious. And the volitional act not to

28 Original: "[…] su poder de transformación y su capacidad para atravesar, subterráneamente, la superficie histórica y reaparecer de nuevo. No se puede enterrar al surrealismo porque no es una idea sino una dirección del espíritu humano" (Paz 1956, 249).

29 Original: "una transformación de la vida en poesía" (Paz 1956, 244), la "socialización de la creación poética" (246). "El surrealismo no se propone tanto la creación de poemas como la transformación de los hombres en poemas vivientes" (245).

intervene contradicts the method's requirements. The arbitrary exercise is a means that already fulfils the aim and thus abolishes poetic writing.[30]

The way Paz criticizes automatic writing indicates that his real concern with surrealism goes far beyond the question of any artistic production or writing technique. It rather constitutes a figure of thought onto which he latches his own poetics. For this reason, the central problem of surrealist creativity for him is *la otredad*. This becomes clear in the chapter on inspiration, in which he explores the latter as an instant of creativity that cannot be directed consciously or voluntarily. For Paz, inspiration always exceeds the poet's control. He thus calls it a "mysterious force" that is set free by an "internal revelation" situated outside of the poet's consciousness (Paz 1973, 154). Considered as an "external revelation", the secret of inspiration also questions the unity of subjective consciousness; "it causes our belief in the [. . .] identity of that same consciousness to waver: there is no self, and within each one of us, diverse voices are in conflict" (154).[31] In Paz's understanding, inspiration remains mysterious, irrational and sacred,[32] but not as something deriving from the unconscious, as in Breton's Freudian reading, but as an integral part of human consciousness. Based on this idea of poetic creation, Paz refers to inspiration as a phenomenon of otherness. Poetry comes into being by confronting and delving into this otherness: by separating oneself from the world and rediscovering it, by being driven outside of oneself in order "to return to Being" (163)—rendered in the original as

30 Evodio Escalante (1997) extensively analyses Paz's critique of automatism.

31 Original: "[La inspiración] hace tambalear nuestra creencia en la [. . .] identidad de esa misma conciencia: no hay yo y dentro de cada uno de nosotros pelean varias voces" (Paz 1956, 172).

32 Paz was very engaged with the sacred as another phenomenon to access reality differently than through rationality. There, his interest differs from Cortázar's who, as an atheist, was not very interested in religion. As already shown, he was more engaged with the supernatural, fantastic and magic appearances of life. In any case, Paz's engagement with the sacred does not imply any religious or confessional commitment.

"*volver a ser*" (Paz 1956, 181): "We can come out of ourselves, *go beyond ourselves to the encounter of ourselves*" (Paz 1973, 161; original emphasis).[33]

Paz relates this personal statement of his writing process to surrealism as an epistemology based on inspiration's otherness: "the true originality of surrealism consists not only of having made of inspiration an idea but, more radically, an *idea of the world*" (Paz 1973, 154; original emphasis).[34] In this sense, it challenges a western vision of modernity that focuses on reason and banishes the supernatural and the divine (Stanton 2015, 407). For Paz, inspiration is the remaining "secret" of the modern age, an age that is still continually trying to bring it under control (Paz 1973, 170). His poetics of otherness is thus closely related to his position as a Mexican writer in search of a broader vision of modernity. This vision derives from an entangled postcolonial history that constantly pushes him to discover different realities and temporalities. For this reason, surrealism has a global significance that goes beyond geographies, histories and cultural identities. For Paz, it embodies the voice of otherness:

> In my understanding, the function of surrealism *is that of not being valid*. Being the other voice. The secret, underground voice, the voice of dissidence. Surrealism is the constitutional disease, the congenital disease of Occidental societies. Its sacred disease. (Paz 1967, 8; original emphasis, my translation)[35]

Considering surrealism as the "voice of dissidence" that western societies need, Paz turns to the metaphor of illness to express how essential and existential the "function" of surrealism as a disruptive factor is to him. As a "sacred disease" it brings disaster, but at the same

---

33 Original: "ir más allá de nosotros mismos al encuentro de nosotros" (Paz 1956, 176).

34 Original: "La verdadera originalidad del surrealismo consiste no solamente en haber hecho de la inspiración una idea sino, más radicalmente, una idea del mundo" (Paz 1956, 172).

35 Original: "La función del surrealismo, a mi juicio, *es no ser vigente*. Ser la *otra voz*, la otra cara de la sociedad. La voz secreta, subterránea, la voz disidente. El surrealismo es la enfermedad constitucional, la enfermedad congénita de la sociedad occidental. Su enfermedad sagrada".

time announces redemption. The religious metaphor is reminiscent of Cortázar (1994a), who, in "Teoría del túnel", considers the adoption of a surrealistic lifestyle as a "lustral task of restitution" (67). For both writers, surrealism appears as the *other* that is able to provide the world view with a "multiple modernity" based not only on control, logic and rationality, but also on inspiration and poetry as driving forces of understanding the self and the world. This re-envisioning of surrealism goes far beyond a historical re-consideration of the movement. Regardless of time and space, the "other voice" of surrealism disturbs dominant and conventional ideas of the world, as it incessantly "opens the door to an interrogation" (Paz 1973, 158) that destabilizes certainties and realities.

Transversal Surrealism from Mexico and Argentina

As the analysis of "Teoría del túnel" and *El arco y la lira* has shown, Cortázar's and Paz's re-envisioning of surrealism as an all-embracing world view does not mean that they enthusiastically follow surrealist doctrines or reproduce the movement's ideas from their "peripheral" position as "belated" Latin American writers. The transversal history of surrealism in Mexico and Argentina even shows that they are not the main protagonists of Latin American surrealism. Their re-envisioning thus cannot be reduced to the unilateral idea that Cortázar and Paz as writers from the Global South assimilated or adapted the supposedly isolated original of European surrealism in the sense of "the west acts and the rest reacts". Neither did they affiliate with the movement as it spread across the Americas. Their critical position towards techniques such as automatic writing reveals that their relationship with surrealism is not that of a unidirectional influence or an adaptation of surrealist style and aesthetics.

The surrealistic world view that both writers connect to an ethics of otherness displays the transformative power of surrealism as it traverses different cultures and geographies, especially those of the Global South. For both writers, surrealism is a figure of thought that reflects on crucial questions concerning Latin America's transcultural entanglements and their individual search for "multiple modernities". Their ethics of otherness also implies the acceptance of an all-embracing reality that incorporates disorder and irrationality, mystery and the abysmal facets of humanity. For this reason, they do not just challenge the "conventional geography and periodization" (Friedman 2012, 509) of surrealism but even go so far as to question its historicity. In their search for an all-embracing world view and alternative models of modernity, they de-historicize and decontextualize surrealism as a European avant-garde movement and reconstitute it as a cosmic necessity to assume its role as "eccentric" in the field of world literature.

In their poetological essays Cortázar and Paz are in search of a radical conception of writing that seeks to overcome the boundary between literature and life. In this context, surrealism's rupture with established literary canons and forms is crucial to them. With regard to "surrealism as world literature" (Ungureanu 2018), their re-envisioning demonstrates that there is no "surrealist norm" that they must adapt to or revolutionize in order to catch up or compete with the conventions of literary centres such as Paris, as Casanova (2004) maintains in her systemic centre/periphery approach in *The World Republic of Letters*. Instead, it is surrealism's task to breach literary or artistic norms as well as resist a normative idea of reality or a "world system". Surrealism's unconventional world view guarantees them the freedom to envision a world order guided by inspiration, in Paz's sense, or even to abolish literature and replace it with life itself, as Cortázar states.

The two poetological essays *El arco y la lira* and "Teoría del túnel" regard it as surrealism's "cosmic" task to destabilize and disturb the idea of literary convention and centricity. Surrealism does not need Breton or Paris as centres from which it spreads into the world. In Cortázar's (1994a) sense surrealism's "cosmovision" (102) involves an all-encompassing responsibility to question any fixed world system of art and literature. Paz claims surrealism as the world's voice of "dissidence" that resists the hegemony of western thought and ideas of world order, as it consists of not conforming to any rule, rejecting any norm or convention. Thus, both writers remind us that surrealism's mandate in the field of world literature is that of being anti-centrical from the very beginning. Cortázar's and Paz's claim for surrealism as a non-conformist world view finally allows us to consider surrealism as world literature beyond the frontiers and asymmetries between the Global North and the Global South, by re-envisioning it as a paragon of the global practice of de-hierarchizing world literature.

Bibliography

Ades, Dawn, Rita Eder and Graciela Speranza. 2012. "Introduction." In *Surrealism in Latin America. Vivísimo Muerto*, edited by Dawn Ades, Rita Eder, and Graciela Speranza, 1–11. Los Angeles, CA: Getty Publications.

Alazraki, Jaime. 2007. "¿Qué es lo neofantástico?" [What is the Neo-phantastic?]. In *Teorías hispanoamericanas de la literatura fantástica*, edited by José Miguel Sardinas, 201–14. Havana: Ediciones Arte y Literatura.

Ashcroft, Bill, Gareth Griffiths, and Helen Tiffin. 1994. *The Empire Writes Back: Theory and Practice in Post-Colonial Literatures*. Abingdon: Routledge.

Breton, André. [1924] 1988. "Manifeste du surréalisme. 1924". In *Œuvres complètes.* Vol. 1, edited by Marguerite Bonnet, Philippe Bernier, Étienne Alain Hubert, und José Pierre, 309–46. Paris: Galimard.

Breton, André. 1969. *Manifestoes of Surrealism*. Translated by Richard Seaver and Helen Lane. Ann Arbor, MI: The University of Michigan Press.

Casanova, Pascale. 2004. *The World Republic of Letters*. Translated by M.B. DeBevoise (Original: *La République mondiale des Lettres*, 1999). Cambridge, MA: Harvard University Press.

Castro-Klarén, Sara. 1975. "Cortázar, Surrealism and Pataphysics." *Comparative Literature* 27 (3): 218–36.

Cortázar, Julio. 1994a. "Teoría del túnel" [Tunnel Theory]. In *Obra crítica*. Vol. 1, edited by Saúl Yurkievich, 31–137. Madrid: Alfaguara.

Cortázar, Julio. [1948] 1994b. "Muerte de Antonin Artaud" [The Death of Antonin Artaud]. In *Obra crítica*. Vol. 2, edited by Jaime Alazraki, 153–55. Madrid: Alfaguara.

Cortázar, Julio. [1956] 1994. "No se culpe a nadie" [Don't Blame Anyone]. In *Cuentos completos*. Vol. 1, edited by Saúl Yurkievich, 293–96. Madrid and Mexico: Alfaguara.

Cortázar, Julio. 1967. *La Vuelta al Día En Ochenta Mundos* [Around the Day in Eighty Worlds]. Vol. 2. Buenos Aires: Siglo XXI Editores.

Cortázar, Julio. 2000. *Cartas (1937-1963)* [Letters (1937–1963)]. Vol. 1, edited by Aurora Bernárdez. Buenos Aires: Alfaguara.

Damrosch, David. 2003. *What is World Literature?* Princeton, NJ: Princeton University Press.

Dickson, Kent. 2019. "Mexico." In *The International Encyclopedia of Surrealism*. Vol. 1, edited by Michael Richardson, Dawn Ades, Krzysztof Fijalkowski, Steven Harris, and Georges Sebbag, 92–100. New York: Bloomsbury.

Eisenstadt, Shmuel. 2003. *Comparative Civilizations and Multiple Modernities*. Vol. 1. Boston, MA: Brill.

Escalante, Evodio. 1997. "La vanguardia requisada" [The Contended Avant-Garde]. *Fractal* 2 (4). http://www.mxfractal.org/F4escala.html.

Friedman, Susan Stanford. 2012. "World Modernisms, World Literature and Comparativity." In *The Oxford Handbook of Global Modernisms*, edited by Marc Wollaeger and Matt Eathough, 499–525. Oxford: Oxford University Press.

Garfield Picón, Evelyn. 1975. *¿Es Julio Cortázar un surrealista?* [Is Julio Cortázar a Surrealist?] Madrid: Gredos.

Gremels, Andrea. 2018. "Dialogando con el surrealismo. Octavio Paz y *El arco y la lira*" [In Dialogue With Surrealism: Octavio Paz's *The Bow and the Lyre*]. *Cuadernos Americanos* 165 (3): 129–44.

Gremels, Andrea. 2016. "*Yo veo, yo imagino*: André Breton y México" [I See, I Imagine: André Breton and Mexico]. *Les Ateliers du SAL*

8: 133–51. https://lesateliersdusal.files.wordpress.com/2016/08/10-lads08-gremels.pdf.

Gremels, Andrea, and Maren Scheurer. 2018. "Intentionally Left Blank: The Empty Page between Signification and Silence." *Comparatio* 10 (1): 39–56.

Lautréamont, Comte de. 2011. *The Songs of Maldoror*. Translated by Russell J. Dent (Original: *Les Chants de Maldoror*, 1868). Chicago, IL: Solar Books—University of Chicago Press.

Moro, César et al. 1938. "Al público de América Latina" [To the Latin American Public]. The André Breton Website. Accessed 3 November, 2021. https://www.andrebreton.fr/work/56600100544560.

Nadeau, Maurice. 1989. *The History of Surrealism*. Translated by Roger Shattuck and Richard Howard (Original: *Histoire du surréalisme*, 1945). New York: Palgrave Macmillan.

Nicholson, Melanie. 2013. *Surrealism in Latin American Literature: Searching for Breton's Ghost*. New York: Palgrave Macmillan.

Nicholson, Melanie. 2019. "Argentina." In *The International Encyclopedia of Surrealism*. Vol. 1, edited by Michael Richardson, Dawn Ades, Krzysztof Fijalkowski, Steven Harris, and Georges Sebbag, 3–5. New York: Bloomsbury.

Paz, Octavio. 1990. *In Search of the Present*. Nobel Lecture. Translated by Anthony Stanton (Original: *La búsqueda del presente*, 1990). Accessed 3 November, 2021. https://www.nobelprize.org/prizes/literature/1990/paz/lecture/.

Paz, Octavio. 1985. *The Labyrinth of Solitude and Other Writings*. Translated by Lysander Kemp and Yara Milos (Original: *El laberinto de soledad*, 1950). New York: Grove Press.

Paz, Octavio. 1956. *El arco y la lira*. Mexico City: Fondo de la cultura económica.

Paz, Octavio. 1973. *The Bow and the Lyre: The Poem, The Poetic Revelation, Poetry and History*. Translated by Ruth L.C. Simms. Austin, TX: University of Texas Press.

Paz, Octavio. 1967. "Octavio Paz en diálogo" [Octavio Paz in Conversation (with Carlos Monsiváis)]. *Revista de la Universidad de México* 21 (3): 1–8.

Paz, Octavio. 1974. *La búsqueda del comienzo: escritos sobre el surrealismo* [In Search of the Beginning: Writings About Surrealism]. Edited by Diego Martínez Torrón. Madrid: Fundamentos.

Pellegrini, Aldo, ed. 1961. *Antología de la poesía surrealista* [Anthology of Surrealist Poetry]. Buenos Aires: Argonauta.

Ramazani, Jahan. 2009. *A Transnational Poetics.* Chicago, IL, and London: The University of Chicago Press.

Richardson, Michael. 2019. "Octavio Paz." In *The International Encyclopedia of Surrealism.* Vol. 1, edited by Michael Richardson, Dawn Ades, Krzysztof Fijalkowski, Steven Harris, and Georges Sebbag, 169–71. New York: Bloomsbury.

Scholz, Lászlo. 1977. *El arte poética de Júlio Cortázar* [The Poetic Art of Júlio Cortázar]. Buenos Aires: Castañeda.

Ščur, Max. 2019. "Julio Cortázar." In *The International Encyclopedia of Surrealism.* Vol. 1, edited by Michael Richardson, Dawn Ades, Krzysztof Fijalkowski, Steven Harris, and Georges Sebbag, 564–66. New York: Bloomsbury.

Spiller, Roland. 2009. "Julio Cortázar." In *Kindlers Literatur-Lexikon.* Vol. 3, edited by Heinz Ludwig Arnold, 211–14. Stuttgart: Metzler.

Stanton, Anthony. 2006. "Paz y Cortázar: Estéticas paralelas" [Paz and Cortázar: Parallel Aesthetics]. *Literatura Mexicana* 17 (2): 213–22.

Stanton, Anthony. 2015. *El río reflexivo: Poesía y ensayo en Octavio Paz (1931-1958)* [The Reflexive Stream: Octavio Paz's Poetry and Essayistic Work]. Mexico City: Fondo de la cultura económica.

Todorov, Tzvetan. 1973. *The Fantastic: A Structural Approach to a Literary Genre.* Translated by Richard Howard (Original: *Introduction à la littérature fantastique,* 1970) Cleveland, OH: Case Western Reserve University Press.

Ungureanu, Delia. 2018. *From Paris to Tlön: Surrealism as World Literature.* New York: Bloomsbury Academic.

Warwick Research Collective. 2015. *Combined and Uneven Development Towards a New Theory of World-Literature*. Liverpool: Liverpool University Press.

Wilson, Jason. 1986. *Octavio Paz*. Boston, MA: Twayne.

Wink, Georg. 2016. "*Prosa Del Observatorio* de Julio Cortázar como crítica epistemológica y manifiesto poético-político: ¿una vislumbre budista?" [*From the Observatory* by Julio Cortázar as Epistemological Critique and Poetic Political Manifesto: A Buddhist Glimpse?]. In *Sur/South: Poetics and Politics of Thinking Latin America/India*, edited by Susanne Klengel and Alexandra Ortiz Wallner, 77–94. Madrid and Frankfurt: Iberoamericana and Vervuert.

Yurkievich, Saúl. 1994. "El encuentro del hombre con su reino" [Man's Encounter with His Kingdom]. Foreword in *Obra crítica*. Vol. 1, by Julio Cortázar. Edited by Saúl Yurkievich, 15–30. Madrid and Buenos Aires: Alfaguara.

Alternative Modernities, Magical Realism and World Literatures of the Global South

Maggie Ann Bowers

Magical realism is made most vulnerable to negative assessment by virtue of its liminal position between the cultures of the Global North and the Global South. From the second half of the 20th century it has been used as a form of expression by writers across the Global South. Yet, it remains a genre that has been embraced by western criticism and has, to a large extent, been defined by it. The gap that exists between the location in which the critical discourse is produced—the cultural position of the literary critics—and the location of the authors and their literary expression, is often commented upon.[1] This sometimes leads to a suspicion of magical realism as a decolonizing mode of writing that is ambivalently associated with the centres of western power. Yet, magical realism most famously is employed by authors from the Global South producing writing resistant to an unquestioned acceptance of western modernity. Seminal magical realist texts from the Global South, such as Colombian Gabriel García Márquez's 1967 *One Hundred Years of Solitude* (*Cien años de soledad*) and Kenyan Ngũgĩ wa Thiong'o's 2006 *Wizard of the Crow* (*Mũrogi wa Kagogo*) interrogate the assumptions of western modernity, with Ngũgĩ's novel seeking to identify possibilities for alternative modernities in decolonized spaces.

This chapter will explore these two novels in a comparative world literature framework to assess their relationship to modernity in the Global South, focused on the shared concern with the relationship between tradition and modernity that also provides the basis for their magical realism. What this chapter reveals is that, while both

1 Further discussion of this can be found in my essay "Magical Realism and Indigeneity: From Appropriation to Resurgence" (Bowers 2020).

texts explore alternative modernities that depart from the western concept, these texts of the Global South propose very different versions of modernity, based on diverging assessments of the role and incorporation of both western and local and indigenous tradition in those modernities.

This chapter is primarily influenced by the theory proposed by Dilip Parameshwar Gaonkar (2001) in his introduction to his book *Alternative Modernities*, as it provides an understanding that shares an affinity with the representations of modernity in the novels under discussion. Gaonkar sees modernity as varied phenomena, specific to location, that develop under both global and local influences. He emphasizes the cultural theory of modernity which "holds that modernity always unfolds within a specific cultural or civilizational context and that different starting points for the transition to modernity lead to different outcomes" (17). In his understanding, Gaonkar recognizes modernity as "inescapable" and firmly links it to origins in Europe and the West, noting it was "born in the West" (1). However, Gaonkar's work emphasizes the development of unique and alternative modernities in non-western locations that move "with and against" the philosophical traditions of Europe. This, he claims, is a form of "double consciousness" wherein western modernity must be acknowledged and interrogated in order to be adopted, adapted, rejected or replaced with new local forms. He explains,

> Whether in vernacular or cosmopolitan idioms, that questioning of the present, which is taking place at every national and cultural site today, cannot escape the legacy of Western discourse on modernity. Whoever elects to think in terms of alternative modernities (irrespective of one's location) must think with and also against the [Western] tradition. (14–15)

Since Gaonkar's introduction of "alternative modernities", there has been resistance among critics to his concept. For instance, Susan Stanford Friedman (2015) comments,

> Positing "other," "alternative," or "minor" modernities ha[s] been important for unthinking Euro/American centrisms, cracking open

> the door to the West's exclusivity, but such categories are insufficient because they leave the West as the measure by which all other modernities are understood. It is not enough to add alternative modernities to the Western instance of modernity. (4)

Friedman goes on to call for a new understanding of "global" modernity and a recognition of the production of varied forms of modernity in non-western contexts. While this may appear to be similar to Gaonkar's aims, Friedman's call to create a "global" framework again risks the elision of the particular complexity of what Gaonkar (2001) calls "creative adaptation", that is, to work with and against western modernity in the process of decolonization (22). Friedman's work, while very useful in linking the specific and particular conditions that create instances of modernity in non-western contexts, does not acknowledge enough the need to negotiate, adapt and work against western modernity. In effect, her work does not reveal the same messy entanglements with western modernity that Gaonkar indicates and which are revealed in these novels. This is significant for the reading of García Márquez's and Ngũgĩ's texts in a world literature framework that takes into account the culturally specific influences upon and the reaction to western modernity, as well as the adaption and creation of alternative modernities in differing contexts within the Global South. Thus, these texts interrogate the concept of modernity to reveal multiple and entangled versions that can impact each distinct cultural context. For the clarity of this argument, the term "modernity" will refer to the overarching concept that can include one or more interrelated, plural, or conflicted versions of "western modernity" and "alternative modernities". The novels reveal that western modernity and alternative modernities can and often do exist in the same location, where alternative modernities are frequently projected in decolonial opposition or negotiation of western modernity.

This chapter explains that it is no coincidence that magical realism is employed in the iteration of such differing expressions of alternative modernities. It too was "born in the West" in the art world of the Weimar Republic of the 1920s and its popularity as a subject of study in western academia has often been noted. Yet, from its most significant development in mid-20th century Latin America, the underlying discourse of magical realism emerges from the tensions inherent in the relationship of modernity to the cultures of the Global South. Thus, the literary expression of the genre of magical realism is closely associated with postcolonial and decolonial discourses that challenge the assumptions of imperial epistemology. As Wendy Faris (2004) observes, its "narrative encoding of alterity" has turned magical realism into "a powerful decolonizing mode" (36). This is attributed to the potential for magical realist narratives to break down conventional western categories of reality and their basis in the scientific understanding of the phenomenal world. In the novels of Ngũgĩ and García Márquez, magical realism is the representation of the extraordinary as mundane, embedded in a realist context. It expands and allows new iterations of "reality" and dismantles categories and limitations of representation associated with European realism. This is inspired by a similar impulse in the creation of "alternative modernities" that are born from innovation and "work against" western imperial assumptions.

Placing these texts into the historical context in which they were written is thus significant and provides an interesting interrogation of the discourse of modernity. Franco Moretti (1996) recognizes the context in which García Márquez wrote his novel in his assessment of this "modern epic". He notes that the 1960s were significant for a changing world order with the removal of colonial power from many countries. Taking an ironic stance, Moretti questions whether the enchantment of western readers with the "classic" *One Hundred Years of Solitude* is partially influenced by the enchantment of the characters of Macondo by "the products of Western technology". His controversial conclusion is a comforting interpretation for a European readership that the novel recounts the years of colonialism as "an adventure filled with wonder" (250). Yet, I contend that this mischievously elides the clear distrust of western modernity that is represented in the novel through the depiction of the central violent episode of the Banana Workers Massacre. Almost two decades later, in his 1982 Nobel Lecture "The Solitude of Latin America" ("La soledad de América Latina"), García Márquez made clear his concerns with the continuing darker side of modernity, reflecting on the violence and poverty he witnessed across Latin America in the 1980s. He portrays Latin American modernity as a result of a continuing difficult relationship between Europe and Latin America, with both sides being implicated in both the positive and negative effects of modernization. Ultimately, García Márquez (1982) claims, "Latin America neither wants, nor has any reason, to be a pawn without a will of its own; nor is it merely wishful thinking that its quest for independence and originality should become a Western aspiration" (n.p.).

Therefore, both the works of García Márquez and Ngũgĩ reveal what Gaonkar observes, that modernity exists in a variety of alternative and distinct forms across the Global South that are more or less influenced by western modernity, in this case in both Latin America and sub-Saharan Africa. These are a result of a continuing complex relationship with the West that cannot yet be dismissed even during a time of decolonization. The novels reveal that modernity has been imposed on both regions through imperial influence, leading to neo-colonial practices by western companies and international aid organisations. The leaders of the communities in both novels seek connection with the wider world and the associated modern influence, but they are both thwarted by local geography and global politics. Of course, the novels were written in different eras and on different continents, with different histories of decolonization. Thus, the novels differ in the extent to which modernity is sought by the wider cast of characters. In the earlier Colombian novel, Macondo remains a closed society where the majority of characters retain their pre-modern attitudes, whereas in the Kenyan novel several characters in Aburĩria look to the West with an aim to make good use of modernity. Hence, where García Márquez represents an unwillingness from both Europe and Latin America to fully unleash modernity in the region during the 20th century, Ngũgĩ's work posits a contemporary indigenous African negotiation and appropriation of aspects of western modernity.

It is no coincidence that magical realism is employed in the iteration of such differing and complex expressions of alternative modernities. Most particularly from its maturation in mid-20th century Latin America, the underlying discourse of magical realism emerges from the tensions inherent in its representation of modernity. The modernist foundation novels of Latin American magical realism are constructed around the sub-text of the uneven development in rural/pre-modern cultures: Miguel Ángel Asturias's *Men of Maize* (*Hombres de maíz*, 1949) draws upon indigenous beliefs and creates a Guatemalan national discourse centred around the character of a coyote-trickster postman; Alejo Carpentier's *The Kingdom of this World* (*El reino de este mundo*, 1949) retells the story of the Haitian uprising from the revolutionary slave perspective. Continuing this theme, yet written slightly later, on the cusp of the arrival of postmodernism, García Márquez's *One Hundred Years of Solitude* is most notably structured around the tensions between imposed capitalist modernity and rural tradition in 19th and early 20th-century Colombia.

Moreover, as world literature has realigned to non-western locations, the study of texts "South-South" across a global literary network has enabled the full recognition of magical realism as a global genre of the South, with shared features emerging from varied and different non-western contexts.[2] However, the political unevenness of the literary world that has been so clearly identified by critics such as those of the Warwick Research Collective is pertinent to the complex

---

2 Since its inception, Magical Realism in Spanish has always been studied comparatively across South-South Latin American texts by influential critics such as Raymond L. Williams. Since Brenda Cooper's (1998) innovative study of West African fiction, there has been an increasing number of studies of transnational English language magical realism across the postcolonial world, and more recently in transnational studies by Maggie Bowers (2020) and Ben Holgate (2019), comparing indigenous texts of North America and Australasia.

cultural position of many magical realist writers. García Márquez and Ngũgĩ are influenced equally in their writing by their vernacular origins and their cosmopolitan writerly context. Thus, they can be interpreted as holding both to a western and a non-western perspective simultaneously. This authorial position problematizes the idea of a clear, single concept of modernity. Although the critics of the Warwick Research Collective adopt Fredric Jameson's concept of a "singular modernity", the tensions concerning modernity in magical realism, as will be revealed, require another understanding that often arises from the indigenous and complicates that assumed singularity of western capitalist modernity. For this purpose, the "alternative modernities" of Gaonkar provide a more effective way to enter into this discussion.

From its European origins, to that of a Latin American and then a postcolonial anglophone and finally a global phenomenon, magical realism, just like world literature, is now more associated with the Global South than any other region. In fact, magical realism as it is currently known has little but lightly traceable influences from the art of the Weimar Republic. Instead, since the 1950s, it became increasingly a genre associated with the articulation of subaltern voices and histories and with the decolonizing strategies of the postcolonial world. Notably, challenges to and revisions of the concept of world literature in the 21st century have followed a similar pattern to that perceivable in the development of the concept of magical realism, moving from European origins and an innate Eurocentrism in the original Goethean concept to being adopted and adapted by writers in the Global South seeking to define world literature within their own context. Mariano Siskind (2015) proposes that magical realism can be understood in terms of a "new" world literature, which he defines through three principles:

> World literature produces new genres, or rather new generic formations, constellations of texts whose identity is defined in accordance with new needs and new critical and aesthetic desires translated into new organizing principles: (1) bridging the different historical and geopolitical ways in which texts are inscribed and classified locally and globally within mappings made

> up of uneven power relations; (2) foregrounding the worldly in world literary texts—in other words, discovering the universalizable potential of akin texts; (3) accounting for the ways in which texts mutate as they travel across cultures and languages, and therefore elude the generic fixity of yesteryear. (n.p.)

His analysis is significant for the assessment of magical realism within a world literature context, as it draws both magical realism and world literature together and posits them as a form of newness—in other words, as an expression of modernity.

Seminal magical realist texts like *One Hundred Years of Solitude* and *The Wizard of the Crow* have developed distinct ways to express modernities in the Global South, which can be explored via the relationship of magical realism to world literature and to modernity in the Global South. Magical realism and world literature are persistently criticized for dangerously straddling the critical approaches of both the North and the South, so that they are seldom viewed without suspicion. A comparison of García Márquez and Ngũgĩ that aligns the specific versions of modernity in both Latin America and sub-Saharan Africa through the association of magical realism and world literature, however, demonstrates that these texts interrogate this ambivalence and represent non-western alternative decolonizing forms of modernity. Hence, this chapter proposes that magical realism is the epitome of world literature of the Global South and, moreover, a product of the alternative modernities that it helps to articulate.

Gaonkar's theory of "alternative modernities", existing in relation to specific cultures and histories in the Global South, is supported by many critics who recognize that modernity is not something static and imposed in entirety but rather something adopted and adapted selectively in equal measure to the rejection of some of its aspects. This is an approach shared by critics considering modernity in both sub-Saharan Africa and Latin America. Senayon Olaoluwa (2008), outlining his approach to modernity in his essay "Between Magic and Logic", notes, "There is neither utter rejection nor outright acceptance of modernity. Instead of pitching tent with either of the extremes, Africa has in a unique way invented her own mode of response to modernity and modernization" (204). For Olaoluwa, this is exemplified by Ngũgĩ's novel *Wizard of the Crow*, in particular in relation to its representation of indigenous and local medical practices in the context of modernity. These are used to treat the psychological illnesses brought on by the internalized racial attitudes of inferiority of African people under the influence of the neo-colonialism of global capitalism and the "slow violence" (Nixon 2011) of the after-effects of European colonialism.

The critic Enrique Dussel (2000) makes the widely accepted observation that "modernity really began in 1492" (474), that is to say, at the moment of contact between Early Modern Europe and the indigenous people of the American continents. The implication of the comment is that modernity is created at the moment when (to use Bhabha's [1994] phrase) "newness enters the world" (212). In this sense "newness" is the moment of the creation of the "other" and is the very first moment of European colonization. This is a broad model of modernity that can be applied transculturally and globally. However, Jorge Larrain (2000) modifies this assertion in his book *Identity and Modernity in Latin America* in order to identify a specifically Latin American understanding of modernity. He claims that it is the way in which Latin America was colonized that has led to a particular relationship with it. He explains that there was a lack of introduction of the institutions, inventions and processes of European modernity until the 19th century, so that while the southern continent of the Americas gained the identity of Latin America in 1492, it did not gain modernity until the end of colonial dependence:

> Latin America was deliberately kept apart from the main processes of modernity by the colonial power. With the process of independence from Spain, Latin America enthusiastically embraced the Enlightenment's ideas, but more in their formal, cultural and discursive horizon than in their political and economic institutional practice, where for a long time traditional and excluding structures were kept in place. (4)

This, Larrain proposes, has led to a particular cultural attitude in Latin America that is based upon a tension between the embrace and suspicion of the "interventions of modernity":

> Hence, it could be said that Latin America was born in modern times without being allowed to become modern; when it could become modern, it became so only in the realm of programmatic discourse; and when it began to be modern in practice, then doubts emerged as to whether this conspired against its identity. (4)

This, famously, is the theme at the heart of the classic Latin American novel, *One Hundred Years of Solitude*. Thus, Ngũgĩ's and García Márquez's novels elucidate "alternative modernities" in their respective contexts. These are revealed with their cultural and historical differences to both European modernity and to each other. Most importantly, García Márquez focuses his novel on the ambiguous influence of modernity in relation to tradition in Latin America, whereas Ngũgĩ's novel exposes the effects of a colonial racialized modernity on contemporary Africa.

In the essay "The Dark Side of Magical Realism: Science, Oppression, and Apocalypse in *One Hundred Years of Solitude*", Brian Conniff asks the important question: is it the introduction of modernity to the village of Macondo that we witness at the beginning of García Márquez's novel, when Melquíades and his band of "gypsies" arrive bringing scientific "wonders", that instigates the apocalypse at the very end? Conniff's interpretation of the text hovers between a recognition of the need for progress and the destructive tendencies of modernity, which are associated with the introduction of influences from Europe and result in the "uneven development" (Warwick Research Collective 2015) of Latin America by the colonial western powers. In his Nobel Lecture, García Márquez (1982) moves to the conclusion that "the interpretation of our reality through patterns not our own [. . .] serves only to make us ever more unknown, ever less free, ever more solitary" (n.p.). Reading *One Hundred Years of Solitude* retrospectively through these later conclusions of García Márquez, we see that the question that he is asking is not whether modernity is progress or destruction (in fact, in this novel, it is both) but whether, even despite its progressive influences, it maintains Latin America in a position of isolation and disempowerment in the global world order. The "patterns not our own" by which Latin America is measured, for instance the visibility of western modernity's institutions and influence, misrepresent the state of the continent that, he infers, should be assessed according to their own value systems. What García Márquez is describing without naming, of course, are the colonial and neo-colonial forces that have crucially shaped Latin America. His focus during the Nobel Lecture is notably political and written with the perspective of the people of the Global South at its heart. Noting instances of poverty and political violence in contemporary Latin America, García Márquez makes clear the influence of colonial explorers and *conquistadores* on the past and current direction of the region.

Although we find many references to local legends and historical events in *One Hundred Years of Solitude*, making this novel's origins in the Caribbean region of Colombia evident (e.g. the Banana Workers Massacre), it is clear from García Márquez's discussion of his work that he places his writing in a broader context. His Nobel Lecture refers to "the unearthly tidings of Latin America" (García Márquez 1982, n.p.) and that region's place in the world. Therefore, while García Márquez is considered to be an iconic figure of Colombia and a canonical writer of Latin America, the perspective from which he writes has always been outwardly facing yet embedded in the local. This was most effectively expressed in Salman Rushdie's (1991) identification of García Márquez's "village world-view" (301). This stance places García Márquez clearly in the position of a writer of world literature from the Global South. Of course, his chosen style for communicating such content is the genre of magical realism. This genre, as has been explored earlier, is clearly associated with world literature, and key figures such as García Márquez, Ngũgĩ wa Thiong'o, Salman Rushdie and Toni Morrison utilize this genre because of its capacity to express the voices of the silenced, oppressed and overlooked. Each of their works contains the representation of seemingly inexpressible horror created through political and colonial violence. In this way, García Márquez (1982) is able to summarize his inclusion of the history of Latin America in his writing during his Nobel Lecture as "a strictly accurate account that nonetheless resembles a venture into fantasy" (n.p.).

In contemporary world literature of the Global South there are repeated images and concepts that are assumed to be connected to the global influence of modernity, with an understanding that this goes hand-in-hand with and is transported by the influence of European colonialism and western neo-colonialism. Moreover, what situates these texts in the Global South is an oppositional stance to the disruption of colonialism and neo-colonialism to the disempowered people and cultures of particular localities as expressed from the perspective of those locations. Michael Bell (2010) explains how this structure is the defining element of magical realism of the Global South: "'Magical Realism' draws on pre-scientific folk belief to subvert the 'Western' commitment to scientific reason, itself associated with both imperialism and a history of realist representation so that the genre is intrinsically oppositional and progressive" (179). The novel is famously structured around a central tension between tradition and scientific progress. Hence, the characters, particularly Úrsula and José Acardio, are in a permanent and unresolved conflict due to her retention of folk belief and tradition and his search for progress through introduced scientific methods. Although Úrsula is proven correct by the end (her prophecy that incest will result in a baby born with a pig's-tail comes true), José Acardio's quest to connect and introduce Macondo to the wider world does bring "progress"—it just happens to culminate in apocalypse.

Yet, *One Hundred Years of Solitude* is not restricted to this oppositional structure. The vast and breathtaking scope of the novel is derived from the intricate exploration of the subtle and conflicting responses, both positive and negative, to the intrusion of modernity in a rural and secluded locality that is representative of the Global South. This is exemplified by the introduction of scientific developments into the community by the Macedonian traveller and revenant Melquíades. Although these inventions come from Europe and are brought into the Latin American context by colonial conquest, they are introduced by a member of a minority ethnic group (one in fact that is marginalized in European society, the Romani people) and from a country that is famous for its ethnic mix due to the invasion of so many nations into its territory. Thus, the influences that direct the development of this community come from near and far, from other locations of the Global South and from the powerful nations of the West. As Moretti (1996) notes in *Modern Epic*,

> the history of Macondo is continually intersected and deflected by other histories: by processes that begin in Europe and in Asia, in 'Colombia', Latin America, the United States. [. . .] This, again, is the geography of the world text: broad, heterogeneous, complex. (243)

Moretti goes on to explain that Macondo is "an isolated community that is caught up in the modern world-system, which subjects it to an unexpected, extremely violent acceleration" (243). For Moretti, as for Conniff, there is an inevitability written into the novel that the introduction of modernity will bring the village of Macondo to its ruin. Yet, the onset of modernity is not a simple process of direct and uninvited influence from Europe that causes nothing but destruction. As Raymond L. Williams (2010) explains in his eco-critical reading of the novel,

> García Márquez is critical of many aspects of the modern progress associated with the rise of the modern capitalistic nation-state. *One Hundred Years of Solitude*, however, is not as unambiguously and consistently supportive of the natural world and unequivocally critical of the modern. (65)

The two characters who are most associated with modernity are José Acardio and Melquíades. They both hold a fascination with scientific progress, but their different approaches to understanding science are complex and surprising. José Acardio is fascinated by science and seeks practical applications to the inventions that Melquíades introduces to the village, but with little success. In his essay "The Plague of Modernity", Martín Camps (2014) explains that "José Acardio Buendía's desire for modernity is evident and his imagination moves him beyond the miracles and magic to use a magnet, in order to find treasures, and a magnifying glass as a weapon" (89). The only treasure that he finds is an old suit of armour, a talisman from the past whose significance he fails to recognize. Melquíades, the European who brings scientific progress with him, on the other hand, only understands science through mysticism and provides non-rational and impractical explanations for the scientific discoveries. Hence, the occurrences of the introduction of scientific progress in the novel only serve, "with the use of magic tricks and alchemy, [to] bring 'civilization' and entice José Acardio with the marvels of the world" (Camps 2014, 89).

Camps's choice of "marvel", a word he reuses later in the same essay, is significant. It brings to mind the use of the word in the discourse of Early Modern European "explorers", communicating the experience of making contact with the unfamiliar New World to an eager audience in Europe. Jerónimo Arellano (2015) explores the emotion of "wonder" in his study *Magical Realism and the History of the Emotions in Latin America*, making a clear connection of this word with European reactions to Latin America, one that could be argued continues to be traceable today in the attitudes of the West towards the poverty and political turmoil associated with Latin America as a region of the Global South. In a cleverly subversive manner, García Márquez twists this association so that it is José Acardio, the Latin American, who "marvels" at the European scientific discoveries, with the same lack of understanding shown by the Europeans towards the "marvels" of Latin America. Arellano expands upon this:

> The collection of wonders that circulates through the novel resists interpretations derived from the internalized assumption of a binary opposition between traditional or indigenous magic and destructive foreign devices, gesturing, rather, to the capacity of scientific discourse and technological innovation to provide a point of departure and an imaginative playground for modes of secular reenchantment. (153)

Arellano refers here to the observation made by García Márquez's narrator that José Acardio has "an unbridled imagination" that goes beyond "the genius of nature and even beyond miracles and magic"

(García Márquez 1972, 2) in order to search for a pragmatic explanation and practical application of the discoveries. As Camps (2014) notes, "The new inventions are seen as artifices that will put to test their capacity to marvel because they cannot distinguish the limits of reality" (92). For the townsfolk, a magical explanation is far more convincing and takes less imagination than a scientific one.

Thus, the magical realist capacity to see beyond the constraints of conventional reality is instigated here by the introduction of science. This is not, as Williams (2010) notes, a simple matter of a binary opposition of the positive natural/traditional versus the negative artificial/scientific, as nature is equally deemed a threat to the lives of the population (65–66). However, this does not mean that the force of modernity, in the guise of scientific progress, is not ultimately the deliverer of destruction. The most violent scene in the novel is a fictionalized representation of the notorious Banana Workers Massacre of 1928 that occurred in García Márquez's home region of Aracataca. This massacre by the Colombian Army of labourers protesting their working conditions, on the orders of a government seen to be under the influence of the United Fruit Company of the United States, is a clear example of neo-colonial involvement in the Colombian economy. In the novel, this event is heralded by the introduction of one of the most iconic aspects of modernity bringing science, communication, speed and capitalist economics to Macondo: the train. It is frequently noted that the train brings the neo-colonialists to the town, takes away their produce to siphon off the economic gains from the region and then takes away the dead "in the same way in which they transported bunches of bananas" (García Márquez 1972, 312). Camps (2014) astutely notes that the arrival of the train "is the first and only time that the word 'modernization' is mentioned in the novel" (92). The description of the train by the townsfolk is reminiscent of the description of the magnet that we see at the beginning of the novel when it is "dragging along in turbulent confusion" (García Márquez 1972, 2). The train, like the magnet, appears to them as "something frightful, like a kitchen dragging a village behind it" (227). Melquíades explains the magnet's power through spiritual lexis:

"'Things have a life of their own,' proclaimed the gypsy with a harsh accent. 'It's simply a matter of waking up their souls'" (2). This explanation speaks to the spiritual and traditional philosophies of the townsfolk, dismissing any attempt to use scientific reason to explain. The train, too, is met with a similar explanation, as they think it must be "some trick of the gypsies" (228). Thus, as Camps (2014) surmises, "Even though the modernization of Macondo is in full throttle, its citizens still believe in the supernatural" (94). Yet, the train remains the herald of modernity in Macondo. This significance of the train is indicated clearly at the end of the chapter, where it is characterized as "the innocent yellow train that was to bring so many ambiguities and certainties, so many pleasant and unpleasant moments, so many changes, calamities, and feelings of nostalgia to Macondo" (228). In fact, this statement exemplifies the ambiguous and complex relationship to modernity in Latin America.

Conniff's analysis of *One Hundred Years of Solitude* indicates a similarly ambiguous and ambivalent relationship of Latin America to modernity, most particularly through its isolation from global systems. The careful examination of time and apocalypse in Conniff's (1990) work leads him to assert that Melquíades's

> theory of the elimination of distance, like his theory of magnetic souls, is a fusion of chicanery and "advanced" science—and it is just as prophetic as José Acardio's accidental discovery of the suit of armor. Even though the natives, José Acardio in particular, are unable to understand the principles of Melquíades' discoveries, they are too willing to assume that it is because they are not "worldly" or "advanced" enough. Melquíades' perspective, unlike theirs, is "global". (173)

Camps (2014) concurs with this line of argument, asserting his own reading that "García Márquez uses magical realism as a strategy to confront Latin American isolation from science and progress, the impossibility of dominating the torrid landscapes and imposing instead an imaginary technology" (94). Although Conniff identifies clearly the isolation of the people of Macondo from the wider world, and with it, its global systems of modernity, I place the emphasis of my interpretation on the "elimination of distance" that underpins the creation of

Melquíades's manuscript. Distance has been eliminated because time, too, is not a recognized concept.

While this would appear to provide an explanation for the downfall of Macondo, it is also true to say that the lack of understanding of the past is another contributing factor. The townsfolk are neither able to understand the future (in the guise of the train) nor the past (as presented in the Sanskrit of Melquíades's manuscript). They are stuck in a never-ending present, unable to gain the perspective of time to connect themselves to future or past generations. This provides an explanation as to why there is a conflation of time periods in the novel such as the simultaneous existence of guns, suits of armour and ancient manuscripts. Moretti (1996) uses this observation to assert the significance of García Márquez's novel as a seminal text of world literature (resonating with the definitions of the Warwick Research Collective): "It is the novel of uneven and combined development" (243). However, I would go further to say there is no distinction between different eras or segments of time. All things exist simultaneously, as the narrator explains regarding his manuscript: "Melquíades had not put events in the order of man's conventional time, but had concentrated a century of daily episodes in such a way that they coexisted in one instant" (García Márquez 1972, 421). This is a concept of time that recurs in magical realist work, including that of Isabel Allende's (1986) *House of the Spirits* and Morrison's (1998) *Beloved*. It undermines authoritarian attempts to control history and, here, undermines the western concept of modernity itself, as a result of historical progress. For this reason, alternative modernities cannot be created in Macondo because there is no future. What seems to be the future is in fact already in the past, as it has been determined and written in the manuscripts of Melquíades. It simply exists in the same dimension of the past and present as everything else recorded by the "gypsy". For the same reason, the inhabitants of Macondo never learn from the past nor can they create a future. José Acardio does not realize the significant connection between the metal suit of armour from Europe that signifies the violence of colonialism and the iron train incurring the violence of neo-colonialism. This inability to learn from the past and move toward the future leaves Macondo with the choice of embracing western modernity (and its destructive neo-colonialism) or rejecting it and accepting inevitable implosion. Thus, the text suggests an allegorical reading that the people of Latin America have responded ambivalently to western modernity, sometimes due to a desire to adhere to pre-modern tradition and other times due to a lack of resources to develop alternatives, but always through complex and entangled patterns of political and economic pressures, resistance, and creativity.

The epic novel *Mũrogi wa Kagogo* by Ngũgĩ wa Thiong'o, translated by the author from Kikuyu as *Wizard of the Crow*, also reveals an ambiguous relationship to modernity that resembles García Márquez's position. The novels are similar in the way in which they simultaneously draw on specific detail from the region and culture of the setting, yet also create narratives that are applicable to their wider regions. It is this that makes them appropriate objects of study through both world literature and postcolonial frameworks. Both writers expose the problematic integration of western modernity into their respective cultures due to its close association with imperialism and neo-imperialism at work in their regions: sub-Saharan Africa (Kenya) and Latin America (Colombia). Representations of these regions reveal similarities in the way that the respective cultures incorporate partial elements of western modernity but are either barred from or reject others. In this respect, both novels reveal that their respective cultures respond to modernity in specific ways yet noting the global systems that link them to a shared western and capitalist modernity that is transposed through imperial and neo-colonial influence. While García Márquez focuses his interrogation of modernity on scientific invention, Ngũgĩ does so through an examination of the role of medicine in contemporary African culture. These are interlinked themes, yet Ngũgĩ also makes clear the prevailing influence from indigenous medicine and practices from Kenya. Therefore, his exploration of an alternative modernity is one that proposes a concept of science that is both western and indigenous.

Elements that make this novel explicitly an exploration of Africa's relationship with modernity begin with the depiction of the political systems at play in the fictional country of Aburĩria. This is a country with a "Ruler" who wields power with a heavy hand, tortures members of the opposition and uses the nation's wealth for his own vanity projects. Most specifically, he plans to have a monument in the form of a staircase built that will act as a modern-day Tower of Babel so that he and his citizens could be "Marching to Heaven" (Ngũgĩ 2007, 17). In order to do this, he seeks international aid from "The Global Bank" (clearly a reference to the World Bank). In this sense, the novel's plot is embedded in modern globalization. While "globalization" and "modernity" are not synonymous, they are closely connected, as Olaoluwa (2008) notes, "the notion of globalization harks back to imperial history and can be appropriately limned as reinforcing the agential dynamics of modernity with the context of colonialism" (202).

What makes the depiction of modernity in this novel distinct is the emphasis placed on oral traditions of communication. The novel notably opens with a comment about gossip. The text has a substantial proportion of dialogue, both direct and reported. The Ruler and his followers use speeches to communicate to the people and each other. In this sense, this novel is laden with a preference for oral communication. For Graham Riach (2020), this preference is fuelled by an understanding that "the power of oral forms is, on the one hand, presented as a tool of contesting power, in accord with an understanding of magical realism in which the oral is coupled with indigeneity and the written with capitalist modernity" (158). Yet, like *One Hundred Years of Solitude*, this is not a novel that rests on a simplistic opposition of tradition versus modernity. The novel exposes an alternative and specifically African version of modernity that is created by constant negotiation of these opposites—what Bruce Berman (2006) calls "selective modernity"—wherein tension and ambivalence remain, contributing to an ongoing conflict between "modernizers and traditionalists" (7).

The position of Africa as identified by Berman in "The Ordeal of Modernity in the Age of Terror" is one of uncertainty. Yet, as Olaoluwa (2008) argues, Ngũgĩ is able to reveal how the mediation of modernity in contemporary Africa is, at least in part, under African control, and contains hope for a more positive future beyond colonial and neo-colonial influence (221). Friedman (2015) observes that tradition should not be held in binary opposition to modernity. She notes, "While ideological or nostalgic reconstructions of past traditions often characterize modernity, traditions also exist in the form of knowledge, values, and practices that are passed down from generation to generation" (Friedman 2015, 322). In fact, Ngũgĩ's work acknowledges that revitalization of tradition can be a mode of modernity wherein it rejuvenates society's connection to its heritage in its contemporary context and thus creates new alternative modernities. This is precisely what the Wizard of the Crow achieves by drawing together his indigenous and western knowledge to provide decolonizing healing.

This is explored by Olaoluwa in his interpretation of the Wizard of the Crow and his powers of healing. Kamĩtĩ is at first unaware of his powers of healing, accidentally falling into a situation where his power is revealed to himself. He becomes, nonetheless, a famous healer who even gains the attention of the Ruler and his cronies—he is, in effect, a man of the people, drawing upon his indigenous knowledge. The relationship of Kamĩtĩ to modernity is a crucial aspect of the novel. He is a city dweller who, having left his rural home region, adopts metropolitan modern life. As Olaoluwa (2008) notes, he is born with a shell in his hand, indicating his potential as a diviner (210). Yet, until he begins to "act" as a healer, he does not recognize or utilize his powers and has lost connection with this aspect of himself. Once he begins to recognize that he is able to see patterns in his patients' lives he acknowledges that he can offer useful advice. His most difficult clients are those from the nation's elite, including the Ruler himself. Their maladies are the embodiment of realized metaphors, a typical trope of magical realism, produced from the complex mixture of psychological damage of corrupting power and the effects of colonialism. The Wizard of the Crow/Kamĩtĩ provides a cure for the upwardly mobile Tajirika who cannot speak and can only utter the word "if". The Wizard is able to reveal to him that his condition is a result of his wish to be white, in other words, to desire the power he associates with white westerners. Tajirika explains, "He showed me that the *if*ness had resulted from my longing to be white. Officer, I wished to become a white man. It was a severe case of white-ache" (Ngũgĩ 2007, 338). The climax of the novel occurs when the Ruler himself is afflicted with the same condition when visiting the Global Bank in New York. He swells up and is only able to say the word "if" over and over. Many western medical doctors are called in an attempt to cure the Ruler, without any effect. Eventually, and against their own judgement due to the Wizard of the Crow's detachment from western medicine, the Ruler's advisers nonetheless call for him. The Wizard is able to cure him by identifying the humiliation that he suffered as an African leader patronized and ignored by the white officials of the Global Bank:

> Now when you saw those two whites walking nonchalantly before the mirror as if they were not aware of your presence or what their kind have done to you, you wanted to give them a piece of your mind, but you got stuck. [. . .] You got stuck at the word *if. IF I had been white, would they have done what they did to me*? (Ngũgĩ 2007, 491; original emphasis)

This is traditional medicine of the mind and spirit that is used to treat the psychosomatic illnesses of those who react to their experience of racialized neo-colonialism.

Hence, the Wizard of the Crow represents indigenous traditional divining as a remedy to global capitalist modernity. However, Kamĩtĩ represents traditional indigenous practices in the guise of cosmopolitan African modernity. Olaoluwa (2008) notes that he is perfectly at home, appearing in a suit and speaking impeccable English, when in New York (217). He is able to command and discuss the Ruler's illness with conventional western doctors. In this way, he reveals, "The Wizard of the Crow packages his art of divination and magic to be consistent with the modern times" (Olaoluwa 2008, 202).

Yet, what his divination exposes is a deeply entrenched racist system at the heart of capitalist modernity. In this way, as Riach (2020) comments, "Ngũgĩ's novel shows how magical realism might mediate the grotesque distortions of global capital" (160). It also serves as a critique of the connection of modernity to the racist assumptions of colonialism in a contemporary African context. What can be gleaned from the text is an illustration of the complex relationship of Africa to western modernity. Olaoluwa (2008) also pursues this aspect stating that "there is a qualified embrace of the ideals of modernity while still preserving a primordial order of African epistemology which does not flinch at the suggestion of collaboration or fusion with practices of western modernity" (204). Ultimately, it appears to me that while Olaoluwa takes a rather optimistic view towards the possibility of collaboration, the Wizard of the Crow rather reveals ways for African people to resist and challenge the racial associations of western modernity by negotiating it and creating alternatives. To return to Berman's assertion, Ngũgĩ's novel reveals the potential for the people of Africa to create their own alternative modernity, one that is "selective" rather than collaborative, and protective of its own traditions.

While the two novels examined in this chapter reveal that there is a clear similarity in the representation of the ambivalent relationship to modernity in the Global South of their respective cultures, it is perhaps the difference in the era in which they were written that leads to the diverging conclusions of the texts. García Márquez's analysis of the apocalyptic effects of both imposed western modernity and lack of a creation of a culturally specific modernity in Latin America are reflective of the region in the 1960s. Ngũgĩ's millennial novel ends with a more positive assessment of the future of sub-Saharan African countries exemplified by Kamĩtĩ's resolution to embrace his magical abilities and bring together both his gifts as a traditional indigenous diviner and his service to the people of the modern metropolis.

What this chapter has revealed is that these are two novels that enchant and disturb by their interrogation of the relationship of the Global South to western modernity. They both provide differing and ambivalent assessments of modernity that are portrayed in parallel with a desire for an emergence of alternative decolonizing modernities influenced by the indigenous and local, with differing success. In effect, these novels remind us that cultures of the Global North and the Global South continue to negotiate their past and their possible collaborative and independent futures both as part of the all-pervasive global capitalist system but also in localized decolonizing processes. The chapter has traced negotiations of modernity that reveal both messy entanglements with the North as well as common concerns in the South that pave the way for an indirect dialogue between the novels. Each South location has its own decolonial priorities, context and methods that produce distinct responses to both western modernity of the Global North and alternative modernities of other locations in the Global South. Thus, it appears that the three elements examined in this chapter—modernity, magical realism and world literature—are all associated with European discourse, but they are experiencing challenges, revisions and adaptations from the Global South that are transforming the literary landscape. What this suggests is that magical realism may well be the most appropriate genre right now for the exploration of the complexities of modernity in the writing of world literature of the Global South. Hence, the regular occurrence of magical realism in world literature creates a network of texts that promote South to South dialogue, that respond to the continuing negotiation of western modernity and the creation of alternatives in the decolonizing process.

Bibliography

Allende, Isabel. 1986. *The House of the Spirits.* Translated by Magda Bogin (Original: *La casa de los espíritus,* 1982). London: Black Swan.

Arellano, Jeronimo. 2015. *Magical Realism and the History of the Emotions in Latin America.* Lewisburg, PA: Bucknell University Press.

Asturias, Miguel Ángel. 1988. *Men of Maize.* Translated by Gerald Martin (Original: *Hombres de maíz,* 1949). London: Verso.

Bell, Michael. 2010. "García Márquez, Magical Realism and World Literature." In *The Cambridge Companion to Gabriel García Márquez*, edited by Philip Swanson, 179–95. Cambridge: Cambridge University Press.

Berman, Bruce J. 2006. "The Ordeal of Modernity in an Age of Terror." *African Studies Review* 49 (1): 1–14.

Bhabha, Homi. 1994. *The Location of Culture*. London: Routledge.

Bowers, Maggie Ann. 2020. "Magical Realism and Indigeneity: From Appropriation to Resurgence." In *Magical Realism and Literature*, edited by Christopher Warnes and Kim Anderson Sasser, 49–63. Cambridge and New York: Cambridge University Press.

Camps, Martín. 2014. "The Plague of Modernity: Macondo, Inc. and the Branding of 'Magical' Latin America." In *Critical Insights: Magical Realism*, edited by Ignacio López-Calvo, 84–96. Ipswich, MA: Salem Press/Grey House Publishing.

Carpentier, Alejo. [1949] 1986. *El reino de esto mundo* [The Kingdom of this World]. Barcelona: Seix Barrel.

Conniff, Brian. 1990. "The Dark Side of Magical Realism: Science, Oppression, and Apocalypse in *One Hundred Years of Solitude*." *Modern Fiction Studies* 36 (2): 167–79.

Cooper, Brenda. 1998. *Magical Realism in West African Fiction: Seeing with a Third Eye*. London: Routledge.

Dussel, Enrique. 2000. "Europe, Modernity and Eurocentrism: The Semantic Slippage of the Concept of Europe." *Nepantla*: *Views from South* 1 (3): 465–77.

Faris, Wendy B. 2004. *Ordinary Enchantments: Magical Realism and the Remystification of Narrative*. Nashville, TN: Vanderbilt University Press.

Friedman, Susan Stanford. 2015. *Planetary Modernisms: Provocations on Modernity Across Time*. New York: Columbia University Press.

García Márquez, Gabriel. 1972. *One Hundred Years of Solitude*. Translated by Gregory Rabassa (Original: *Cien años de soledad*, 1967). London: Penguin.

García Márquez, Gabriel. 1982. "Nobel Lecture: The Solitude of Latin America." (Original: "La soledad de América Latina," 1982).

Accessed 3 November, 2021. https://www.nobelprize.org/prizes/literature/1982/marquez/lecture.

Gaonkar, Dilip Parameshwar. 2001. *Alternative Modernities.* Durham, NC: Duke University Press.

Holgate, Ben. 2019. *Climate and Crises: Magical Realism as Environmental Discourse.* London: Routledge.

Larrain, Jorge. 2000. *Identity and Modernity in Latin America.* Cambridge: Polity Press.

Moretti, Franco. 1996. *Modern Epic: The World-System from Goethe to García Márquez.* Translated by Quintin Hoare. (Original: *Opere mondo: Saggio sulla forma epica dal Faust a Cent'anni di solitudine,* 1994). London and New York: Verso.

Morrison, Toni. 1988. *Beloved.* London: Picador/Chatto and Windus.

Ngũgĩ wa Thiong'o. 2007. *Wizard of the Crow.* Translated by Ngũgĩ wa Thiong'o (Original: *Mũrogi wa Kagogo,* 2004). London: Vintage.

Nixon, Rob. 2011. *Slow Violence and the Environmentalism of the Poor.* Cambridge, MA: Harvard University Press.

Olaoluwa, Senayon. 2008. "Between Magic and Logic: Globalization and the Challenge of Medical Collaboration in Ngugi's *Wizard of the Crow.*" *Perspectives on Global Development and Technology* 7: 201–22.

Riach, Graham. 2020. "Myth, Orality and the African Novel." In *Magical Realism and Literature,* edited by Christopher Warnes and Kim Anderson Sasser, 148–63. Cambridge and New York: Cambridge University Press.

Rushdie, Salman. 1991. *Imaginary Homelands: Essays and Criticism 1981–1991.* London: Granta/Viking.

Siskind, Mariano. 2015. "The Genres of World Literature: The Case of Magical Realism." In *The Routledge Companion to World Literature,* edited by David Damrosch, Theo D'Haen, and Djelal Kadir, n.p. Abingdon Oxford, New York: Routledge and Boston, MA: Credo Reference.

Williams, Raymond L. 2010. "An Eco-Critical Reading of *One Hundred Years of Solitude.*" In *The Cambridge Companion to Gabriel García*

Márquez, edited by Philip Swanson, 64–77. Cambridge: Cambridge University Press.

Warwick Research Collective. 2015. *Combined and Uneven Development: Towards a New Theory of World-Literature.* Liverpool: Liverpool University Press.

What's in a World? Rerouting World Literature with *Lotus* and the Afro-Asian Writers' Association

Lucy Gasser

The widely-cited turn towards World Literature Studies has been accompanied by a number of disciplinary debates about how best to understand that "world literature" which it might make its object of study. In this chapter, I propose to read the Afro-Asian Writers' Association and its trilingual quarterly journal *Lotus* at the intersection of these discussions, as manifesting a world literature in-the-making premised on South-South relations. Scholars increasingly seem to agree that amongst the things world literature *shouldn't* be is an unexamined reproduction of Eurocentric literary canons. In the work of scholars such as Gayatri Spivak (2005) and Emily Apter (2013), an awareness for structural inequalities undergirds a cautioning "against world literature" when the feasibility of a World Literature Studies entails steamrolling over difference and over-confidence in the presumption of translatability. Eric Hayot (2012) and Franco Moretti (2013) are amongst those to seek methodological innovations in the pursuit of restructuring how scholars might "do" world literature. Hayot (2012) critiques the remedy of merely inserting non-western writings into western scholarly frameworks as inadequate: "The furniture changes; the foundation is unmoved" (5). Moretti's suggested alternatives include the quantitative bent of analyses performed under the sign of "distant reading". Pheng Cheah (2016), in turn, has argued for world literature to be understood as a site and agent of "world-making activity" (2). Systemic inequality across the globe suggests, for him, that the need for the "opening of other worlds [. . .] is most acute in postcoloniality (11–12).[1]

1 I would like to extend my gratitude to Alain Féry and the editors of this volume, for their constructive comments on an earlier draft of this paper.

Many of these arguments have in common that they call for recognising, or crafting alternatives to, the historical Global North bias in formulations of world literature and ways of reading it. Such a call speaks to a possible motivational alignment with scholarship that has long been produced under the auspices of Postcolonial Studies, even as the pivot towards World Literature Studies has been criticized as entailing a depoliticization of "the ailing non-identical category of postcolonial literature" (Robbins 2012, 383). By contrast, when read as institutional successor to a fatigued Comparative Literature Studies, the turn towards world literature has been framed "as the remaking of comparative literature after the multicultural debates and the disciplinary critique of Eurocentrism" (Warwick Research Collective 2015, 4).

Though much is made of their differences, all three disciplinary categories—Comparative Literature, World Literature, and Postcolonial Studies—have in common that the discussions they produce have historically tended to be routed via the colonial metropole, or its successor "centres" in the Global North. In Postcolonial Studies, this emerged in the figuration of a literature of riposte, or rebuttal—perhaps most astutely formulated as "the empire writes back" (Ashcroft, Griffiths, and Tiffin 1989). One of the pre-eminent examples of writing in this mode might be Chinua Achebe's *Things Fall Apart*, a once counter-canonical text that has since achieved a canonical status of its own. Fundamentally, though, when literatures of the postcolonial South are articulated in this way, they are—despite the certainly emancipatory energy such texts often had—still being given meaning in relation to a figure of Europe. As such, they are defined in negative or derivative terms: as not-Europe; as repudiating European colonial epistemological and cultural violence.

The Eurocentric leanings of Comparative Literature Studies are well-attested to by now and form part of the grounds from which an interest in world literature has emerged. Traditional Comparative Literature syllabi and anthologies produced in the Global North have frequently indicated a very limited understanding of the literatures that warrant "comparison". Scholars have critiqued the terms in which texts from beyond this traditional scope have been read when they do enter the conversation, with readers "likely to impose domestic literary values on the foreign work" (Damrosch 2003, 4) and approaches taken that produce "literary value by placing authors and artists into an already existing theory" (Hayot 2012, 5). In an early intervention in these debates, Moretti (2004) posited that the "way we imagine comparative literature is a mirror of how we see the world" (81). Many iterations of institutionalized Comparative Literature Studies would thus suggest an extremely restricted sense of "the world" that merits mirroring. This entails implicit ascriptions of marginality, which emerge from and are perpetuated by systems of knowledge production historically determined by coloniality to produce the marginalization of some (in the Global South) to the benefit of others (in the Global North). As Aamir Mufti (2016) puts it in his critique of English as overwhelmingly the language that mediates so much of "world" literature, the "ability to think 'the world' itself, whether in literary-critical thinking or other discourses and practices, is hardly distributed evenly across the world" (10). These are structures in which I—as a scholar writing in English and situated in the Global North—am implicated, too.

For many thinkers, the turn towards world literature, then, has taken its impulse from a desire to be more inclusive of marginalized voices. Nonetheless, World Literature (Studies) is far from unencumbered by Eurocentric legacies. It is very often constructed as genealogically indebted to a European literary tradition, as evidenced in oft-cited references to Goethe's coining of *Weltliteratur* in conversation with Eckermann in 1827 (Goethe and Eckermann 1984). As Alexander Beecroft (2010) puts it,

> theories of world literature, then, are in fact frequently theories of European literature and only secondarily of the ways non-European literatures find themselves integrated into the European world system, leaving little room to discuss, for example, inter-Asian literary relations, which from the perspectives of the world system are seen as minor links between peripheries. (266)

This chapter draws to the fore precisely such "minor links between peripheries" in its delineation of a world literature routed through Afro–Asian relations. Indeed, reading such calls alongside an upsurge in the demand for an increased study of South–South relations (wa Ngugi 2012; Mwangi 2009) suggests that it might be useful to look for resources for reimagining and re-triangulating the "world" of world literature with historically elided relations in mind. What kind of world, and what kind of world literature, emerge from cultural exchanges that are not routed via the colonial metropole, or Eurocentric renditions of World Literature? Whose world, and whose world literature, might thus be configured?

In this chapter, I read the Afro-Asian Writers' Association (AAWA), and specifically its quarterly literary journal *Lotus,* as the crystallisation of its participants' efforts to produce a world literature of their own: a world literature predicated on South–South exchange and relations. These practices of producing and, to some extent, studying world literature do not entail wilfully excising Europe from the equation altogether, but often enough render it peripheral or incidental: one possible but not compulsory reference point. This is ultimately in harmony with the call to "provincialize" Europe, perhaps most audibly voiced in Dipesh Chakrabarty's (2000) influential work, which sought not to remove or erase European epistemology, but constitute it as one amongst many. In this sense, for Chakrabarty, "provincializing Europe cannot ever be a project of shunning European thought" (255). Mukoma wa Ngugi's (2012) formulation is essentially in agreement with this understanding of a desirable relationship to the west: "The goal is not to sublimate or ignore the West [. . .]. The goal is to be in relation with the West as with everyone else" (3). While Chakrabarty is concerned with "Europe" and wa Ngugi with the "West", I put a closer discussion of the distinction between the two to the side for the moment, since further elaborating on Europe or the west is not a focal point of this chapter, although they remain in its peripheral vision. What these terms refer to emerges as a relatively indistinct agglomeration in the texts I read below. The point is to focus on lateral—or what are sometimes called "horizontal" (Yoon 2015,

234; Lewis 2018, n.p.)—relations within the Global South not predicated on a presumptive primary or prior relationship to the Global North. I propose to read the Afro-Asian Writers' Association and *Lotus* as instructive manifestations of such lateral relations.

The Afro-Asian Writers' Association and *Lotus*

At the silver jubilee conference of the AAWA held in Tashkent in 1983, then Secretary General of the Association Alex La Guma (1984) dated the origins of the movement to a conference held in India in 1956 (50). The brief history of the movement printed in *Lotus* the following year takes the same starting point: "In 1956 Delhi hosted the first ever international meeting of Eastern writers in which 17 Asian countries took part. [. . . This] gave birth to the idea of creating a movement of Afro-Asian writers" (Faizi 1984, 11). The AAWA officially emerged from the Permanent Bureau of Afro–Asian Writers, founded at the first Conference of Afro–Asian Writers hosted in Tashkent in October 1958. This congress had its precursor in the first meeting of the Afro-Asian People's Solidarity Organisation (AAPSO) held in Cairo from December 1957 to January 1958. Further conferences of the AAWA were held in Cairo (1962), Beirut (1967), New Delhi (1970), Alma Ata (1973), Luanda (1979), Tashkent (1983), and Tunis (1988).

The precursor publication to *Lotus* was the journal *Afro-Asian Writings*, which appeared between 1967 and 1970. The AAWA issued *Lotus* from 1971 until 1991 in English, French and Arabic (Halim 2012, 565). The Arabic edition was published first in Beirut and then in Tunis (due to the bombing of the Beirut offices in 1982), and the English and French editions were printed by the Solidarity Committee of the German Democratic Republic in East Berlin (Faiz 1983, 16). According to translators who worked for the journal, it would have been available "to writers' unions and through subscription to libraries [and] was also sold in some bookstores in African and Asian countries" (Halim 2017, n. p.). Annual subscription cost $8.00 including postage. From 1968 to 1983, the Association also awarded the Lotus Prize for literature, which has been described as an "Afro-Asian Nobel at a time when very few writers from these continents were awarded an actual Nobel" (Djagalov 2019, n. p.).

The AAWA and *Lotus* manifest the making of a world literature premised on South–South relations as an exchange of equals. Differences in what is construed as "development" do signal an idea that some of the interlocutors of these South–South conversations might be "further along" than others. Yet the participants can be read as equals in the sense that, in contradistinction to the colonial set-up, there is no figuration of naturalized inferiority of any of the parties. This is not to represent either the AAWA or *Lotus* as a utopian accumulation of the "Bandung Spirit", with its hopes and dreams for what was at the time called the Third World—although certainly the genealogy of the Association and its publication have their roots in the conference that took place in Indonesia in 1955. At the subsequent conference in Cairo two years later, AAPSO framed itself as the embodiment of the principles formulated at Bandung (Yoon 2015, 240), and La Guma in his address of 1983 placed the AAWA's work in a lineage with Bandung, too (1984, 50).

Scholarly interest in Bandung has surged in recent years, arguably as a result of a similar injunction that has emerged in other disciplines, to reconfigure histories of the Cold War in ways that don't relegate its Global South participants to the role of peripheral, passive onlookers. As Christopher Lee points out, also of tendencies in Area Studies,

> Afro-Asian relations have been marginalized until quite recently by conceptual frameworks that have either centred historical change as emanating from Europe—world systems theory being a key example—or emphasized the local and regional dynamics of African and Asian communities making their own history, if not always under conditions of their choosing. (Lee 2010, 20)

The Bandung conference's celebrated "spirit" had an invigorating effect on the "Third World", which, with Vijay Prashad (2007), was "not a place. It was a project" that was always worldly in its aspirations as its participants "dreamed of a new world" (xv) and sought alternatives to being bullied or co-opted by the Cold War superpowers. At the same time, scholars like Chakrabarty (2005) have warned against overstating the cohesion of the "movement" represented by Bandung, with its "shallow intellectual unity" (4814).

Despite the repeated invocation of avowedly worldly intentions and a commitment to "Third-Worldism", the AAWA, like Bandung before it, failed to meaningfully include Latin America in its efforts to unite those invested in its anti-imperial project (Halim 2017, n. p.). This was the case both within the ambit of writers published, and of texts addressed. It is, indeed, due to this elision that Robert Young (2001) places the birth of postcolonialism, which others have seen at Bandung, rather with the *Tricontinental* journal established by the Afro-Asian Latin American People's Solidarity Organization, or *Organización de Solidaridad con los Pueblos de Asia, África y América Latina* (OSPAAAL), after the Havana conference of 1966 (213). While *Lotus* included occasional contributions from and discussions of Latin American writers, they are exceptions rather than the rule, and Latin America remains, for the most part, a blind spot in the journal and its exchange networks (see also Halim 2012, 578–82).

There is no disputing that the AAWA was, against the grain of the non-alignment espoused at Bandung, very much implicated in Cold War power struggles. The Association and its work were certainly cynically co-opted by the Soviet Union (Schulze-Engler 2020, 122), which was fundamentally involved in its constitution and furnished it with financing. The failure of non-alignment is not least signalled by the founding conference having taken place in Uzbekistan, and the Charter of 1983, for one, was published not only in the three languages of *Lotus*, but also in Russian; the English and French editions of the journal, as previously mentioned, were printed in the GDR. The Soviet Union's involvement was not covert, and its support was fondly remembered by some of the AAWA's members well after the Union's dissolution. Bhisham Sahni (2015), in his memoirs published in the original Hindi in 2004, would write of this time:

> The Soviet Union was definitely instrumental in bringing the Afro-Asian nations closer to one another, for building world peace, and for the common goals of those nations. It encouraged feelings of

> mutual cooperation, but once the Soviet Union was dissolved, the alliance of the Afro-Asian nations also fell apart. I think that it was very unfortunate. It was for the benefit of everyone to have kept the unity of the Afro-Asian nations intact. (n. p.)

All the same, Global South actors who participated in the Association and its publication asserted their agency in myriad ways and conjugated their participation in Cold War power plays according to national and personal interests. The AAWA and *Lotus* provide documents of these various interventions and indicate negotiations of the given geopolitical situation that were more often than not pragmatic and strategic.

The first issue of *Lotus* was published in 1968, a year after revelations broke about the CIA-backing, through the Congress for Cultural Freedom, of journals *Encounter* and *Hiwar* (Halim 2012, 569). The Association should also be read within the context from which it emerged, and *Lotus* be understood as not just implicated in the Cold War's cultural front, but likely born of it—without this rendering Global South participants as passive objects in the historiography of the Cold War.

The participants of the AAWA were to a large extent held together by an understanding of sharing a history of colonial oppression. This echoes precisely those configurations, described above, which are routed via the erstwhile colonial "centre". The cohesion of the AAWA is articulated in terms of, or as derived from, a relationship to the colonial metropole; solidarities thereby furnished are fundamentally hinged to an understanding of shared victimhood (Schulze-Engler 2020, 119). The AAWA's charters repeatedly testify to members' understanding of themselves and their coherence as a group in these terms: "The Association unites [. . .] all writers who stand for the struggle against imperialism, colonialism, neocolonialism" (Afro-Asian Writers Association 1980, 1; 1983, 1).

While united, then, as a result of understanding themselves as sharing pasts of colonial oppression, the cultural production embodied by *Lotus* is fuelled by a sense of common objectives and thus often enough essentially forward-looking. These writers also understood themselves as participating in the fashioning of a new canon of world literature going forward. As La Guma wrote in a piece published in 1973, the journal was bringing Afro-Asian literature "into the arena of world literature" (1973, 132–33). His formulation implies a pre-existing world literature, but as my discussion will show, many of the contributions to *Lotus* suggest a more fundamental restructuring of what is understood as constituting world literature, and the "world" manifested therein. They are, in the first place, concerned with building a new canon of world literature, but, beyond this, their exchanges and discussions stage re-triangulated ways of making, reading, and relating to literary worlds.

The charters and publications of the AAWA were put together by an extremely heterogeneous array of individuals, who by no means produced a uniform understanding of what the priorities of *Lotus* were or should be. Nonetheless, as a set of publications that moved through the world as a unit of sorts, I read *Lotus* as a cumulatively produced text that circulated in and through the global South with a certain influential power.

On Configurations of World

In the first component of my argument, I pursue a discussion of world literature in a more or less descriptive, canonical sense: as a body of writings that travel and circulate beyond the context of their own production. Scholars such as David Damrosch (2003) have gone to lengths to reject the understanding of world literature as merely a "set canon of texts" (281). The AAWA's investment in enlarging and augmenting such a "set canon" indicates that these goals were not at odds with also restructuring the formation of such a canon more fundamentally. The configuration of world literature the AAWA and *Lotus* participate in producing denies the adequacy of the existing "set" canon, in the sense of a body of works deemed to "qualify" for inclusion. They expose the insufficiency of a canon in which cultural production of the Global North enjoys the greatest representation and sets the terms of discussion. They also contest the conception of "world" this presumes. Their modulation of the "world" in their world literature differs structurally from established canons in that Africa and Asia are the nodes that determined the exchanges along which this world literature is routed. What was at stake was not an expansion to include texts which received Euro-American canons long deemed "peripheral", but a reshuffling of that presumptive peripherality.

This is not to say that these writers and their texts don't also engage with a figure of Europe in a mode perhaps better described as writing *against* than "writing back". They do this by putting Europe's supposed desirability up for scrutiny, as in William Saidi's (1975) "Study from Zambia". In the article, Saidi comes out in favour of "a break with all things 'Western'", not least because "the country is faced with challenging economic struggle against the racist regimes, which would love to see us sink in expensive scotch whisky and caviar" (11). This entails a critique of the wicked west's decadence, certainly—but its primary concern is with domestic Zambian politics. This prefigures trends Evan Mwangi has identified in contemporary African novels, which

> engage in a politics that is more scathing in its attack on wayward Africans than on the imperial West [...] indicating that Africans can contribute to a resolution to their own problems rather than blaming colonialists and outsiders for all the problems on the continent. (Mwangi 2009, 2)

This is, again, a figuration in which the role played by the Global North is peripheral.

One of the early critiques levelled at a literature of riposte in the postcolonial South was that it implicitly appealed for European legitimation, not least when it was penned in a colonial language (wa Thiong'o 1986). In the world literature in-the-making of the AAWA and *Lotus*, there was certainly a measure of authentication at play, in terms of the participants fashioning processes that sought to establish their writings as legitimately constituting a canon worth reading and writing about. However, this validation was happening between Afro-

Asian discussants and, as I will go on to show, at least partially beyond consecration from the Global North.

Harking back to what is often positioned as the European fountainhead of "world literature", Beecroft points out that when Goethe announces that the time of national literatures is passing,

> it is in fact only through the recent construction of the "national literature" that Goethe's *Weltliteratur* will be possible and will have to be understood. Only once literature has been broken down into national units can those units be recombined to constitute a "world literature". [...]
> It is only when literature begins to be "national" that it can yearn to transcend those bonds, and to belong to the world. (Beecroft 2013, 3)

These concerns refract differently when moved into Afro-Asian contexts in which national borders and national literatures, as Europeans had come to know and develop them, were a foreign import (and often enough a violently imposed one). In this framing, European *Weltliteratur* is cast as the origin point of a transcendence that its own epistemological structures rendered necessary.

In what follows, I seek to understand world literature beyond these confines because the relations and exchanges drawn forward here are refigurations of literary-cultural circuits that in some cases precede colonial and European intervention. All the same, it is absolutely the case that contributors to *Lotus* more often than not appear to have understood themselves as representatives of their nations. A recurring emphasis on the importance of fostering "indigenous" literatures is for the most part pinned to such nation-based, and often enough nationalist, constructions.

Lotus and the AAWA understood themselves as building and intervening in world literature from their earliest conceptions. This was expressed at the Tashkent conference in 1958, as evidenced in the permanent bureau's documentation of the proceedings: "We the writers of Africa and Asia, have come together here in Tashkent and have discussed issues of importance to us, writers, and to world literature" (Permanent Bureau of Afro-Asian Writers 1970, 23). Formulations like La Guma's (1973) previously cited call to enter "the arena of world literature" (132–33) seem to strive for the inclusion of Afro-Asian writings into a pre-existing canon of world literature which has previously ignored or excluded them. In this sense, a number of the AAWA's participants were doing advocacy work for the "value" of their own national literatures as constituting world literature too. For example, Clariss Ratsifandriamahanana (1984) urgently pleaded for the need to translate Malagasy literature, because "our literature matches some of the best of world's literature [. . .]. We could contribute to the world treasure house of literature" (70).

Nonetheless, contributions to *Lotus* frequently also indicate a rewriting of the understanding of how that world literature should be constituted. This world literature, significantly, was reconfiguring marginality in the scope of what "counted" as world literature. An example would be a piece written by Lodongiyn Tudev (1975) in a special issue on Mongolian literature: "Today, the spiritual life of Mongols is inseparable from the treasures of world literature" (153). Tudev calls on a long-lived legacy of cultural production and exchange for his country, "a land of ancient culture [and] centuries-old traditions of literary contacts" (152) to produce an interconnected literary history that would deny the attribution of either belatedness or peripherality to Mongolia and its cultural production. The writers involved in the AAWA and *Lotus* were actively participating in configuring their own canon of world literature whose content and frames of reference were Afro-Asian. As Duncan Yoon (2015) notes of an anthology published by the bureau in 1963, "it is one of the first anthologies of world literature compiled exclusively with non-Western contributions" (246).

For Rossen Djagalov, in fact, the cultural production fostered by the association and its journal represent a postcolonial canon in-the-making. He points particularly to the winners of the Lotus Prize, a list of literary luminaries who are today likely to appear in many a syllabus of must-read postcolonial cultural production, including Sembène Ousmane (1971), Ngũgĩ wa Thiong'o (1973), and Chinua Achebe (1975). Significantly, Djagalov (2017) indicates that "many of the recipients received the award well before they acquired a significant literary reputation among Western publics" (n. p.). This demonstrates that what was under construction was a world literature in a canonical sense beyond approval and/or consecration from the Global North.

A Russian-language transcript of the discussion that took place in Cairo in 1970 amongst jury members for the Lotus Prize of that year, found in the Russian State Archive for Literature and the Arts and translated by Djagalov, is indicative of the varying views on how this legitimation should be achieved. It suggests that the participants of this conversation were quite consciously and strategically negotiating political and literary aspects in their deliberations. General Secretary at the time, Youssef El-Sebai, indicates the value of having the then Prime Minister of India—the conference host that year—Indira Gandhi conduct the prize-giving in Delhi as it "will help raise the prestige of the conference and the prize" (quoted in Djagalov 2019, n. p.). He goes on to suggest that they consider awarding a Lotus Prize to writers whose nations are currently in the throes of liberation struggles. Doudou Gueye, Senegalese representative for the Permanent Bureau, in contrast, takes the view that awarding the prize on the basis of a political agenda without recourse to the literary merits "will reduce the stature of the prize" (quoted in Djagalov 2019, n. p.). Soviet representative Anatoly Sofronov, in his turn, proposes the Uzbek poet Zulfiya, on the grounds that she "represents the Soviet East, and [is] not only a major poet, but also, importantly, a female writer" (quoted in Djagalov 2019, n. p.). This is in keeping with an oft-propagated narrative of the Soviet Union's progressiveness in combatting sexism—but it is worth noting that by and large, the AAWA and *Lotus* appear to have been overwhelmingly a boys' club.

The jury's deliberations make clear that the members are strategically negotiating the canonization of their prize and of the literature it is supposed to honour. With the prize, they aim to increase the visibility and prestige of a world literature whose foundations and determining co-ordinates are Afro–Asian. In the sense that the selection of Lotus Prize-winners prefigured a canon of postcolonial writers now well-established, the canonization under construction was to some extent successful. In 1983, Faiz Ahmed Faiz, then editor-in-chief of *Lotus*, delineated the as-yet-unfulfilled projects of the AAWA, suggesting that the Association's intentions lay with developing their own canonization mechanisms. These included

> the setting-up of a publishing house of Afro-Asian literature, compiling a biographic dictionary of Afro-Asian writers, publication of translations of Afro-Asian classics into major European languages, introducing departments of Afro-Asian literature into national universities. (Faiz 1984, 56)

The AAWA's plans thus clearly included building their own legitimating infrastructure around the literature and writers they were weaving into a world literature in-the-making. A further strain of these canonization practices emerges in the commemoration implicit in much of the mourning work done by the journal and by speeches given at the Association's various gatherings. These include many elegiac articles and special issues dedicated to the memory of deceased participants, of whose presence "the ranks of world literature have been deprived" (Editor 1984, 4).

But more than rearticulating a descriptive canon, the writers contributing to *Lotus* show themselves to be actively grappling with the normative dimensions of a world literature, and with that "world" which a world literature was to be constituted by. Their confrontations with these questions entailed implicit and explicit critiques of colonization and its imperial epistemologies. While they often speak to a definition in terms of the Europe they were rejecting, they also construct alternative temporalities and histories that are deeply rooted in Africa's and Asia's *pre*colonial pasts. Crucially, rich histories of ancient civilizations and cultures that predate European colonial invasion are something the two continents are constructed as having in common. As such, they serve as grounds for connection and alliance between them prior to their being united solely in rejection of colonial oppression. In Faiz's (1984) artful phrasing at the 1958 conference, "It was a festival of reunion between old friends who had never met before, between ancient lovers parted over the centuries" (53). As he describes it, the Afro-Asian writer has

> covered, on the one hand, ancient cultural links with his Asian and African neighbours penned off by imperialist enclosures. On the other hand, the community of suffering and humiliation, of struggle and liberation, brought the peoples of our continents close together in mind and spirit. (56)

Alignment on the basis of anti-imperialism finds its counterweight in alignment on the basis of "ancient cultural links". Contributions that voice the latter as grounds for community between Africa and Asia are commonplace in articles in *Lotus,* and in the speeches made at the AAWA's meetings, which were sometimes printed in the journal. Bhisahm Sahni (1983), in his address configures those he speaks to as united by just such histories: "Most of us have come from many an ancient city of Asia and Africa which have been cradles of great civilizations and culture. We convey to Tashkent, on behalf of all those ancient cities, warm, sisterly, fraternal greetings" (63). At a meeting of the Executive Council in Vietnam in 1982, local representative, To Khyu (1983) describes those present "as true literary representatives of our two giant continents in the homeland of the world's oldest civilisations, one of the places where history dawned and where man first used the wonderful idioms of art and poetry" (127). He too names histories of colonial oppression, but as with Faiz, the history of what links these continents starts earlier. Sharing histories of ancient civilizations and cultures also prepares the ground for the Association's shared present and forward-looking concerns, as the forum furnished by the congress "enriches us by bringing us into closer contact with the great literary inheritance of our respective countries of Asia and Africa and with our present day literary endeavours" (Sahni 1983, 63).

In the cultural imaginary thus cumulatively produced by contributors to *Lotus*, a duty to the future is being configured—and this is also what serves to unite the AAWA's participants. This forward-looking cause for alignment and community finds frequent expression: "Asia and Africa are truly rich—in natural resources, cultural legacy, good will and in their efforts for the future" (Khyu 1983, 128); "We, the writers [. . .] are responsible for the future" (Rashidov 1983, 10); "Wc are all of us responsible for the future" (Ozerov 1984, 22). As anxieties about a possible nuclear war mount and nuclear disarmament becomes a recurring concern, there is also an increase in voicing these forward-looking duties in terms of a planetary future, with the Association members naming a responsibility "to ensure a peaceful future for humanity" (Executive Council of AAWA 1983b, 141). Shared pasts of ancient interconnected civilizations, colonial oppression, and future-oriented duties combine with the canonization work the AAWA had been participating in during the years of its existence to produce a sense that "through joint action [. . .] a new type of writer has come to the fore, the writer who loves his country and works for both his native culture and for world literature" (Ozerov 1984, 18).

The understanding of the world constituted in world literature thus produced, then, speaks to precolonial histories, and does so with a particular emphasis on the valence of interconnectedness in those histories. In a piece called "The Role of Classical Afro-Asian Peoples' Heritage, and Particularly the Arab Heritage, in the Development of Contemporary World Culture", dubbed a "Study from Syria", Salah Dihni (1975) makes an argument for the significance of Arab cultural heritage in shaping "world culture". Explicitly criticizing the definition of contemporary world culture as the "exclusive output of Europe and America" (60–61), Dihni emphasizes that this construction depends on eliding "the role played by the ancient and noble nations of Asia and Africa in shaping world culture" (61). He describes a history when "Europe, then living in darkness, was receiving the cultural heritage of the ancient world through the Arab peoples of North Africa and Western Asia" (61), and includes cultural contributions of "Black African peoples who also studied the stars, and who had their own beliefs, gods and culture" (65). Like Tudev in his delineation of Mongolian "world" literature, he calls on circuits of trade and cultural exchange that predate Europe's self-fashioning as the centre of the civilized world.

Dihni's critique of the European narrative of world culture lies in its presumption of exclusivity. He describes how cultures change and evolve:

> No cultural flourishment can be born from nothingness, just as no flower can grow in a barren desert. All cultures must borrow from and strive on their predecessors, then they develop and change into their own characteristic entities. (Dihni 1975, 62)

This emphasis on exchange carries through a great deal of the AAWA's writing. It is evident in the agenda agreed on in Vietnam in 1982 for the conference to come in Tashkent, which named a desire to foster the "contribution of the Afro–Asian writers' movement to broaden interaction and cross-fertilization between the literatures of East and West" (Executive Council of AAWA 1983a, 146). It appears in commitments to "rejecting the division of cultures into lower and higher, eastern and western" and "build[ing] up the interconnection between all of them with a view to preserving the treasury of world culture as a whole" (Rashidov 1983, 10). It recurs tellingly in the plenary session speech given by Anna Lilova (1984), president of the International Federation of Translators, at Tashkent: "All nations today realise that the development of national cultures and literatures depends to a remarkable degree on how available the cultural heritage of a society is to the members of another society" (67). As in Dihni's understanding, cultural development (putting aside the question of how precisely this is conceived) depends on interaction and sharing. As such, even as the nation as unit of cultural production prevails, it is not viewed as static, and the configuration of a world literature at play is essentially set on transcending its artificial barriers. An understanding of the importance of cultural crosspollination is integral to the type of world literature thus triangulated.

Such historical delineations as emerge here obviously repudiate imperial epistemologies of the beginning of history for colonized territories as the point of colonial contact; of the arrival of colonists on *terra nullius*; of the culture of the European colonial metropole as the apex of human civilization sui generis. They indicate grounds for alliances that predate colonial oppression. More than this, they act as sharp critique of the epistemological arrogance entailed by presuming such a small selection of cultural contributions to suffice for harnessing thc label of "world". This echoes the reconfiguration of international relations represented by Bandung for Quỳnh N. Phạm and Robbie Shilliam (2016) in that it seeks to "redefine [...] the very idea [...] of who constitutes the global" (16). What is at stake here is what can adequately and meaningfully be understood as constituting the "world"—in formulations like world literature and world culture—and when it begins. *Lotus* repeatedly puts up for scrutiny the use of "world" in an exclusive mode. The configurations of world represented in the journal are characterized by their inclusivity and their mutual constitution. Between Sahni's (1983) enunciation of the "galaxy of poets and writers" (63), Dihni's ancient African star studies, and a cumulatively produced concern for a future endangered by nuclear proliferation, these worldly dimensions are sometimes even discursively invoked in planetary and cosmic terms.

Constitutive of this quality of inclusive worldliness is an emphasis on relations and exchange. In this way, AAWA and *Lotus* manifest an array of practices of world literature which sees their contributors understanding world literature and its "world" as something they are participating in making and studying. These reading practices are primarily invested in South-South relations.

South-South Ways of Reading: Translations and Networks

South-South reading practices crystallize in translational work and networks of cultural production. The problem of routing via the colonial metropole is to some extent mirrored in the predominant trajectories of translation in *Lotus*. Published in English, French and Arabic, it is likely that contributions were oftentimes translated to and from Arabic via one of the colonial languages, English and French (Halim 2012, 572). The problem of translation is a long-standing and much-discussed one in countries of the postcolonial South, which flowered in debates whose key proponents in Africa were once represented on opposite sides by Ngũgĩ wa Thiong'o and Chinua Achebe.

These are debates with which the contributors to *Lotus* are familiar and consciously grappling. As Rosette Francis (1975) writes in a review of a collection published by Ngũgĩ wa Thiong'o:

> Ngugi who cherishes his African name writes mainly for an African public. The problems of language and publication in Africa and the desire to reach the biggest number of readers have made many African writers address non-African readers and meet the demands of western publishing houses looking for the exotic. (146)

In a "Study from the Philippines" F. Sionil Jose (1983) laments the marginalization of his native language Ilokano and critiques the literary output of "the Illustrados", whom he dubs the first educated Filipinos (in western terms). As he sees it, "most of the writing was an effort to prove that Filipinos had a glorious past, that men of achievement such as the Illustrados deserved seats in the Spanish parliament" (86). European-colonial legitimation is again what is at stake here, and Jose is quite pragmatically reconciled to the fact that colonial languages continue to figure large, for the moment, in Afro-Asian cultural production. In a "Study from Tanzania", J.P. Mbonde (1975) points to the intersection of such pragmatic concerns with questions of class and education: "as far as the situation of the reading public in my country is concerned it is basically the same class that can read foreign languages" (27).

In postcolonial contexts, translation has been marked by an implicit insistence on the necessity of a European language as a determining node or transit point, with translation mostly occurring *from* languages indigenous to colonial territories, *into* a European language, and much more rarely in the other direction, let alone between indigenous languages (Bassnett and Trivedi 1999, 5). This is certainly affected by pragmatic concerns of reaching the largest audience possible and structures of a literary market which sees scant profit in the latter—as La Guma (1975) notes in an article on South African literature under apartheid: "the English-speaking South African [. . .] has a world language at his disposal. It is partly a question of economics. Book production for a tiny market is unprofitable" (18). In his discussion of world literature, Aamir Mufti (2016) gives cause to be critical of the reverberations of the ubiquity of English: "European 'world' languages, above all English, seem to be the not-quite-invisible ether that permeates" (xi) the spaces in which World Literature (Studies) happen.

Djagalov (2017) points out that amongst the Association's key goals was an attempt to reroute the prescriptive trajectories of this literary market, "to forge an international alliance among the literatures of the two continents aimed at consolidating their forces and achieving independence from the publishing centres of Paris, London, and New York" (n. p.). This goal was, of course, entangled in the Soviet Union's cultural agenda in the theatre of Cold War spheres of influence. It also served to carve translational routes that did not necessarily go through the erstwhile colonial metropoles of western Europe.

The AAWA and *Lotus* were keenly attuned to, and invested in, issues surrounding translation. This is evidenced as early as the Cairo conference, whose participants expressed a commitment to "translation to and from the languages of the member countries, and the establishment in every member country of a planning body to coordinate the translation movement" (Afro-Asian Peoples' Solidarity Conference 1958, 60). It is sustained in the Association's charters, which consistently name "encouraging literary exchange and translation on the widest scale" (Afro-Asian Writers Association 1980, 2 and 1983, 2) amongst their "Aims and Objectives".

Hala Halim (2012) has argued for the importance of the fact that, beyond being produced in the colonial languages of English and French, *Lotus*'s publication "in Arabic, a Third World language, in and of itself contests the hegemony of imperialism's linguistic legacy" (572). Arabic animated the journal's capacity to reroute its world literature without necessary recourse to a language of the colonial metropole—though, as previously indicated, translation to and from Arabic was often executed via one of the colonial languages.

Halim's (2012) interviews with journal editors Al-Kharrat and al-Sha'rani indicate that "producing *Lotus* in other indigenous languages [. . .] was not pursued" (572). An Editor's Note by Youssef El-

Sebai in 1975 suggests that, while such a project was not necessarily attempted in any centralized or consistent capacity, there were instances of such lateral translations taking place:

> The Permanent Bureau, in cooperation with member states, tries to publish "Lotus" and the series in local languages. Up till now, publication of selections from the magazine and series in local languages has been possible in India, Bangladesh, Sri Lanka, the German Democratic Republic, Malaysia and Japan. (4–5)

Tudev's (1975) delineation of Mongolian translational history casts Mongols as having "seven centuries' experience of literary contacts and translation to lean on" (153). This historical lineage of literary translation has germinated such that now

> the Mongolian family library also has on its shelves books by various Afro-Asian writers [. . .]. If, a few years ago, Mongolian writers and translators were mainly working from Russian translation of foreign books, they now translate directly from the following languages: French, English, Spanish, Hindi, Arabic, Japanese, Korean and others. (155)

Though clearly colonial languages like English and Spanish still figure, these lists deny the inevitability of their centrality. Similarly, a delegate from Mauritius, Deepchand Beehari (1984), points out in a plenary speech the historical linguistic richness of his native land: "In my country French, English, Chinese, Urdu, Hindi, Tamil and Arabic were spoken" (79), but for a long time literature was only produced in French. Yet post-independence, Mauritian writers now also work in English, Hindi, Urdu and Creole languages, as he relates. El-Sebai's and Tudev's examples disrupt the established one-way trajectory of translation between dominant colonial languages and marginalized indigenous ones and create the impression of a markedly interconnected translational network whose nodes are not necessarily colonial. Beehari suggests that despite ever-present market concerns, non-colonial languages might be becoming more viable as vehicles for literary transfer.

Lotus serves to make visible networks of cultural production—which include translational work—premised on South-South relations. Whether or not readers of the journal could access it in their own indigenous language (for the most part unlikely), many of them are likely to havc gained a sense of the value of indigenous cultural production and the existence of networks that sought to foster it. La Guma (1975), reporting on South Africa, describes that "political resistance of the African people was kept alive [. . .] also through literature produced from African-owned printing presses [. . .] publishing in African languages. This meant that all literary productions were available to the general African populace" (14). He signals the emancipatory power inherent in the use of indigenous languages even as he grants the pragmatic necessity, as previously mentioned, of writing in English to make use of its currency as a "world language". He reads the Xhosa poet Mghayi as having managed, "by using double meanings [. . .] to compose virulent satires on the regime and the British empire" (14); his satire gets through the censors because they do not speak indigenous languages well enough to grasp the nuances in which the parody inheres.

In a review of the novel *The Marabi Dance* by Modikwe Dikobe, Ali Shalash (1975) describes how it

> appeared in 1973, part of the "Series of African Books" established and edited by the famous Nigerian novelist Tshinwa Etohebi [likely Chinua Achebe] and published by Heinemann in London, the house that gave us around 140 works by African authors from both North and South of the continent. (180)

Graham Huggan (2002) has pointed out that the esteem in which much African literature in English is held today "would be unthinkable without the momentum provided by Heinemann's promotional enterprise, worldwide distributional networks and financial support" (50). All the same, the Heinemann African Writers Series to which Shalash refers, established in the early 1960s, can be charged with marketing "African authenticity" for and to a European and American audience (Huggan 2002, 52–53; see also Lizarríbar 1998). The British-based Heinemann Books, in consciously catering to both African and western readers, does not perform the prioritisation of South-

South relations *Lotus* does. Its ambivalence notwithstanding, the Series certainly speaks to another cultural network that contributors to *Lotus* were increasing the visibility of, as they consecrated the viability of such works of literature from the Global South as a world literature of their own making.

Rerouting World Literature: South-South Relations

Lotus provided a platform for South-South practices of reading. The journal lends insight into how cultural producers and intellectuals from the Global South were talking to each other during this time: what they were reading of each other's work, and how they were conducting conversations about what they read. Though these discussions occasionally make reference to European cultural production, they are still first and foremost concerned with South-South exchange and, as indicated earlier, dubbing these relations South-South should not hinge on a wilful excision of Europe altogether. A primary impression a reader of the journal is likely to walk away with is of the dense networkedness of many of these intellectuals and writers. These networks and the agents who represent their nodes contribute to telling histories of independence struggles and the Cold War that are not primarily routed via the erstwhile colonial centre, nor necessarily via the superpower blocs.

For instance, a 1981 special issue of *Lotus* in commemoration of Tajik poet Mirzo Tursun-zadeh, published under the editorship of Faiz Ahmed Faiz, gives an account by a friend of the poet, Mirza Ibragimov, of a journey to India in 1947. Ibragimov relates how the two are invited to a meeting of a Muslim organization in Calcutta and are asked how they view the setting up of an independent state of Pakistan. Tursun-zadeh's response, which his friend lauds for its diplomacy, is that this is to be determined by Indian Muslims and Hindus themselves. The frames of the conversation conducted here, and the agents of history brought into focus, are triangulated according to Indian Muslims and Hindus, and Muslims in Central Asia (Ibragimov 1981, 31). British colonialists are peripheral to the rendition.

A similarly commemorative piece written by Mulk Raj Anand (1975) tells of his long-term friendship with Sajjad Zaheer, who passed away during the 5th Afro-Asian Writers' Conference in Alma Ata in 1973 (44). Anand's essay relates their meeting as students in London in the early 1930s, their collaborative authorship of the Progressive Writers' Association manifesto, their participation in the struggle for Indian independence upon their return to the sub-continent, and their subsequent separation due to Partition. In 1958, they attended the Tashkent conference together, and in 1970 they worked together to host the AAWA conference held in New Delhi that year. Not only did the AAWA and its publication serve as a platform for building networks and relations between Africa and Asia, it also did this work within the continents. This is explicitly noted, for instance, by Assefa Gabre-Mariam (1983) from Ethiopia in his address to the conference in 1983: the AAWA "strengthened the friendship and solidarity not only among Afro-Asian writers but also among African writers themselves" (65).

Halim (2017) has called the interactions represented in *Lotus* examples of "South-South comparatism", and has suggested that "various articles in the 'Studies' section [. . .] perform *regards croisés*, or intersecting gazes; i.e.: a text by an intellectual from a given African or Asian country addressing another country's culture(s), sometimes with comparatist references" (n. p.). A reader of the journal wouldn't have to look far for examples of this, and the readings and discussions thus communicated could aptly be described as a "network of affinity and awareness" (Lewis 2018, n. p.). The frames of reference for these "studies" are telling of the particular inflections of these networks. For instance, a study from India by Ashis Sanyal (1975) on "Points of View in African Poetry" draws on Léopold Sédar Senghor, Jean-Paul Sartre, Lewis Nkosi and Rabindranath Tagore (32) in order to conduct its wide-ranging assessment of trends in poetry on the African continent. The reviews section provides a stage for similar reading practices, where, in one example, the review of the Ngũgĩ collection addressed earlier—which tells stories and histories of the Kenyan independence struggle—is followed by a review of a Vietnamese collection, *The*

Watchmaker of Dien Bien Phu, by Abdel Moneim Selim (1975), which describes the Vietnamese struggle against US imperialism (151).

Perhaps most tellingly, Ali Shalash's (1975) review of *The Marabi Dance* begins: "Stendahl once remarked that a novel is a streetwalker" (180). The piece thus implicitly starts via an articulation in terms of an established figure of the traditional European canon. The misspelling of the name, though, opens to the possibility of what, to echo Harold Bloom (1997) with a difference, might amount to a productive misreading which serves to "clear imaginative space" (5) for the networks of South-South relations under construction. Mukoma wa Ngugi's (2012) call for rethinking such relations delineates that part of the problem that needs to be addressed is that "the periphery is always located in the third world and the centre is always the west. The European is never the visitor, never in need of hospitality, and never the 'other'—even when in the Global South" (1). Perhaps, however, the *Marabi Dance* review is latently just such a moment when the misspelt European is momentarily an "other", and, as a reference point, is very much relegated to the periphery.

The discussions represented in the charters and protocols of the AAWA and its journal indicate abundant critical self-reflection on the part of their participants about how they want to understand themselves in relation to figurations of the Global North. Or rather, they indicate a capacity to position themselves in no particular or primary relation to Europe, the colonial metropole, or a figure of the west—which I have here allowed to agglomerate into an amorphous accumulation precisely because this is very much how it appears in the social-cultural imaginaries with which *Lotus* is suffused.

In describing her experiences of drawing up an undergraduate survey course in "World Literature", Vilashini Cooppan (2004) proposes world literature as

> not something you are given in full or get by proxy. Not a pre-packaged canon that differs from the traditional one only in its inclusion of a handful of unfamiliar names. Rather, world literature is a way you learn to think, a mode in which you learn to read, and a collective agreement you make to lose something in translation in order to gain something in transformation. (30)

The world literature in-the-making configured in the writings of the AAWA and *Lotus* might serve as training in thinking along different lines and reading in different modes. Drawing forward the Afro-Asian relations and exchanges manifested by the Association and its journal, reroutes a productive conception of world literature that denies the necessity or inevitability of the Global North as a decisive node. The determining coordinates of this world literature are discussants in the Global South, who thus re-triangulate the peripherality which they have too often been assigned.

Bibliography

Afro-Asian Peoples' Solidarity Conference. 1958. *Afro-Asian People's Conference 26 December 1957-1 January 1958. Principal Reports Submitted to the Conference.* Cairo: Permanent Secretariat.

Afro-Asian Writers Association. 1980. *The Charter of the Afro-Asian Writers' Association.* 1. Beirut: Afro-Asian Writers' Association.

Afro-Asian Writers Association. 1983. *The Charter of the Afro-Asian Writers' Association.* 3. Tashkent: Afro-Asian Writers' Association.

Anand, Mulk Raj. 1975. "Some Reminiscences of Sajjad Zaheer." *Lotus* 4 (26): 44–51.

Apter, Emily. 2013. *Against World Literature: On the Politics of Untranslatability.* London: Verso.

Ashcroft, Bill, Gareth Griffiths, and Helen Tiffin, eds. 1989. *The Empire Writes Back.* London: Routledge.

Bassnett, Susan, and Harish Trivedi, eds. 1999. *Post-Colonial Translation: Theory and Practice.* Translation Studies. London: Routledge.

Beecroft, Alexander. 2010. "When Cosmopolitanisms Intersect: An Early Chinese Buddhist Apologetic and World Literature." *Comparative Literature Studies* 47 (3): 266–89.

Beecroft, Alexander. 2013. "Greek, Latin, and the Origins of 'World Literature'." *CLCWeb: Comparative Literature and Culture* 15 (5): 1–9.

Beehari, Deepchand. 1984. "Plenary Session Speech." *Lotus* 54: 78–79.

Bloom, Harold. 1997. *The Anxiety of Influence: A Theory of Poetry*. New York: Oxford University Press.

Chakrabarty, Dipesh. 2000. *Provincializing Europe: Postcolonial Thought and Historical Difference*. Princeton, NJ: Princeton University Press.

Chakrabarty, Dipesh. 2005. "Legacies of Bandung: Decolonisation and the Politics of Culture." *Economic and Political Weekly* 40 (46): 4812–18.

Cheah, Pheng. 2016. *What Is a World?: On Postcolonial Literature as World Literature*. Durham, NC: Duke University Press.

Cooppan, Vilashini. 2004. "Ghosts in the Disciplinary Machine: The Uncanny Life of World Literature." *Comparative Literature Studies* 41 (1): 10–36.

Damrosch, David. 2003. *What Is World Literature?* Princeton, NJ: Princeton University Press.

Dihni, Salah. 1975. "The Role of Classical Afro-Asian Peoples' Heritage, and Particularly the Arab Heritage, in the Development of Contemporary World Culture." Translated by Nihad A. Salem. *Lotus* 2–3 (24/25): 60–69.

Djagalov, Rossen. 2017. "The Afro-Asian Writers Association and Soviet Engagement with Africa." *Black Perspectives*, 2 November. https://www.aaihs.org/the-afro-asian-writers-association-and-soviet-engagement-with-africa/.

Djagalov, Rossen. 2019. "The Lotus Prize for Afro-Asian Literature (1969–1988)." *Afro-Asian Visions: New Perspectives on Decolonisation, the Cold War, and Asian-African Connections*, 6 November. https://medium.com/afro-asian-visions/the-lotus-prize-for-afro-asian-literature-1969-1988-4ee1d2f8bad1.

Editor. 1984. "In This Issue." *Lotus* 55: 4.

El-Sebai, Youssef. 1975. "Editor's Note." Translated by Rosette Francis. *Lotus* 2–3 (24/25): 4–5.

Executive Council of AAWA. 1983a. "Agenda of the 7th Jubilee Conference of Afro-Asian Writers Tashkent, October 1983." *Lotus* 52: 146.

Executive Council of AAWA. 1983b. "Appeal to Writers All Over the World." *Lotus* 52: 141.

Faiz, Faiz Ahmed. 1983. "15 Years of Lotus." *Lotus* 53: 15–17.

Faiz, Faiz Ahmed. 1984. "Address at Inaugural Session of Tashkent Conference 1983." *Lotus* 54: 53–58.

Faizi, Rakhmat. 1984. "About the Movement of Afro-Asian Writers: A Brief History." *Lotus* 54: 11–16.

Francis, Rosette. 1975. "Book Review: Secret Lives." *Lotus* 4 (26): 146–50.

Gabre-Mariam, Assefa. 1983. "Plenary Session Speech." *Lotus* 54: 63–64. Tashkent: Afro-Asian Writers' Association.

Goethe, Johann Wolfgang von, and Johann Peter Eckermann. 1984. *Conversations with Eckermann, 1823–1832*. Translated by John Oxenford (Original: *Johann Peter Eckermann: Gespräche mit Goethe in den letzten Jahren seines Lebens*, 1836). San Francisco, CA: North Point Press.

Halim, Hala. 2012. "Lotus, the Afro-Asian Nexus, and Global South Comparatism." *Comparative Studies of South Asia, Africa and the Middle East* 32 (3): 563–83.

Halim, Hala. 2017. "Afro-Asian Third-Worldism into Global South: The Case of Lotus Journal." *Global South Studies: A Collective Publication with the Global South*, 22 November. https://globalsouthstudies.as.virginia.edu/key-moments/afro-asian-third-worldism-global-south-case-lotus-journal.

Hayot, Eric. 2012. *On Literary Worlds*. Oxford and New York: Oxford University Press.

Huggan, Graham. 2002. *The Postcolonial Exotic: Marketing the Margins*. Abingdon: Routledge.

Ibragimov, Mirza. 1981. "Reason and Talent." *Lotus* 2 Special Issue: "Mirzo Tursun-zadeh—In Commemoration of His 70th Birthday." 30–34.

Jose, F. Sionil. 1983. "The Writer in a Changing Society." *Lotus* 53: 83–90.

Khyu, To. 1983. "We Have a Great Common Duty to Independence, Freedom, Peace, Civilization, Literature and Culture: Statement at Session of Executive Council of AAWA 1982." *Lotus* 52: 127–29.

La Guma, Alex. 1973. "On Short Stories." *Lotus* 17: 132–33.

La Guma, Alex. 1975. "South African Writing Under Apartheid." *Lotus* 1 (23): 11.

La Guma, Alex. 1984. "Address at Inaugural Session of Tashkent Conference 1983." *Lotus* 54: 50–52.

Lee, Christopher J. 2010. *Making a World After Empire: The Bandung Moment and Its Political Afterlives.* Athens, OH: Ohio University Press.

Lewis, Su Lin. 2018. "A Manifesto by the Afro-Asian Networks Research Collective in Radical History Review 131." *Afro-Asian Visions: New Perspectives on Decolonisation, the Cold War, and Asian-African Connections*, 22 June. https://medium.com/afro-asian-visions/a-manifesto-by-the-afro-asian-networks-research-collective-30857823579f.

Lilova, Anna. 1984. "Plenary Session Speech." *Lotus* 54: 67–68.

Lizarríbar, Camille. 1998. *Something Else Will Stand Beside It: The African Writers Series and the Development of African Literature.* Ann Arbor, MI: University of Michigan Press.

Mbonde, J.P. 1975. "The Importance of Translation in the Development and Consolidation of Relations between Writers and Peoples." *Lotus* 2–3 (24/25): 24–29.

Moretti, Franco. 2004. "Conjectures on World Literature." In *Debating World Literature*, edited by Christopher Prendergast, 148–62. London: Verso.

Moretti, Franco. 2013. *Distant Reading.* London and New York: Verso.

Mufti, Aamir R. 2016. *Forget English! Orientalism and World Literatures.* Cambridge, MA: Harvard University Press.

Mwangi, Evan. 2009. *Africa Writes Back to Self: Metafiction, Gender, Sexuality.* Albany, NY: State University of New York Press.

Ngũgĩ wa Thiong'o. 1986. *Decolonising the Mind.* Portsmouth: James Currey/Heinemann.

Ozerov, Vitali. 1984. "Responsibility for the Future." *Lotus* 54: 17–22.

Permanent Bureau of Afro-Asian Writers. 1970. "Appeal to the Writers of the World." In *12 Years, Afro-Asian Writers.* Vol. 23. Cairo: Afro-Asian Writers' Permanent Bureau.

Phạm, Quỳnh N., and Robbie Shilliam, eds. 2016. *Meanings of Bandung: Postcolonial Orders and Decolonial Visions.* London and New York: Rowman and Littlefield International.

Prashad, Vijay. 2007. *The Darker Nations: A People's History of the Third World.* New York: The New Press.

Rashidov, Sharaf. 1983. "Return to Tashkent." *Lotus* 53: 10–14.

Ratsifandriamahanana, Clariss. 1984. "Plenary Session Speech." *Lotus* 54: 69–70.

Robbins, Bruce. 2012. "Uses of World Literature." In *The Routledge Companion to World Literature*, edited by Theo D'haen, David Damrosch, and Djelal Kadir, 383–92. New York: Routledge.

Sahni, Bhisham. 1983. "Plenary Session Speech." *Lotus* 54: 63–64.

Sahni, Bhisham. 2015. *Today's Pasts: A Memoir.* Translated by Snehal Shingavi. New Delhi: Penguin.

Saidi, William. 1975. "Literature in Zambia and the Liberation Struggle." *Lotus* 4 (26): 9–11.

Sanyal, Ashis. 1975. "Points of View in African Poetry." *Lotus* 2–3 (24/25): 31–41.

Schulze-Engler, Frank. 2020. "Entangled Solidarities: African–Asian Writers' Organisations, Anti-Colonial Rhetorics and Afrasian Imaginaries in East African Literature." In *Reconfiguring Transregionalisation in the Global South*, edited by Ross Anthony and Uta Ruppert, 117–39. Cham: Springer International Publishing.

Selim, Abdel Moneim. 1975. "Book Review: *The Watchmaker of Dien Bien Phu.*" Translated by Rosette Francis. *Lotus* 4 (26): 151–53.

Shalash, Ali. 1975. "Book Review: The Marabi Dance by Modikwe Dikobe." Translated by Ahmed Attia. *Lotus* 1 (23): 180–82.

Spivak, Gayatri Chakravorty. 2005. *Death of a Discipline.* New York: Columbia University Press.

Tudev, Lodongiyn. 1975. "World Classics in Mongolia." *Lotus* 2–3 (24/25): 152–53.

Wa Ngugi, Mukoma. 2012. "Rethinking the Global South." *The Journal of Contemporary Thought* 35: 1–6.

Warwick Research Collective. 2015. *Combined and Uneven Development: Towards a New Theory of World-Literature*. Liverpool: Liverpool University Press.

Yoon, Duncan M. 2015. "'Our Forces Have Redoubled': World Literature, Postcolonialism, and the Afro-Asian Writers' Bureau." *Cambridge Journal of Postcolonial Literary Inquiry* 2 (2): 233–52.

Young, Robert J.C. 2001. *Postcolonialism: An Historical Introduction*. Oxford and Malden, MA: Blackwell Publishers.

Bwana Goethe and the Remaking of World Literature: Afrasian Imaginaries in M.G. Vassanji's *The Magic of Saida*

Frank Schulze-Engler

In an intriguing passage in M.G. Vassanji's novel *The Magic of Saida* (2013), the narrator figure, a moderately successful publisher in today's Tanzania, muses about the decision of Omari bin Tamim, a celebrated early-20th-century Swahili poet who composed a long epic poem on "The Coming of the Modern Age", to collaborate with the colonial regime in what was then German East Africa and to write poetry celebrating the power and might of the German colonizers:

> Why that poem, why such abject flattery of the Bwana Mkubwa, the German overlord? Every such falsehood he wrote and uttered was a betrayal of those Kilwa warriors and all the others who had hanged for resisting; it was a betrayal of his language and its beautiful poetry, so much so that it embarrassed; it was a betrayal of his people. Omari knew all that. But he had resolved that there was no alternative to bending to the new order. Who could deny its superiority, its achievement, its strength? Instead of fighting it blindly and arrogantly, and be vanquished, why not take from it? Why not learn to recite a few lines of Bwana Goethe, appreciate the German lied? And as for telling the truth, surely there would come a time; there would come a time to explain, to revoke this Faustian pact. After all, how could a subject's simple-minded homage to the Kaiser be taken at face value? (Vassanji 2013, 150–51)

The idea of "Bwana Goethe", the founding father of the concept of world literature, does not play a major role in *The Magic of Saida*; it is, in fact, evoked just once more in Vassanji's novel, when the slightly drunk German commissioner von Rode, who has taken a liking to Omari and acts as his patron, asks him "have you composed any new verse for us, O Goethe of Ostafrika?" (160). In these instances "Bwana Goethe" clearly stands for a stark cultural hierarchy installed by the

German colonial regime and is invoked as an icon of cultural and literary superiority, in much the same way that Shakespeare was invoked throughout the British Empire (Marcus 2017). To be (ironically and somewhat patronizingly) addressed as "Goethe of Ostafrika" means to be inserted into a hierarchically ordered notion of world literature, where the great name from the Centre is conferred as a badge of honour on a literary subject whose emulation of the Centre's standards is deemed satisfactory by those who are apparently in control of "world literature". It could also be read as a sign of "bending to the new order" of modernity, instigated by German colonialism: a literary practice of submission located somewhere between blatant treason and what Homi Bhabha (1994) has termed "sly civility" (132–44); an "art of the contact zone" (Pratt 1991) that is predicated on the *not yet* before the Faustian Pact with the devil of colonialism can be revoked; a poetics of the waiting room (Chakrabarty 2000, 8–9), where those not yet modern enough according to Eurocentric normative models of modernity, prepare to join world literature as the narrative construction site of mature modernity.

All of this seems very much in tune with major currents in the contemporary world literature debate focussing on a hermeneutics of suspicion regarding the continuing hegemony of the "west" over the "rest", economic structures of literary production that reflect the inequities of the modern world system, and the "world" in "world literature" (Cheah 2016)—and "Bwana Goethe" undoubtedly serves as a reminder that categories like "world literature" are by no means innocuous and mark contested histories as well as territories. Behind this deceptive façade, however, Vassanji's *The Magic of Saida* unfolds a literary world of its own that provides a powerful antidote both to the flood of world-weary critique that would have us believe that the renewed interest in the concept of world literature depoliticizes our understanding of "postcolonial" literature as "a literature of resistance" (Young 2011, 216) and to the allure of catch-all economistic cosmologies invoking the capitalist world-system as "the matrix within which all modern literature takes shape and comes into being" (Warwick Research Collective 2015, 20). This antidote, I will argue, is provided by a worldly literature generated by and grappling with South-South connectivities and Afrasian imaginaries that widen the narrow scope not only of epistemological anti- or decolonialism but also of economistic fantasies of seemingly eternal "centres" and "peripheries". As I hope to show in the main part of this chapter, *The Magic of Saida* contributes both to provincializing Eurocentric notions of world literature (including Goethe's iconic presence in virtually all arenas of the global world literature debate) and—in an ironic twist—to remaking world literature in such a way that Goethe can re-enter the contemporary debate on eye-level: "Bwana Goethe" thus finally stands for a new, decentred understanding of world literature no longer predicated on "comparing back to the centre".

World Literature: Out of the Fortress

As Robert J.C. Young (2011) has rightly remarked, world literature "makes up more a heterogeneous field of critical debate than a constituted canon" (215). The following section of this chapter will take a closer look at two influential strands in this critical debate that Amir Mufti (2016) has characterized as "those who employ a 'centre-periphery' conceptual framework and those more reliant on 'empire-colony'" (32). While Mufti sees the tension between these two rival frameworks as a *productive* one, I am much more sceptical of either of them and believe that literary studies need to break out of this double aporia of World Systems economism on the one hand and postcolonial nostalgia for the moment of anticolonial revolution on the other if they wish to stay attuned to the transformational dynamics produced by contemporary world literature—and if they are indeed to contribute something original to the understanding of the contemporary world through their exploration of the role of literature in processes of globalization.

I would like to begin with a critique of the idea that world literature should be seen in terms of the capitalist world system as theorized by Immanuel Wallerstein (1974–88). This idea was first explored by Franco Moretti in his famous "Conjectures on World

Literature" (2000), reiterated in Pascale Casanova's *The World Republic of Letters* (2004) and has been most systematically unfolded to date in the book publication *Combined and Uneven Development: Towards a New Theory of World-Literature* by the Warwick Research Collective (2015). Here is their definition of world literature:

> We propose [. . .] to define "world literature" as *the literature of the world-system*—of the modern capitalist world-system, that is. (8; original emphasis)
>
> In proposing a definition of world-literature as literature that "registers" the (modern capitalist) world-system, we [. . .] are not suggesting that only those works that consciously define themselves in opposition to capitalist modernity be considered world-literary [. . .]. Our assumption is [. . .] that the effectivity of the world-system will *necessarily* be discernible in any modern literary work, since the world-system exists unforgoably as the matrix within which all modern literature takes shape and comes into being. (20; original emphasis)

The Wallersteinian matrix invoked in this passage assumes that the world is constituted by centres, semi-peripheries and peripheries; these in turn are seen by the authors of *Combined and Uneven Development* to predetermine the structure of world-literature as a global system engaged in "registering" the capitalist world system.

There are many points one could raise and debate here: for example, whether Wallerstein's historical model is a useful and plausible guide to the historical emergence of global capitalism as well as its current state (which might be answered with a guarded "yes" to the first part, but with an emphatic "no" to the second part), or why a theory of literature would wish to entangle itself in what is undeniably an economistic and reductive theory of culture. All of this would lead too far for the purposes of this chapter, however, so I would just like to focus on the scathing critique of non-hierarchical models of world-literature offered in *Combined and Uneven Development*:

> The premise of "combined unevenness" developed here repudiates at a stroke the idea—linked, presumably, to the political mantra that "globalisation" is a tide lifting all boats—that the "world" of world-literature is a "level playing-field", a more or less free space in which texts from among the globe can circulate, intersect and

> converse with one another. (Warwick Research Collective 2015, 22)

Here we find ourselves at the centre of the epistemological citadel this theory has erected in order to maintain its hold on world literary realities: the unwavering belief in the perennial world-systemic structures of centres, peripheries and semi-peripheries walls itself in to ward off the challenges posed by the emergence of a decentred globalized modernity. What is performed as an allegedly "materialist" critique ends up firing sarcastic mockery from the ramparts of theory on all those who have sought to explore the serrated terrain of a changing world order, libelling them as adherents to the neoliberal mantra of the world as a wishful "level playing-field". Edward Said (2000) addressed this terrain when he asserted that

> the world's geography has changed so definitely [. . .] as to allow now for almost the first time a new geographical consciousness of a decentered or multiply-centered world, a world no longer sealed within watertight compartments of art or culture or history, but mixed, mixed up, varied, complicated by the new difficult mobility of migrations, the new independent states, the newly emergent and burgeoning cultures. (471)

Caryl Phillips (2001) also dared to venture into this puzzling territory when he talked about a "new world [. . .] in which it is impossible to resist the claims of the migrant, the asylum seeker, or the refugee" (5) and affirmed:

> The old static order in which one people speaks down to another, lesser, people is dead. The colonial, or postcolonial, model has collapsed. In its place we have a new world order in which there will soon be one global conversation with limited participation open to all, and full participation available to none. In this new world order nobody will feel fully at home. (5)

I would like to take my cue from these two incisive formulations and argue that the usefulness of new definitions of world literature depends centrally on the degree to which they are able to meet this challenge of thinking of the world of globalized modernity (and of the role of literature in that world) beyond a deeply engrained hierarchical view of the world that continues to pervade a wide array of academic disciplines, including cultural and literary studies. Neither Said nor Phillips can be swept aside, I believe, with the simplistic and reductive idea that they are advocating a neoliberal level playing-field credo; what is at issue is whether theories of world literature are capable of moving beyond the notion of a world eternally frozen into a hierarchy of centres and peripheries. In this respect, the good intentions of these theories are irrelevant. Whether they believe themselves to be speaking on behalf of the wretched of the earth, the victims of capitalism, or a socialist revolution infinitely rehearsed and deferred into the future: what counts is the performative outcome of their analysis here and now—whether they perpetuate or undermine a hierarchically structured understanding of the world (and world literature).

Let's briefly visit the other fortress, manned mainly by adherents of different strands of postcolonial theory, built around the notion of the "postness" of the present and the firm belief that what is at issue in current world literature debates are power structures built on discursive legacies reaching back to the era of colonialism. Mufti (2016) has argued that his

> *Forget English!* [. . .] enters the ongoing discussion about the globalization of literary relations from a sharply critical angle, discovering in the contemporary world structures and relations whose genealogy takes us to national, linguistic, continental, civilizational, and racial definitions, asymmetries, hierarchies, and inequalities of the colonial era. (51)

Young's essay "World Literature and Postcolonialism" is another salient case in point. Young (2011) postulates a categorical difference between "world literature" and "postcolonial literature" and regards "world literature" as a body of texts constituted by "emphasizing 'classic' historical rather than contemporary writing" (215); by contrast, he sees "postcolonial literature" as defined by the fact that "postcolonial would always refer to relatively recent writing" (215). Here is Young's contrastive definition of postcolonial literature as opposed to world literature:

> It is in this context that postcolonial literature as a literature of resistance takes on its significance. Many works of postcolonial literature—and of criticism, moreover—involve what Ashcroft et al. term "writing back," [. . .]. Part of the way in which postcolonial literature "resists" has thus been its rewriting of the colonizer's own classics, making them truly worldly. (216)

What is perhaps most surprising about Young's definition of postcolonial literature as the subversive "other" of world literature is its defensive reiteration of a classical proposition that is now more than thirty years old: the idea that postcolonial literature is to be defined by its "writing back" to the centre (Ashcroft et al. 1989), which locks so-called postcolonial literature into a seemingly perennial relationship to Europe and the west and encourages a victimological perspective on cultural and literary production.[1]

This postcolonial impasse confirms the urgency of moving beyond postcolonial critical routines focussing exclusively on North-South interactions and taking South-South relations seriously in any attempt to come to terms with global literary dynamics. An interesting perspective eschewing both the reiteration of centre-periphery models and the recycling of the writing back-paradigm can be found in Ngũgĩ wa Thiong'o's essay "The Globalectical Imagination" (2012a). Far from setting up a contrast between world literature and the postcolonial, Ngũgĩ sees the postcolonial as an indispensable constituent of an understanding of world literature that translates Goethe into a contemporary world of globalized modernity: "The postcolonial is at the heart of the constitution of Goethe's world literature, and even in theory, it indeed constitutes the nonimperial heart of the modern and postmodern" (55).

Ngũgĩ's definition sees world literature not so much as a distinct body of texts—as suggested, for example, in David Damrosch's (2003) famous definition of world literature as encompassing "all literary works that circulate beyond their culture of origin, either in translation or in their original language" (4), as well as in Young's differentiation between "postcolonial" and "world" literature discussed

1 See, for example, Mwangi (2009) and wa Ngugi (2012).

above—but rather as the inevitable condition of literature in a globalized world. He suggests a "globalectical reading" of world literature that breaks up former modes of hierarchical thought and allows a decentred reading of literature in "a world of shared intellectual property" (55):

> Globalectics becomes the way of reading world literature. Globalectical reading means breaking open the prison house of the imagination built by theories and outlooks that would seem to signify the content within is classified, open to only a few. This involves declassifying theory in the sense of making it accessible—a tool for clarifying interactive connections and interconnections of social phenomena and their mutual impact in the local and global space, a means of illuminating the internal and external, the local and the global dynamics of social being. This may also mean the act of reading becoming also a process of self-examination. (61)[2]

Ngũgĩ's focus on "interactive connections and interconnections" (61) points the way towards a more productive assessment of world literature that remains attentive to the ways in which literature engages with a changing world and at the same time engages in a remaking of world literature itself. What is at issue are literary practices that generate perceptions of worldliness beyond Eurocentric imaginaries of modernity: whether advocated or rejected, these perceptions have remained dominant modes of making sense of an increasingly globalized social world. These new imaginaries are not primarily focussed on notions of "alternative modernities" (Gaonkar 1999) or "postcoloniality"—that, paradoxically enough, often remain conceptionally tied to what they challenge[3]—but give literary shape

---

2 This emphasis on world literature as acts of reading recalls Damrosch's (2003) second major definition of world literature as "not an infinite, ungraspable canon of works but rather a mode of circulation and of reading, a mode that is applicable to individual works as to bodies of material, available for reading established classics and new discoveries alike" (5).

3 See Mukoma wa Ngugi's (2012) critique of the principle of "triangulating ideas [. . .] through the West" prevalent in postcolonial theory: "Indeed, the major limitation of the otherwise courageous post-colonial enterprise has been a theoretical and conceptual inability to escape the West-

to more relevant visions of the world that leave behind unilateral accounts (such as those generated in the wake of a European unipolarity or the bipolarity of the 20th-century Cold War period). A renewed attentiveness to South-South connections is vital for this remaking of world literature, not because the writing exploring these connections promises to reveal a Third Worldist, postcolonial or decolonial "truth" to be set against the "falsehood" of "western" views,[4] but because it explores new dimensions of a "poetics of relation" (Glissant 1997) generating a multipolarity of vision. As the last part of this chapter will argue, this multipolarity not only allows for imaginaries of "convivial worlds" (Steiner 2021) to emerge, but also generates fictional self-reflexivity: echoing the notion of "implicated subjects" (Rothberg 2019), the chapter will conclude on the notion of "writing implications"—a literary practice exploring embarrassing and unacknowledged past and present entanglements, let-downs and betrayals—as an important dimension of contemporary world literature.

Beyond Bandung: Afrasian Imaginaries in the 21st Century

In recent years, one area of these South-South connections—transregional relations between Africa and Asia—has received particular attention both in the humanities and the social sciences. This attention has often focussed on Afro-Asian anticolonial politics initiated at the famous Bandung Conference in 1955 which has been hailed as a model of South-South cooperation and invoked in visions of "Reviving Bandung" (Pham and Shilliam 2016) and a renewed "Global Solidarity" (Wardaya 2005). These debates are also echoed in a spate of recent publications on the Afro-Asian Writers' Association (AAWA), an organization set up under the auspices of the Afro-Asian

South South-West framework. [. . .] Unable to escape this locked and unequal dialectic, many postcolonial thinkers end up affirming the very relationships they are trying to undermine" (5).

4 For a critique of the persistent presence of "the west" in postcolonial discourse see Meighoo (2016).

People's Solidarity Organization (AAPSO) that had considerable international impact, not least through its journal *Lotus*, in the 1970s and early 1980s.[5]

Yet anticolonial political solidarity constitutes only one dimension of a long history of Afrasian transregionalism that also rests on a millennium of extensive interactions between Africa and Asia predicated on trade (including the trafficking of millions of enslaved people from Africa) across the Indian Ocean (Bose 2006, Gupta, Hofmeyr and Pearson 2010, Desai 2013), the emergence of Indian Ocean Cosmopolitanisms (Hawley 2008) and "Connective Afrasian Sea Memories" (Karugia 2018) as well as equally long histories of Asian diasporas in Africa (Pirbhai 2009), African diasporas in Asia (De Silva Jayasuriya and Pankhurst 2003, Bhatt 2018) and personal entanglements between Africans and Asians (Ngũgĩ 2012b).

A helpful framework for navigating this puzzling terrain of South-South connectivities may thus be the concept of transregionalism that constitutes a challenging middle ground between the "global" and the "local". Such a transregional perspective is arguably helpful in coming to terms with some of the economic, social and cultural dynamics to be encountered in a world that is becoming more and more decentred and multipolar (Clegg 2009, Hiro 2010), and to understand South-South relations (such as those between Africa and Asia) as key moments in these dynamics. The term "Afrasia" employed in this chapter, based on incisive "Afrasian" publications (Pearson 1998, Adem and Mazrui 2013, Desai 2013, Karugia 2018) as well as on the research work of the "Africa's Asian Options" project,[6] thus seeks to move beyond both a "post"-posture characterized by a perennial hermeneutics of suspicion of empire and its legacies and the temptations

5 See Halim (2012). For a discussion of Lotus and the AAWA in terms of world literature, see Yoon (2015) and Lucy Gasser's contribution to the present volume; for a more sceptical view of AAWA's history and present significance see Schulze-Engler (2019).

6 Africa's Asian Options (AFRASO) was a major interfaculty research project at Goethe University Frankfurt from 2013 to 2019; see www.afraso.org.

of a catch-all economism that is increasingly out of sync with the realities of the 21st century. What is at issue is a framework that encompasses real changes in the social world based on economic shifts, political realignments, migration dynamics and cultural flows as well as necessary transformations in academic knowledge production:

> Afrasia thus neither denotes a new territorial container nor marks off a new geopolitical mega-area, but stands for an emerging space of connective interaction and a new heuristics for coming to terms with entangled areas and intertwined histories in a decentred world that can no longer be grasped through the Eurocentric categories that dominated the theory and practice of area studies for so long. (Achenbach et al. 2020, 3)

Transregional connectivities are thus a salient feature of the contemporary world, of important changes in academic knowledge production and, last but not least, of contemporary world literature.

Afrasian Imaginaries at Work: Entangled Histories

In the third part of this chapter, I would now like to turn to narratives "drawing on a lateral imaginary of a history of South-South circulation of goods, people and ideas between Africa, South Asia and the Arabian Peninsula which cannot be subsumed under the colony-metropole axis" (Steiner 2021, 151) and to a striking novel from East Africa that challenges literary studies to come to terms with the Afrasian complexities outlined above.

Three dimensions of transregional worldliness are particularly important in *The Magic of Saida*: (a) entangled Afrasian histories based on and shaped for over a thousand years by the settlement of Asians and Arabs in Africa and Africans in India as well as trade, slavery, Arab (and later European) colonization, religion (particularly Islam), anticolonial struggles and post-independence history; (b) complex individual identities generated "in the thick of multiplicity" (Vassanji 1996) that relate to specifically Afrasian afterlives of slavery and that blur clear-cut "African", "Asian" and "Arab" ascriptions and designations; and (c) a constitutive self-reflexivity eschewing unconditional nationalist, socialist, racial, ethnic, religious and post- or decolonial solidarities that gives rise to a multipolar imagination undermining ideals of individual or collective purity.

"The past is a dangerous business", warns Akilimali, an Islamic traditional healer in *The Magic of Saida* called in to investigate the mysterious death of Mzee Omari who was found hanging from the very Mango tree where numerous rebels against German colonial rule (including Mzee Omari's brother Abdulkarim) were executed in the ancient Tanzanian coastal town of Kilwa, "it is best to keep it buried" (Vassanji 2013, 114). In many ways, Vassanji's novel confirms Akilimali's diagnosis, if not his prescription. *The Magic of Saida* is built upon a quest plot (featuring the successful African-Indian-Canadian doctor Kamal Punja who returns to Tanzania, where he was born and grew up, to find Saida, the love of his youth) that intertwines "public" and "private" histories and unearths a large number of puzzling and often embarrassing insights into entangled individual and collective pasts that many would like to keep out of sight.

On the collective side, many of these pasts hinge on ancient Afrasian connections and the imaginaries they generate in subsequent generations. A central feature of these connections are the Sidis, descendants of Africans that came to India "as policemen, traders, bureaucrats, clerics, bodyguards, concubines, and soldiers from different regions of Africa" (Shroff and Mehtab 2020, 409), but were also brought to India during many centuries of an Arab-run slave trade central to the burgeoning commercial universe linking up Africa, Arabia and Asia across the Indian Ocean:

> Africa was not entirely foreign to the western ports of India; since olden times ships had plied the ocean between the two continents, carrying a small but steady trade. [. . .] But Singpur, lying in the hinterland, had a different connection to Africa. It was home to the Sidis, the dark people whose ancestors had travelled the other way, from Africa to India, some centuries before and never returned. Their saint, Sidi Sayyad, was known widely for his magical powers. (Vassanji 2013, 123)

It is at the shrine of Sidi Sayyad, the historical Afrasian saint,[7] in fictional Singpur that Punja Devraj, a young enterprising adventurer from one of Western India's many port cities, has an epiphanic vision:

> Punja heard it said that the ancestors of the dark curly-headed folk of Singpur had come originally from a wonderful island called Jangbar in Africa. [. . .] It was as he heard these tales of the spice island of opportunity and its friendly sultan, away from anything he'd known, that the revelation struck Punja: [. . .] He would go to Jangbar. The Pir of Jangbar, Sidi Sayyad himself, had beckoned him. This is what he would always relate, Sidi Sayyad had sent him to Africa to take his greetings to his people. (Vassanji 2013, 125)

Punja Devraj's journey from India to East Africa in the 1870s, one of the central fictional events in Vassanji's novel, is thus arguably based on an act of the Afrasian imagination drawing on centuries of transregional South-South connections: Punja sees himself as "returning" to Africa at Sidi Sayyad's behest, and thus completing a centuries-old circular movement of Africans to India and now back to Africa. Furthermore, although Punja travels from British-dominated India to East Africa, his migration is not that of a colonial subject, but that of an Indian adventurer bound for a powerful independent African state, the rulers of which actively encouraged Indian migration to and settlement in Zanzibar and the vast East African territories controlled by the Zanzibar Sultanate in order to promote Indian Ocean commerce and strengthen their own power base.

One strand of the novel follows the exploits of Punja in East Africa where the entanglement of African and Asian pasts generated new complexities in the late 19th century. In the 1880s, particularly after the notorious Berlin Conference of 1884, the Zanzibar Sultanate was increasingly under pressure by the German and the British Empire, and it is in this turbulent phase of history when a centuries-old

---

7 For an account of the contested role of Sidi Sayyad and his shrine in Ahmedabad in contemporary Indian memory politics (and particularly the attempts by the current Hindu fundamentalist government under Narendra Modi to turn Sidi Sayyad into an emblem of Indian diversity and open-mindedness while cold-shouldering local Sidis and Sidi culture), see Shroff and Mehtab (2020).

Arab Empire in Africa and a large number of African territories struggling for their sovereignty became the hub of a first phase of modern anticolonial resistance that Punja arrives in East Africa. Vassanji tackles this multiply entangled history by creating a complex factional scenario where fictional characters based on historical personalities (such as Punja) interact with historical figures turned into fictional protagonists (such as Hassan bin Omari who led an armed uprising against German colonial rule). Punja—who has now settled for good in East Africa—turns into "Punja the Lion", a famous protagonist of the struggle against the encroaching German Empire,[8] and fights alongside famous African anticolonial heroes:

> Punja was now a man of the coast, a respected Indian trader and honorary Swahili who was convinced by now that Sidi Sayyad of Singpur had sent him to Africa with a noble purpose: to help his people, the Africans, resist the onslaught of the Europeans. [...] He was that saint's emissary and gift to his ancestral homeland. He would do all he could to help resist the invasion of his adopted land. (Vassanji 2013, 139)

By the time Punja is eventually captured by the Germans and, together with Hassan bin Omari and other insurgents, is hanged on the notorious mango tree in the town centre of Kilwa,[9] he has indeed become a widely acknowledged African freedom fighter. Yet the intricate interplay of Afrasian imaginaries in Vassanji's novel also registers the historical ironies generated by the transregional blurring of "African", "Asian" and "Arab" pasts and presents:

> Punja's great-grandson, a century and some years later now, wonders whether Sidi Sayyad, if we grant him his supernatural powers, lying in Singpur under a mound of fragrant flowers, was aware of this singular irony, that those leading the fight against the foreign invasion on the east coast of Africa were eminent traders in slaves

8 For a historical account of the German war against Hassan bin Omari, the role of Indian businessmen in that war, and the trial of the leaders of the uprising see Miehe et al. (2002, 21–22).

9 The mango tree where Hassan bin Omari was hanged stood in Kilwa as a historical site until 1991; the historical Indian supporters of the uprising were sentenced to death, but "their death sentences were transmuted into imprisonment and high fines" (Miehe et al. 2002, 21).

> too; that it was slavers of this ilk who had brought at least some of his people all the way to India. (Vassanji 2013, 139)[10]

However, Punja the Lion is by no means the only character in *The Magic of Saida* who combines an active role in the anticolonial struggle with a transregional imaginary predicated on South-South relations. Wasim, one of Punja's co-conspirators, "a tall, charismatic figure in the crisp white kanzu and white kofia of a pious Muslim [...] more African than Arab" and "a follower of Sheikh Ayesi of Somalia" (132) tells Punja about the intricate political agenda of his brand of Islam:

> The aim of the Sufi orders in Africa and India and the Middle East was also to preserve Islamic ways from corruption by the Europeans, and therefore to take measures to throw off the yoke of foreign colonialism, and moreover to spread Islam in regions where it had not taken root. (131)
> "When you get to the mainland," said Wasim, "be sure to give support to our people who are resisting the white man. This is a jihad. Soon we may be able to drive the infidel out." (132)

Another intriguing transregional imaginary emerges in the present-day strand of the novel where Kamal Punja meets Dr. Navroz Engineer whose life trajectory combines a thousand-year-old history of a Persian diaspora across the Indian Ocean and a fascination with radical anticolonial nationalism:

> Dr. Navroz Engineer had come to Tanzania as a child in the 1960s with his Communist Indian parents, both of them doctors and disenchanted with India but ardent admirers of Julius Nyerere, Tanzania's president, and his brand of African socialism. (221)
> "And what are you?" Kamal asked Navroz, more to test him.

10 Another historical irony registered by Vassanji's novel lies in the fact that it is both the late 19th-century hegemonic drive of European Empires in East Africa and the early 20th-century emergence of African nationalism that weakened the Afrasian connectivities of an East African coastal town like Kilwa and led to their eventual parochialisation: "The old Muslim towns on the coast [...] changed from pivots of commercial and cultural exchange into margins of territorial states seeking their economic well-being in peasant commodity production" (Becker 2014, 114).

> "Me? It's difficult, as you say. I am called a Tanzanian Asian." Then he added with a chuckle, "Do you know Kilwa was settled by Persians more than a thousand years ago?" [. . .]
> "My own ancestors went from Persia to India," Navroz said. "I am Parsi, as you've no doubt guessed. A complete circle, you see. My DNA would tell you that I am ethnically related to the Swahili. Amazing world we live in, isn't it?" (222–23)

Afrasian Afterlives of Slavery and the Emergence of Complex Identities

It is not only collective political, religious and ethnic visions that are refracted through an Afrasian lens in *The Magic of Saida*, however, but also private histories and individual identities. If the story of Punja Devraj's 19th-century life often hinges on "grand" politics and memories of collective pasts, Kamal Punja's 20th-century tale mainly focuses on his complicated individual past, his diasporic voyage out of Africa to Canada and his struggle with his own brand of Asian Africanness. In many ways, Punja Devraj's and Kamal Punja's stories mirror each other: both have a circular dimension with regard to "origins" (Indian-born Punja Devraj as well as African-born Kamal Punja "return" to Africa, the former to begin a new life there, the latter to reconnect to his childhood and youth), both blur clear-cut definitions of "Africa" and "Asia", and both are decisively shaped by South-South interactions ranging from transregional solidarities to racist xenophobia that cannot possibly be reduced to confrontations with European colonialism or economistic tales of "centres" and "peripheries".

A particularly powerful Afrasian imaginary utilized in *The Magic of Saida* is slavery, which is invoked both at the level of "big" (collective) history and with regard to Kamal's individual identity tribulations. By contrast to "Atlanticist" understandings of slavery that have given rise to a "middle passage epistemology" (Wright 2015) often employed in contemporary post- and decolonial theory, the idea of slavery in *The Magic of Saida* is saturated by very different transregional histories and social realities predicated on long histories of Asian-Arab-African interactions rather than European-African ones.[11] Early on in the novel, Kamal is introduced to the complexities of slavery by his African mother, whose grandmother was brought to Kilwa as a slave: "The sea holds many secrets, you understand? Kilwa is an old town. Slaves were brought here, from the south. Many died. Others?—sent off to Zanzibar, Bagamoyo. Arabia. India. Know this. Those are the bones of our ancestors" (Vassanji 2013, 51).

The story of slavery in *The Magic of Saida* is not only a diasporic one, however: Kamal's ancestors include Punja the Lion on his father's side, and possibly Afro-Arabian slave traders such as Hassan bin Omari (also widely known by his Swahili name Makunganya) who fought—and was killed alongside—Punja the Lion in the anticolonial uprising against the Germans on his mother's side:

> "Mama, that Makunganya—he was a great man, a jitu, who fought the colonialists—sio?"
> "That he was. But he was also a slaver who captured and sold my grandmother. Or it was his men who did that."
> "Could he be my ancestor, eti?"
> "Maybe." (Vassanji 2013, 86)

Kamal grows up in Kilwa as an African boy raised by an African mother, until the latter decides to send him to Dar es Salaam to his father's Indian relatives, plunging him into an Afrasian identity crisis

11 Isabel Hofmeyr (2010) has summarized this contrast between "Atlantic" and "Indian Ocean" epistemologies of slavery in the following manner: "As transnationalism and associated models like oceanic studies gain momentum in the academy, the Indian Ocean obliges us to extend our axes of investigation. It requires us to relativize the Atlantic, which has become normative, especially in slavery and African diaspora studies. Analyses of domination and resistance, colonizer and colonized arise from postindependence revisions of colonial history. These in turn draw on Atlantic readings of slavery where the boundary between enslaved and free is unequivocally demarcated and racialized. In the Indian Ocean this boundary blurred, and race and slavery were not associated in any marked form [. . .]. At every turn the Indian Ocean complicates binaries, moving us away from the simplicities of the resistant local and the dominating global and towards a historically deep archive of competing universalisms" (721–22).

that turns out to be "the riddle of his life" (38):

> "But I'm an African," he protested with vehemence. Ni Mwafrika! "I don't speak Indian, I don't eat Indian! They eat daal and they smell!" "Mhindi, tu." An Indian. That's what she wanted for him. But why? So he too could be a sultan. (29)

It is against this complex background of contradictory memories and experiences that Kamal's own puzzling attitude to the notion of "slave" can be understood, not as a result of colonial brainwashing, but as part of Kamal's complex struggle for Africanness:

> Everyone had a nickname at school, and his was Golo. It was friendly; even to this day, Kamal said, some of his friends knew him as Golo. It meant, in its original sense, servant, or slave. In a strange way, he was proud of it. There was nothing to be ashamed of, he was living in Africa, his continent. And later, it was just a moniker. Later in life, in Edmonton, his wife Shamim would detest it. *How could you allow yourself to be called a slave? Where is your pride?*
> [...]
> But that's what he was in Dar es Salaam: Golo, the African; the chotaro, the half-caste Indian. (195; original emphasis)

The peculiar constellation in which Kamal is confronted with—and largely accepts—the nickname Golo is once more an Afrasian rather than a Eurafrican one: having been sent to Dar es Salaam to become an "Indian", Kamal soon realizes "that of the Asians who all seemed the same, some were Shamsis, others Ithnasheris, and still others Hindus, which was why there were several prayer houses in the neighborhood" (Vassanji 2013, 193). The diversity of East African "Asians" in *The Magic of Saida* thus runs parallel to the internal differentiation of East African "Muslims": Kamal's family belongs to the Shamsi community that figures in several of Vassanji's novels, a community "both closely factual and broadly fictional" (Jones 2007, 29) and modelled on the transnational Ismaili branch of Shiite Islam headed by the Aga Khan. Kamal's family in Dar es Salaam support his education and enable him to study medicine in Uganda and eventually become a successful doctor in Canada, but the "Asian" environment he now lives in (particularly the school he is sent to) is saturated with a racism of its own:

> Until he could prove otherwise, for Golo to get top marks in the predominantly Asian school was thought to be impossible, no less by him. He was African, the Indian part didn't matter. He couldn't speak the Indian language correctly, and his English sounded African, was often brutally imitated. He was the dark bonehead. (Vassanji 2013, 227)

Kamal eventually sheds the idea that "Africans are the most stupid and uneducated in the world" and that he is "a mshenzi, the most uncivilized of Africans" whose "grandmother was a mtumwa, a slave" (228), but earlier on his role as "Golo" operates on a thin line between "positive" and "negative" racism and serves both as a self-designation rejecting "Asian weakness" and reaffirming his Africanness and as a projection foil for Orientalist fantasies generated by his "Indian" family:

> As any African would tell you, it was the daal they ate that softened them. He was Golo, he did not eat daal. And he was a hero to his young cousin Azim, who once explained his prowess: "You know, you know, my brother Kamal has the blood of an African warrior—like, like, like... Tarzan! You should see him finish a bone—like, like, like... a lion!" (201)

The invocation of Tarzan, the King of the Jungle, in Azim's eulogy on Kamal's African ferocity echoes a similar anecdote in Vassanji's *The Book of Secrets* (1994) where Tarzan also forms the cornerstone of an exotic image of Africa "culled from the likes of Rider Haggard, Tarzan, and Sanders of Africa" (Vassanji [1994] 1997, 238) harboured by a Goan teacher travelling to East Africa to "civilize the natives". Such passages provide a salutary reminder that the complex Afrasian imaginary of slavery at work in *The Magic of Saida* does not operate in a self-contained social universe. The South-South connectivities this chapter seeks to explore as the foundation of a specific form of worldliness that is changing the contours of contemporary world literature do not stand apart from, but are interlaced with cultural flows that link Africa and Asia to other parts of the world; the "Global South" should thus not be understood in terms of a territorialized, closed container—or in a binary demarcation of "North" (or "West") and "South" such as that attempted by the so-called "Brandt Line" in the

1980s (Independent Commission 1980)—, but rather in terms of a renewed attentiveness to South-South social, cultural and literary relations. These relations are often enough transnational, transregional and transcultural and contribute to the emergence of cultural complexity, both on a collective and an individual level, rather than cultural purity or a homogenous national identity. As Kamal Punja says of himself:

> Well, I am of here and these are my people, and yet I have a life and family elsewhere. In Canada, I've thought of myself as African—though not African Canadian or African American—attractive illusions for a while. It becomes difficult to say *precisely* what one is anymore. Isn't that a common condition nowadays? (Vassanji 2013, 222; original emphasis)

Self-Reflexivity and the Predicament of Past Betrayals

In *The Magic of Saida*, this attentiveness to cultural complexity is inextricably intertwined with a constitutive self-reflexivity that casts a wary eye on nationalist, socialist, ethnic or racial appeals to collective identity and their potential for further social exclusion or even murderous violence. As discussed above, colonialism—and particularly the confrontation with the German Empire in East Africa—is part of this scenario (as the space given to colonial violence and various anticolonial insurgents including the Maji-Maji Movement amply testifies to), but the main thrust of this self-reflexivity (which places it beyond the confines of anticolonial binarisms and their latter-day post- and decolonial incarnations) is directed towards "writing back to self" (Mwangi 2009) and to an unflinching confrontation with the social, political and ideological deformations that have come to bedevil East African societies after independence. When Kamal wonders in a conversation with the publisher-narrator what has happened to the pride in the newly-won nationhood of Tanzania he witnessed as a young man, the latter muses:

> The answer is that it didn't last long after he left. That idealism and pride, the hope of independence that some of us remember so wistfully as the heyday of uhuru, was taken to ideological extremes that

> finally brought us to this state. All this bustle that you see in our capital, the wonderful dollar consumerism, runs on the rails of foreign aid. I could have told him my personal truth—that I happen to be one of those ideologues who railed in the past against capitalists and imperialists. Even in those shrill days my publishing business could survive only on foreign generosity, and it's still foreign patronage that keeps me in comfort. That's what became of our pride. We swallowed it, along with all the gifts we received. (Vassanji 2013, 59)

Ethnically defined African nationalism and racism against "Indians" and "Arabs" receives its share of critique in Vassanji's tour d'horizon, both on a micro-level, when African prejudices against Afrasian and Afrabian "Others" surface in Kamal's lifeworlds in Kilwa and Dar es Salaam, and on a macro-level, when the novel pinpoints the ethnic hatred emerging after the Zanzibar revolution of 1964 (Vassanji 2013, 264) and—at much greater length—Idi Amin's expulsion of the "Indians" in Uganda in 1972 (255–66). As a Tanzanian student at Uganda's prestigious Makerere University, Kamal is a first-hand witness of this expulsion, which leads to his decision to emigrate to Canada, but Vassanji takes great care not to paint a one-dimensional picture of "Southern" racism. Identifying with his African side ("[a] half cheer from a half-caste", 262), Kamal at first feels sympathies for the new populist black leader ("an African who was utterly natural, who didn't have to assume English manners [. . .] [who] could talk back with utter insouciance to anybody in the world, including the British prime minister", 260) and remembers the many large and small acts of Anti-African racism he witnessed in Tanzania:

> It was the Golo in him who sent up the partial cheer for Idi Amin. It was the half-caste who had identified with the house servants ("boys"), flinched at their abuse and humiliations, and suffered his own share of them in school. It was the boy who had cried for his African mother and his special friend in Kilwa. He recalled his horror and shame when he saw a young African woman coming out of his uncle's back room. (260)

Yet Kamal eventually comes to realize that the populist panache of Uganda's military dictator and his fanning of ethnic hatred serves his own rather than "his people's" interests. Kamal also understands that the anticolonial rhetoric on which this populism feeds is hard to reconcile with Amin's own military track record:

> But there was this other side of him that saw through the cynical reverse racism that was at work. The Asians had overnight become "aliens" and "foreigners," objects of hate and derision. [...] It looked much too easy, pointing fingers at a minority of a different colour too frightened to defend itself. [. . .] And Idi Amin had served as a soldier for the British, hunting Mau Mau in Kenya. Nothing was straightforward. (261)

The constitutive self-reflexivity in *The Magic of Saida* is thus a deliberately non-partisan one that cuts across ethnic, religious and racial divides and confronts powerful myths of collective identity with discomfiting insights into complex, entangled histories. One of these myths is the nationalist invocation of a homogenous or "pure" body politic from which all those deemed "alien" or "sick" may easily be excised. This myth, Vassanji's novel points out, played a major role in the expulsion of "Asians" from Uganda, but it also persists in the demonized figure of the "traitor" who becomes emblematic of an unwillingness to engage—in collective memory as well as in contemporary politics—with the internal rifts that characterize African societies as much as those anywhere else in the world:

> Meanwhile, we in this—and other—nations must face a conundrum: How do we accept those who collaborated with our colonizers? Worked for them; put on boots and uniform and took up arms on their behalf against fellow Africans. Were they traitors or simply practical and realistic? This was the dilemma put to me by Kamal. It is the shameful part of the history of any nation that is often glossed over in silence. The policemen who brought down their sticks on the skulls of Gandhi's followers were fellow Indians; those who hunted the Mau Mau in Kenya and the ANC in South Africa were in large numbers fellow Africans. (100)

The Afrasian imaginary at work in this passage is predicated neither on a shared history of anticolonial resistance nor on long histories of trade and communication across the Indian Ocean, nor indeed on the transcultural entanglements generated in individual lives unfolding in transregional lifeworlds (although, as shown above, all of these also feature in Vassanji's novel). What is at issue here is the shared burden of internal conflict in Asian and African societies acknowledged through "narrative recognition of local historical responsibility in facilitations of major political incursions" that "depicts local characters as implicated and involved in these processes, which are now seen as messier and murkier than in former clear-cut accounts that apportioned blame almost exclusively to foreigners" (Gagiano 2019, 5). If, as Annie Gagiano (2019) has argued, the emergence of literary illuminations of past betrayals "signpost possible political and moral growth in formerly colonized societies that are beginning to take ownership *also* of periods and processes of colonial or imperial invasion" (4–5; original emphasis), this growth is of a decidedly Afrasian kind in *The Magic of Saida*. Vassanji's writing self-reflexively explores the discomfitures and embarrassments of public and private African and Asian histories and their transregional connectivities—from the manifold legacies of the Indian Ocean slave trade in India, Arabia and East Africa to Idi Amin's expulsion of the "Asians", from Indian and Arab racism against allegedly "inferior" Africans during and after colonialism to African connivance with or support for the violent excision of alleged "Arabs" and "Asians" from post-independence societies in East Africa, and from Omar bin Tamim's betrayal of anticolonial insurgents, including his own brother, to Kamal Punja's let-down of his juvenile love Saida. In this manner, Vassanji provides the imaginative groundwork for an "ethics of possibility" generating "ways of thinking, feeling and acting [. . .] that expand the field of the imagination, that produce greater equity [. . .], and that widen the field of informed, creative and critical citizenship" (Appadurai 2013, 295).

Coda: Writing Implications—Mzee Omari, M.G. Vassanji and Bwana Goethe Do World Literature

M.G. Vassanji's *The Magic of Saida*—just like many of his other writings and those of many other contemporary African writers—is thus full of characters that cannot simply be designated as "victims" or "perpetrators" and that may, as Michael Rothberg (2019) has recently suggested, more productively be addressed through the category of the "implicated subject". Focussing on "the one who participates in injustice, but in indirect ways" can indeed contribute to providing "a more complete picture of the workings of violence, exploitation, and domination" (20), but to make this category truly productive for coming to terms with the contemporary remaking of world literature, it needs to be eased out of the conceptual constraints that Rothberg seems to place it in by suggesting that it is mainly "we citizens of the Global North" (12) who are the prime examples of such implicated subjects.[12] This epistemological preponderance of the "Global North" in planetary scenarios of self-reflexivity may emerge from the best of intentions (such as wishing to highlight historical patterns of exploitation and injustice and their legacies for the contemporary world), but it inevitably clashes with the political and cultural necessity to self-reflexively confront new scenarios of oppression, marginalization and injustice in a heterogenous, multipolar and rapidly transforming "Global South" and echoes some of the binary thinking that a few decades ago produced the juxtaposition of "First" and "Third World".

In the field of African literature, to take the most immediately relevant example in the context of the present chapter, this self-reflexive confrontation of "Africa Writing Back to Self" (Mwangi 2009) has long since supplemented if not supplanted older modes of "Writing Back to the Centre" as "colonial discourse is increasingly overshadowed by more than half a century of post-independence literary production that far outweighs, in its experimental generativity, much

12 "Privileged consumers in the Global North are not [...] best described as 'perpetrators' of exploitation, but rather as implicated subjects, participants in and beneficiaries of a system that generates dispersed and uneven experiences of trauma and well-being simultaneously. Such an approach also helps us to conceptualize collective responsibility in the age of what many have called the Anthropocene: we citizens of the Global North are not precisely perpetrators of climate change, yet we certainly contribute disproportionally to current and future climate-based catastrophes and benefit in the here and now from the geographically and temporally uneven distribution of their catastrophic effects" (Rothberg 2013, 12).

of what preceded it" (West-Pavlov 2020, 555). In this setting, implication is surely as multidirectional as memory (Rothberg 2009) and needs to be taken as seriously in the "Global South" as in the "Global North". If one hallmark of the remaking of world literature explored in this chapter is the gradual emergence of a truly global network of relations beyond the older North-South trajectories which so much of world literature theorizing has moved along, literature's capacity to explore a wide array of implications (including its own) across and beyond the confines of national literary spaces and to acknowledge "contested ownerships" of what Edward Said (1993) some three decades ago diagnosed as "overlapping territories" and "intertwined histories" (3) is of primary importance. As Russel West-Pavlov (2020) has written about Vassanji's *The Book of Secrets*,

> Vassanji's parable suggests that rather than rejecting colonial discourse, a strategy which naively assumes that the past can be simply shaken off, its ongoing effects must be acknowledged in all their ambivalence, and "owned" by the various stakeholders who are drawn into its ambit. The "post-colonial" tenor of such a literary archive increasingly fades in the course of these various and often conflicted ownerships [. . .]. It is above all in the networked, matrix-like procedure, which works as much or even more along South-South axes than along the rather tired axes of coloniser-colonised relationships (North-South encounters) that it remains possible to continue to negotiate the manifold cultural connections in a constructive manner. (555)

Yet, literature not only "mirrors" or "registers" the emergence of South-South axes forming part of a wider matrix of cultural relations in a world of globalized modernity, but actively co-produces these axes which serve as trajectories of conviviality (Steiner 2021) as well as of conflict. A novel like *The Magic of Saida* can thus productively be read as a text "writing implications": a medium that offers striking images of the complex role of South-South connectivities in the world and at the same time critically scrutinizes the role of (world) literature itself. This is why finally this chapter returns to Vassanji's text one more time—to examine how the Swahili poet Mzee

Omari, the anglophone novelist M.G. Vassanji, and last but not least Bwana Goethe "do" world literature.

Omari bin Tamim, or Mzee Omari as he becomes known later in life, is easily the most bewildering embodiment of world literature in *The Magic of Saida*. As a young man, he throws in his lot with the German colonizers, accepts the literary patronage of a German district commissioner and passes on important information that leads to the capture of a whole group of anticolonial insurgents; later he doubly betrays his brother by being instrumental in his arrest (leading to his subsequent execution) and passing his brother's poetry off as his own; even later he turns into the celebrated elder poet who is considered the "voice of his people" but finally kills himself because he cannot live with his guilt:

> How to judge, then, the poet who yielded, who took up his pen and praised our oppressors, and gave them legitimacy? To resist was heroic; but was it better for some to create, to record, to learn and to survive? [. . .]
> "As a boy I was moved by Mzee Omari's stories of resistance," said Kamal. [. . .] And so how to explain the old man's pride in his association with the German colonizers? He was a man of great dignity, much loved. It was impossible to imagine that under that venerable, ancient exterior of our poet-historian there lurked something else, so fragile—and guilty?" (Vassanji 2013, 100)

Omari's personal guilt in the novel may be extreme, but the implicatedness of his writing is not: most Swahili poets writing about German colonial rule in East Africa were encouraged by Europeans to compose their poetry (Miehe et al. 2002, 31) and often—at least on the surface—wrote in praise or at least in awe of German colonial power, which in the 1970s sparked off a lively debate in Tanzania about this corpus of texts as a product of "bootlickers" (Miehe et al. 2002, 87–89). Yet, given Vassanji's interest in the fragility and guilt of literary practice, it comes as no surprise that sections from Mzee Omari's epic prose poem "The Composition of the Coming of the Modern Age" (modelled on a number of historical Swahili poems)[13] take up considerable space in the text. Allegedly written in Swahili, later preserved by British scholars and rendered in English in Vassanji's novel, this nested narrative is a remarkable instance not only of "implicated writing", but also of "linguistic hospitality" (Steiner 2021, 153) that opens up a literary continuum between an anglophone text originating in India, East Africa and Canada and read throughout the world—and that is obviously "world-literary" by most definitions currently available—and an imaginary Swahili text modelled on a corpus that has largely been forgotten today and that at first sight seems thoroughly "local" and way beyond the discursive turf of "world" literature.

Yet even the original Swahili poems Vassanji draws on were already very much products of a newly emerging world literary constellation: focusing on European incursions into East Africa, they were written in a seemingly "traditional" style that varied considerably from the prescriptive frameworks of classical Swahili writing (Miehe et al. 2002, 31–44), and—although originally handwritten to be locally recited—they were collected and translated by (mostly German) administrators and scholars who published them in specialized publishing houses and scholarly publications in Europe (Miehe et al. 2002, 94). The transcultural entanglements of this corpus (that has long since become part of the literary landscape of "anglophone" Tanzania) are further enhanced by the fact that "most of the originals of the poems got lost in the course of time" (Miehe et al. 2002, 94)—just as Mzee Omari's handwritten papers in *The Magic of Saida* "were used a long time ago to wrap things" (Vassanji 2013, 303)—and now only survive as published translations or in bilingual scholarly editions.

If Mzee Omari can be said to be "doing world literature" in Vassanji's text, he does so beyond naïve assumptions of cultural and linguistic purity. His story does not unfold as a triumphant chronicle of liberation, but as a bewildering story of implication and—just like

13 The first part of Mzee Omari's prose poem, for example, shows remarkable parallels to Hemdi bin Abdallah bin Said bin Abdalla bin Masudi al Buhriy's Swahili epic "The Poem about the German Conquest of the Swahili Coast" (reprinted in Miehe et al. 2002, 118–88).

The Magic of Saida as a whole—against the background of a long history of "East Africa as a literary and linguistic contact zone" (Diegner and Schulze-Engler 2015) where, as Yvonne Owuor (2015) has suggested, Swahili and English can be seen as

> vehicles of transportation—metaphorically, *matatus* (there is subtle order to the seeming chaos)—through which symbols, experiences, messages, meanings, maps, and archetypes of one cultural zone not only visit one another but oftentimes hop aboard and contribute to the blend of passengers. (142)

A second perspective on doing world literature emerges through an encounter Kamal Punja has as a high school student in Tanzania. The headmaster of his school, Mr. Palangyo (modelled on the historical Tanzanian writer Peter Palangyo who, like the headmaster, wrote only one novel during his literary career), invites an internationally renowned (entirely fictitious) Ghanaian writer to speak to his students about the importance of African literature. Having read some of the students' work, the writer comments:

> "But I have one overall comment to all budding African writers. Write about what you know. Why write about England? What do you know about living in New York? Write about Dar es Salaam, write about Tanzania. Those are the stories we need." He looked around at the faces before him. "By all means read about London and New York, but let those in Europe and America, and indeed Nigeria and Ghana, read about your Dar es Salaam. That's what Africa needs." (Vassanji 2013, 238–39)

This nationalist model of developing African literature as a critical encounter with local realities in order to widen the scope of world literature and set up a dialogue with readers in other parts of Africa and the world is one that many writers in the final phase of colonialism and the first decades of independence followed with considerable success, but Vassanji's mode of "doing world literature"—like that of many African writers in recent decades—has clearly followed a different trajectory. While transnational connections, migration and transcultural entanglements can be traced to the very beginnings of African literature, they have become an increasingly salient feature both in the production and the critical reception of contemporary African writing. This is demonstrated, for example, by the lively debate on the theory and practice of "Afropolitanism" (Wawrzinek and Makokha 2011; Coetzee 2017): it is certainly true that the question "what do you know about living in New York?" will be answered differently by many 21st-century writers from Africa.

Yet the worldliness of Vassanji's writing extends beyond the orbit of "Africa and the west" which still seems to circumscribe many contemporary critical debates. As the editors of *The Transnational Imaginaries of M. G. Vassanji* have rightly warned:

> As Vassanji's work has developed—and as the world around him and all of us has changed—[. . .] there is a need to determinedly stress the location of Vassanji's work and the ways it should be read, in a transnational space that connects people, places and issues across the world, rather than issues and problems of settlement in the West. (Murji and Sayed 2018, 3)

"Doing world literature" in *The Magic of Saida* and other writings by Vassanji thus takes up the original impetus of modern African literature to put Africa on the world literary map, yet it not only enlarges, but also complicates and transforms that map by exploring the manifold and often puzzling multidirectional relations that connect individuals and collectives to national, continental, transregional and global spaces and histories. Relations to Europe and the west via colonialism and its aftermaths as well as migration are part of this scenario, but they are embedded in a much wider matrix in which—as has been shown above—Afrasian imaginaries play a prominent role. These imaginaries signal towards conviviality and "transnational horizons of hope" (Steiner 148), but also to scenarios of conflict and implication, where yesterday's rallying cries for liberation and inclusion can easily become tomorrow's idioms of oppression and exclusion and self-reflexive writing becomes weary of "unconditional" solidarities and turns instead to "solidarities in a minor key" (Amin 2008, 16), "disenchanted" or "entangled solidarities" (Schulze-Engler

2015 and 2019). The problem of "home" in *The Magic of Saida*[14] is thus arguably not just an issue for "diasporic tourists" and "native strangers", but the signum of the "new world order" introduced earlier in this chapter in which, according to Caryl Phillips (2001), "nobody will feel fully at home" (5).

This, finally, brings us back to Bwana Goethe. At a first glance, the question of how he might be doing world literature in Vassanji's novel may seem absurd, as he has no agency of his own in the text, but only makes two fleeting appearances as an emblem of German colonial "soft power". For readers in Europe, and particularly in Germany where demands to acknowledge the full extent of colonial crimes such as the genocidal war against the Herero and Nama in today's Namibia and the brutal suppression of the Maji Maji uprising in today's Tanzania have—more than a century after the event—moved into the centre of an intensifying debate on the legacies of German colonialism, these fleeting appearances linking the world literary icon to colonial atrocities committed by the land of poets and thinkers in Africa may nevertheless have a salutary effect. Of course, Goethe was not complicit with colonial wars fought many decades after his death, but the fact that he was instrumentalized in Germany's early 20th-century imperial ventures is an important facet in a long history of culture and imperialism in Germany which also includes the inevitable implicatedness of 18th- and 19th-century culture and literature in a world dominated by European colonialism.

But *The Magic of Saida* was neither created to "write back to the centre" nor to "decolonize Goethe". The most important function of Bwana Goethe in terms of world literature may thus well be his virtual absence in Vassanji's novel—a space-clearing gesture that leaves room for the literary exploration of new ensembles of contemporary world literature in an increasingly decentred and multipolar world. The Afrasian imaginaries mobilized in *The Magic of Saida* testify to the waning hegemonic power of Europe in a world where the idea that

14 "The urge to return home remains an irresistible pull factor in Vassanji's work but now, articulating where and what that home is seems more complicated than ever" (Rollins 2018, 132).

there is a "Greenwich meridian of world literature" and that this meridian runs through Paris (Casanova 2004, 88) is about as plausible as the belief that French maritime power remains a cornerstone of 21st-century global security architectures in the Indo-Pacific region. But they also open up new, surprising and puzzling spaces of negotiation that are important far beyond the transregional context they originated in.

If world literature, following Ngũgĩ wa Thiong'o, is the condition of literature in a world of globalized modernity as well as a cypher for the necessity to come to terms with this condition, focussing on South-South connections between literatures may help literary studies to get better access to the puzzling dynamics of a world in which power hierarchies and relations between East, South, West and North are undergoing new realignments. To do so, they will need to leave the conceptual fortresses, however, that have been erected both to contain the contradictory multiplicity of world literary practice and to bolster up the waning explanatory power of old and new critical orthodoxies, and they will have to follow literature onto the contested and serrated terrain where the social imaginaries of a globalized world are produced, negotiated, and transformed. On that terrain, Goethe today is neither "Bwana Mkubwa, the German overlord" nor the towering beacon illuminating the topography of world letters, but he may still have his part to play in the global conversation that has been remaking world literature ever since its inception.

Bibliography

Achenbach, Ruth, Jan Beek, John Njenga Karugia, Rirhandu Mageza-Barthel, and Frank Schulze-Engler. 2020. "Afrasian Transformations: An Introduction." In *Afrasian Transformations: Transregional Perspectives on Development Cooperation, Social Mobility and Cultural Change*, edited by Ruth Achenbach, Jan Beek, John Njenga Karugia, Rirhandu Mageza-Barthel, and Frank Schulze-Engler, 1–17. Leiden: Brill.

Adem, Seifudein, and Ali Mazrui. 2013. *Afrasia: A Tale of Two Continents.* Lanham, MD: University Press of America, 2013.
Amin, Ash. 2008. "Collective Culture and Urban Public Space." *City* 12 (3): 5–24.
Appadurai, Arjun. 2013. *The Future as Cultural Fact: Essays on the Global Condition.* London: Verso.
Ashcroft, Bill, Gareth Griffiths, and Helen Tiffin. 1989. *The Empire Writes Back: Theory and Practice in Post-Colonial Literatures.* London: Routledge.
Becker, Felicitas. 2014. "Islam and Imperialism in East Africa." In *Islam and the European Empires,* edited by David Motadel, 112–28. Oxford: Oxford University Press.
Bhabha, Homi K. 1994. "Sly Civility." In *The Location of Culture,* by Homi K. Bhabha, 132–44. London: Routledge.
Bhatt, Purnima Mehta. 2018. *The African Diaspora in India: Assimilation, Change and Cultural Survivals.* Milton Park, Abingdon: Routledge.
Bose, Sugata. 2006. *A Hundred Horizons: The Indian Ocean in the Age of Global Empire.* Cambridge, MA: Harvard University Press.
Casanova, Pascale. 2004. *The World Republic of Letters.* Translated by M.B. DeBevoise. (Original: *La République mondiale des Lettres,* 1999). Cambridge, MA: Harvard University Press.
Chakrabarty Dipesh. 2000. *Provincializing Europe: Postcolonial Thought and Historical Difference.* Princeton, NJ: Princeton University Press.
Cheah, Pheng. 2016. *What Is a World? On Postcolonial Literature as World Literature.* Durham, NC: Duke University Press.
Clegg, Jenny. 2009. *China's Global Strategy: Towards a Multipolar World.* London: Pluto Press.
Coetzee, Carli, ed. 2017. *Afropolitanism: Reboot.* Milton Park, Abingdon and New York: Routledge.
Damrosch, David. 2003. *What Is World Literature?* Princeton, NJ: Princeton University Press.
Desai, Gaurav. 2013. *Commerce with the Universe: Africa, India and the Afrasian Imagination.* New York: Columbia University Press.
De Silva Jayasuriya, Shihan, and Richard Pankhurst. 2003. *The African*

Diaspora in the Indian Ocean. Trenton, NJ: Africa World Press.

Diegner, Lutz, and Frank Schulze-Engler, ed. 2015. *Habari ya English? What about Kiswahili? East Africa as a Literary and Linguistic Contact Zone*. Matatu 46. Leiden: Brill.

Gagiano, Annie. 2019. "Postcolonial Illuminations of Past Betrayals in Tan's *The Gift of Rain* and Owuor's *Dust*." *The Wenshan Review of Literature and Culture* 12 (2): 1–27.

Gaonkar, Dilip Parameshwar, ed. 1999. *Alternative Modernities*. Durham, NC: Duke University Press.

Glissant, Edouard. 1997. *Poetics of Relation*. Translated by Betsy Wing (Original: *Poétique de la relation*, 1990). Ann Arbor, MI: University of Michigan Press.

Jones, Stephanie. 2007. "Merchant-Kings and Everymen: Narratives of the South Asian Diaspora of East Africa." *Journal of Eastern African Studies* 1 (1): 16–33.

Halim, Hala. 2012. "*Lotus*, the Afro-Asian Nexus, and Global South Comparatism." *Comparative Studies of South Asia, Africa and the Middle East* 32 (3): 563–83.

Hawley John C., ed. 2008. *India in Africa, Africa in India: Indian Ocean Cosmopolitanisms*. Bloomington/Indianapolis, IN: Indiana University Press.

Hiro, Dilip. 2010. *After Empire: The Birth of a Multipolar World*. New York: Nations Books.

Hofmeyr, Isabel. 2010. "Universalizing the Indian Ocean." *Publications of the Modern Language Association of America* 125 (3): 721–29.

Independent Commission on International Development Issues. 1980. *North South: A Programme for Survival*. London: Pan Books.

Karugia, John Njenga. 2018. "Connective Afrasian Sea Memories: Transregional Imaginaries, Memory Politics, and Complexities of National 'Belonging'." *Memory Studies* 11 (3): 328–41.

Marcus, Leah S. 2017. *How Shakespeare Became Colonial: Editorial Tradition and the British Empire*. Milton Park, Abingdon: Routledge.

Mazrui, Ali A., and Seifudein Adem. 2013. *Afrasia: A Tale of Two Continents*. Lanham, MD: University Press of America.

Meighoo, Sean. 2016. *The End of the West and Other Cautionary Tales.* New York: Columbia University Press.

Miehe, Gudrun, Katrin Bromber, Said Khamis, and Ralf Grosserhode, ed. 2002. *Kala Shairi: German East Africa in Swahili Poems.* Köln: Rüdiger Köppe.

Moretti, Franco. 2000. "Conjectures on World Literature." *New Left Review*, New Series 1: 54–68.

Mufti, Amir. 2016. *Forget English! Orientalisms and World Literatures.* Cambridge, MA: Harvard University Press, 2016.

Murji, Karim, and Asma Sayed. 2018. "Introduction: Locating M.G. Vassanji in a Transnational Context." In *The Transnational Imaginaries of M. G. Vassanji*, edited by Karim Murji and Asma Sayed, 1–16. New York: Peter Lang.

Mwangi, Evan. 2009. *Africa Writes Back to Self: Metafiction, Gender, Sexuality.* Albany, NY: State University of New York Press.

Ngũgĩ wa Thiong'o. 2012a. "Globalectical Imagination: The World in the Postcolonial." In *Globalectics: Theory and the Politics of Knowing*, by Ngũgĩ wa Thiong'o, 44–62. New York: Columbia University Press.

Ngũgĩ wa Thiong'o. 2012b. "Asia in My Life." *Pambazuka News*, 17 May. https://www.pambazuka.org/governance/asia-my-life.

Owuor, Yvonne Adhiambo. 2015. "O-Swahili—Language and Liminality." In *Habari ya English? What about Kiswahili? East Africa as a Literary and Linguistic Contact Zone*, edited by Lutz Diegner and Frank Schulze-Engler, 141–52. Matatu 46. Leiden: Brill.

Pearson, Michael N. 1998. *Port Cities and Intruders: The Swahili Coast, India, and Portugal in the Early Modern Era.* Baltimore, MD: Johns Hopkins University Press.

Phạm, Quỳnh N., and Robbie Shilliam. 2016. "Reviving Bandung." In *Meanings of Bandung: Postcolonial Orders and Decolonial Visions*, edited by Quỳnh N. Phạm and Robbie Shilliam, 3–19. London and New York: Rowman and Littlefield.

Phillips, Caryl. 2001. "Introduction: A New World Order." In *A New World Order: Selected Essays*, by Caryl Phillips, 1–6. London: Secker and Warburg.

Pirbhai, Mariam. 2009. *Mythologies of Migration, Vocabularies of Indenture: Novels of the South Asian Diaspora in Africa, the Caribbean, and Asia-Pacific.* Toronto: University of Toronto Press.

Pratt, Mary Louise. 1991. "Arts of the Contact Zone." *Profession*: 33–40.

Rollins, Jonathan. 2018. "Roots/Routes and Rhizomes: Diasporic Tourism and the Return of the Native Stranger." In *The Transnational Imaginaries of M. G. Vassanji*, edited by Karim Murji and Asma Sayed, 119–34. New York: Peter Lang.

Rothberg, Michael. 2019. *The Implicated Subject: Beyond Victims and Perpetrators.* Stanford, CA: Stanford University Press.

Said, Edward. 1993. *Culture and Imperialism.* New York: Knopf.

Said, Edward. 2000. "History, Literature, and Geography." In: *Reflections on Exile and Other Essays*, by Edward Said, 453–73. Cambridge, MA: Harvard University Press.

Sayed, Asma, and Karim Murji. 2018. "Introduction: Locating M.G. Vassanji in a Transnational Context." In *The Transnational Imaginaries of M.G. Vassanji: Diaspora, Literature, and Culture*, edited by Asma Sayed and Karim Murji, 1–16. New York: Peter Lang.

Schulze-Engler, Frank. 2015. "Once Were Internationalists? Postcolonialism, Disenchanted Solidarity and the Right to Belong in a World of Globalized Modernity." *Reworking Postcolonialism: Globalization, Labour and Rights*, edited by Pavan Kumar Malreddy, Birte Heidemann, Ole Birk Laursen, and Janet Wilson, 19–35. London and New York: Palgrave Macmillan.

Schulze-Engler, Frank. 2019. "Entangled Solidarities: African-Asian Writers' Organizations, Anti-Colonial Rhetorics and Afrasian Imaginaries in East African Literature." In *Reconfiguring Transregionalization in the Global South: African Asian Encounters*, edited by Ross Anthony and Uta Ruppert, 117–39. Cham: Palgrave Macmillan.

Shroff, Beheroze, and Sonal Mehtab. 2020. "Sidi Voices and the Sidi Sayyid Mosque: Narratives of Space and Belonging." *South Asian History and Culture* 11 (4): 407–20.

Steiner, Tina. 2021. *Convivial Worlds: Writing Relation from Africa.* Milton Park, Abingdon: Routledge.

Vassanji, M.G. [1994] 1997. *The Book of Secrets*. New York: Picador.

Vassanji, M.G. 1996. "Life at the Margins: In the Thick of Multiplicity." In *Between the Lines: South Asians and Postcoloniality*, edited by Deepika Bahri and Mary Vasudeva, 111–20. Philadelphia, PA: Temple University Press.

Vassanji, M.G. [2012] 2013. *The Magic of Saida*. New York: Vintage.

Wa Ngugi, Mukoma. 2012. "Rethinking the Global South." *Journal of Contemporary Thought* 35: 5–10.

Wallerstein, Immanuel. 1974-1988. *The Modern World-System*, [1.] 1974. *Capitalist Agriculture and the Origins of the European World-Economy in the Sixteenth Century*. San Diego, CA: Academic Pr.; [2.] 1980. *Mercantilism and the Consolidation of the European World-Economy, 1600-1750*. San Diego, CA: Academic Pr.; [3.] 1988. *The Second Era of Great Expansion of the Capitalist World-Economy, 1730-1840s*. San Diego, CA: Academic Press.

Wardaya, Baskara T. 2005. "Global Solidarity against Unilateralism." *Inter-Asia Cultural Studies* 6 (4): 476–86.

Warwick Research Collective. 2015. *Combined and Uneven Development: Towards a New Theory of World-Literature*. Liverpool: Liverpool University Press.

Wawrzinek, Jennifer, and J.K.S. Makokha, ed. 2011. *Negotiating Afropolitanism: Essays on Borders and Spaces in Contemporary African Literature and Folklore*. Amsterdam and Atlanta, GA: Rodopi.

West-Pavlov, Russel. 2020. "Towards a Global South Literary Genealogy: M. G. Vassanji and Joseph Conrad as Secret Sharers in *The Book of Secrets* and *Heart of Darkness*." In *Taking Stock: Twenty-five Years of Comparative Literary Research*, edited by Norbert Bachleitner, Achim Hölter, and John A. McCarthy, 539–55. Leiden and Boston, MA: Brill Rodopi.

Wright, Michelle M. 2015. *Physics of Blackness: Beyond the Middle Passage Epistemology*. Minneapolis, MN: University of Minnesota Press.

Yoon, Duncan M. 2015. "'Our Forces Have Redoubled': World Literature, Postcolonialism, and the Afro-Asian Writers' Bureau." *The*

Cambridge Journal of Postcolonial Literary Inquiry 2 (2): 233–52.
Young, Robert J.C. 2011. "World Literature and Postcolonialism." In *The Routledge Companion to World Literature*, edited by Theo D'Haen, David Damrosch, and Djelal Kadir, 213–22. New York: Routledge.

Notes on Contributors

Maggie Bowers is a Senior Lecturer in English Literature at the University of Portsmouth, UK. Her research focuses on indigenous and multi-ethnic writing of the Americas as well as the postcolonial writing in English of India and Southern Africa. Her particular specialism is the genre of magical realism in literature from across the globe. Her works include *Magic(al) Realism* (2004), the co-edited journal edition *Native North American Literature and Literary Activism* (2017) and the essay collection *Imaginary Europes: Literary and Filmic Representations of Europe from Afar* (2016). She has published articles on writers such as Toni Morrison, Louise Erdrich, Salman Rushdie, Tomson Highway and Thomas King.

Ottmar Ette is Chair of Romance Literature at the University of Potsdam. He has published widely on Francophone and Hispanophone literatures, *TransArea Studies*, and the poetics of movement. He is Honorary Member of the Modern Language Association of America (MLA), a regular member of the Academia Europaea, and director of the research project *Travelling Humboldt—Science on the Move* of the Berlin-Brandenburg Academy of Sciences and Humanities. His latest publications include the monographs *Literatures of the World: Beyond World Literature* (2021) and *Mobile Prussia: Views Beyond the National* (2021).

Lucy Gasser is lecturer in Anglophone literary and cultural studies at the University of Potsdam, where she completed her doctorate in 2019. She was a visiting researcher at Delhi University in 2017, and holds a Master's from the University of Cape Town. She is a founding editor of poco.lit., a platform for postcolonial literatures, and has published in various fields, including Postcolonial Studies, World Literature Studies, and translation. Her monograph *East and South: Mapping Other Europes* was published in 2021.

Andrea Gremels is a researcher and lecturer of Francophone and Hispanic Literatures and Cultures at the Department of Romance Languages and Literatures at Goethe University Frankfurt am Main. She has published widely on Francophone and Latin American literature, film, and other media, Transcultural Studies, and global surrealism. She is Executive Board member of the International Society for the Study of Surrealism (ISSS) and a former Alexander von Humboldt Fellow in Paris and Berlin. Her monograph *Die Weltkünste des Surrealismus: Netzwerke und Perspektiven aus dem Globalen Süden* will be published in 2022.

Eduardo Jorge de Oliveira is Assistant Professor of Brazilian Studies (Literature, Culture, Media) at the Institute of Romance Studies of the University of Zurich (UZH). He is a member of the Center for Latin America (LZZ) and the Center for Arts and Cultural Theory at the same university. He is the author of *A invenção de uma pele: Nuno Ramos em obras* (2018) and *Signo, sigilo: Mira Schendel e a escrita da vivência imediata* (2019). His research and key interests are in literature and the visual arts, and the boundaries between literary theory and Ethnographic Studies.

Delphine Munos is a Visiting Professor of English Literature at Ghent University, and she lectures in the Modern Languages Department at the University of Liège, Belgium, where she is a member of the postcolonial research group CEREP. The author of *After Melancholia* (2013), a monograph on Jhumpa Lahiri, she specializes in Anglophone postcolonial literatures, with a special focus on "minor-to-minor" interactions between different postcolonial places and minority histories. She is co-editor of the book series "Cross/Cultures: Readings in Post/Colonial Literatures and Cultures in English" at Brill and has co-edited journal issues for *South Asian Diaspora* (2014; 2018) and *Journal of Postcolonial Writing* (2018; 2019).

Jan Rupp is an adjunct professor at Heidelberg University and has served as interim professor at the universities of Frankfurt, Giessen, and Wuppertal. He is the author of *Genre and Cultural Memory in Black*

British Literature (2010) and *Pageant Fictions* (2016). Among his co-edited volumes are two essay collections on intermedial storytelling in the novel and on new narrative genres on the internet. His research interests include Cultural Memory Studies, narrative theory, ritual in literature, and (Neo-)Victorian Studies. He has published widely on diasporic British as well as on postcolonial Anglophone writing and theory. Among his current work is a project on figurations of world writing and environmental memory in literatures of the Global South.

Maren Scheurer is a researcher and lecturer at the Department for Comparative Literature at Goethe University Frankfurt. She is the author of *Transferences: The Aesthetics and Poetics of the Therapeutic Relationship* (2019) and co-editor of *Narratives of the Therapeutic Encounter: Psychoanalysis, Talking Therapies and Creative Practice* (2020), *Serienfragmente* (2021) and *Amputation in Literature and Film: Artificial Limbs, Prosthetic Relations, and the Semiotics of "Loss"* (2021). She has published essays on psychoanalysis, literature, and other media as well as late-nineteenth-century transformations of realism in a wide range of journals and edited collections. With Aimee Pozorski, she serves as executive co-editor of *Philip Roth Studies*.

Frank Schulze-Engler is professor of New Anglophone Literatures and Cultures at the Institute of English and American Studies at Goethe University Frankfurt. He has published widely on African, Asian and indigenous literature and culture, Indian Ocean literatures and cultures, postcolonial theory, and transculturality in a world of globalized modernity. He was joint project leader of "Africa's Asian Options" (AFRASO) funded by the German Federal Ministry of Education and Research. He serves as co-editor of *Matatu: Journal for African Culture and Society*; his most recent publications include a co-edited special issue of *Matatu* on "Afrasian Connectivities" (2021).

Ana Sobral is an educator and cultural mediator in the fields of postcolonial studies, critical race studies and hip hop studies. She was Assistant Professor of Global Literatures in English at the English Department of the University of Zurich and is currently project manager of Weiter Schreiben Schweiz, a platform for exiled authors in Switzerland. She regularly gives workshops in schools and cultural institutions on the topics of racism, anti-colonialism and cultural globalization and she has an ongoing podcast on the globalization of rap music.

Jarula M.I. Wegner is adjunct lecturer at the Institute of English and American Studies at Goethe University Frankfurt, Germany. He is editorial board member of the Festival Culture Research and Education network, co-founder and speaker of the Global Memories Working Group at the Memory Studies Association and co-founder of the Interdisciplinary Memory Studies Group at the Frankfurt Humanities Research Centre. He holds degrees in Chinese (BA), German (MA) and English (MA and PhD). His work has been published in international, peer-reviewed journals, such as, *ARIEL, Caribbean Quarterly, Journal of Aesthetics and Culture, Journal of West Indian Literature* and *Memory Studies.*